The Occult Diaries of
R. Ogilvie Crombie

Gordon Lindsay

The Occult Diaries of R. Ogilvie Crombie

Copyright © 2011 Gordon Lindsay

Gordon Lindsay has asserted his right to be identified as the author of this work. All rights are reserved, including the right to reproduce this book, or portions thereof, in any form.

Edited by David Spangler
Book Design by Jeremy Berg

ISBN: 978-0-936878-39-3

Lindsay, Gordon
The Occult Diaries of R. Ogilvie Crombie/ Gordon Lindsay

First Edition: September 2011

Printed in the United States of America

9 8 7 6 5 4 3 2 1 0

Starseed Publications
2204 E Grand Ave.
Everett, WA 98201

Dedication

This book is dedicated to the memory of Ogilvie, friend and teacher, with the hope that his writings may lead my readers to experience the enlightenment that has come my way through association with this truly remarkable mystic.

Acknowledgements

I am indebted to my wife, Jean, for the patience and forbearance she displayed over the years when my time was inevitably split between attempting to support her and our burgeoning family and at the same time pursue the esoteric with Ogilvie. Coping with two young children and running the household with a partner who had one foot in this world and the other in the next was never going to make for an easy life.

I would also like to extend my thanks to all those presently and formerly associated with the Findhorn Community who have helped to bring this book to fruition, and especially to my editor, David Spangler, for his inspired commentary and suggestions.

Contents

Introduction 1

Part 1: Life Between Lives (LBL) 3

Part II: Introduction 27

    Chapter 1: The Ages of Man 28
    Chapter 2: Jungian Dream Sequences 51
    Chapter 3: Supranormal Abilities.. 59
    Chapter 4: Who was ROC?... 67
    Chapter 5: Spiritual Teachers 85
    Chapter 6: The Channelled Message 99
    Chapter 7: Nature Kingdoms... 107
    Chapter 8: The Space Connection 203
    Chapter 9: The Thought Responsive Universe..................... 215
    Chapter 10: Duality: Light and Dark 231
    Chapter 11: Music.. 239
    Chapter 12: Power Points 247
    Chapter 13: Conclusions 257

Bibliography 262

R. Ogilvie Crombie

Introduction

Robert Ogilvie Crombie is probably best known as one of the seminal figures in the history of the Findhorn Foundation community in northern Scotland. He was the elderly Scottish gentleman who spoke with nature spirits and whose exploits are chronicled in books such as *The Gentleman and the Faun*, (published as *Meeting Fairies* in North America), *The Magic of Findhorn* and the *Findhorn Garden Story*. But there was much more to this man's life and work than just his association with Findhorn. As a scientist, hermetic magician, and a researcher of the psychic realms, he was in many ways a key figure in the history of esotericism in the twentieth century. His story is less-well known than it could be simply because he worked in solitude and privacy. He did not write books and did not take students or attempt to found a group or an esoteric school. When he was guided to share some of his inner work with the world at large, he did so through the lens of the Findhorn community. In so doing, he exerted a powerful influence on the imagination and spiritual work of thousands of people around the globe, particularly in how they view humanity's relationship and responsibility to the natural world.

I always had it in mind to provide an account of Ogilvie's life, but it has taken me nigh on 35 years since his death in 1975 to put pen to paper. Viewed in retrospect, this tardiness is perhaps no bad thing, as so much has developed in recent years in the realms of psychic research, leading to a much greater awareness and understanding of the nature and workings of the unseen worlds. Where appropriate, I have therefore drawn on this more recent life-between-life (LBL) evidence, unavailable to Ogilvie during his lifetime, as many parallels exist between these and his own experiences; many of the aspects that puzzled him can now be more easily explained.

Part I of this book, therefore, is devoted solely and unashamedly to a consideration of the fundamentals and discoveries of this life-between-life (LBL) research, as first and foremost it has such primary applicability to all of our lives, as well as forming a framework for Ogilvie's. I would urge my reader to give this topic particular attention as it will be referred to regularly throughout the remainder of the book and underpins many of the discussions. Further supportive evidence for the LBL findings is also presented in this section from the many reports from those having had near-death-experiences (NDE), and out-of-body experiences (OOB).

Throughout his 75 year life, and especially in his latter years, Ogilvie had many truly remarkable experiences of an other-worldly nature. By good fortune, he committed an account of most of these to paper, and I have now

The Occult Diaries of

transcribed the vast bulk of them into print, largely for ease of reading as his handwriting at times verges on the illegible. In addition, much of the material was spread over a disparate collection of diaries and notebooks, and chronological order had become somewhat blurred. Part II, therefore, is comprised entirely of extracts from these journals, together with relevant descriptions, background information and comments. Part II is Ogilvie's story.

The first chapter in Part II summarises Ogilvie's life—his outer life, that is—while the remainder of the book is devoted to his inner dealings which were highly varied and extensive. With material of this nature, it is extremely difficult to follow a strict chronology, or even to tightly categorise by topic, and I would ask my reader to be patient when I inevitably stray now and again from conformity.

Where literal extracts are taken from Ogilvie's saga, these are presented in inset format. The accompanying date is shown but in the order of year, month, and day (for example, 730421 would be the 21st April, 1973). Not particularly user friendly, but it computer sorts nicely. Where the date is immediately followed by an 'a', 'b' or 'c' and so on, it indicates different extracts from the same date. Within the extracts themselves, where I have added explanatory notes or comments, these are shown in square brackets, [......].

Latterly Ogilvie, particularly through his involvement with the emergent Findhorn Community, was nicknamed ROC after the initials of his name. Although it has a bit of a harsh ring about it, it does convey an impression of solidity and reliability. Its adoption in the text, however, makes annotation much less cumbersome, and it can be quickly spotted. I have therefore used this abbreviation fairly liberally.

… R. Ogilvie Crombie

Part 1
Life Between Lives (LBL)

LBL investigation is accomplished through deep hypnosis of the subject. This approach has the considerable advantage that the "between world" — the ethereal state between death in one life and incarnation in a subsequent one — can be examined in fine detail over a period of many hours (or from many such sessions amounting to days for that matter). The technique is similar in many respects to that used by the practitioners of past life recall with the exception that the hypnotic state of the subject needs to be deeper.

In the case of the hypnotised subject, it would seem that an active connective channel is established from the conscious mind, through the person's unconscious, and into the superconscious realm, allowing a two-way conversation or question and answer dialogue to take place with a minimum of information colouration; memory recall tends to be both extensive and accurate. As with all hypnosis, however, it is important for the hypnotist to frame questions in such a way that it will avoid leading the subject or creating false scenarios that the subject can build on. This situation does not appear to be such a major problem as normally believed; subjects can in fact be quite vehement in their refutation of certain suggestions which do not accord with "the truth" as they are witnessing it.

Early pioneer of research into life-between-life, Dr Michael Newton, following some thirty years of LBL investigation, published two treatises, *Journey of Souls* in 1994, followed by *Destiny of Souls* in 2000. Other pioneers and investigators such as Ian Lawton and Andy Tomlinson have confirmed his findings. His first essay into LBL occurred by accident while regressing one of his hypnotised subjects. Newton formulated a question which the subject misunderstood and then commenced to describe events which were clearly occurring in a between-life context. The detailed description he gave from this perspective so intrigued Newton that he was stimulated to spend virtually his entire life to date after this momentous event examining the LBL in detail.

Perceived knowledge at the time indicated that if reincarnation was the order of the day, then the time spent in the limbo, holding or Bardo state between lives would only be for a matter of days or weeks, but as discovered in LBL, in general this period turned out to be anywhere from tens to thousands of years! Given the nature of the subject, Newton has nonetheless been successful in treating it in a highly scientific and analytical manner.

In the description of the various consciousness states, our normal waking life may be classified as the Beta stage. This is followed by the first hypnotic condition described as the Alpha state, which ranges from its lightest, such as that achieved in meditation, through a medium state (suitable for recovering childhood memories), and then to the deepest Alpha, where past-life memory may be recovered. To achieve good between-life results, however, a further deepening of hypnotic state to the so-called Theta level is required. This is the deepest that may be achieved prior to the onset of the Delta state which corresponds to deep sleep.

With the subject in this required level of hypnosis, progressive regression to childhood and then still further into the womb is carried out and memories elicited. Instead of continuing the regression still further backwards into the immediately prior between-life state, the subject is switched into the immediately previous lifetime itself, and asked to describe his or her last moments on earth in that particular body i.e. his death in that former life. This then leads smoothly into the life-between-life condition and ensures that the chronology moves in the more natural forward, rather than reverse direction.

LBL research offers information on the various stages from dying in one life, soul existence in the between-life, and rebirth into the next.

Leaving the Body

As with the NDE, the subject, following death, first becomes aware that he is outside his physical body and viewing the physical scene he has just left from a short distance away. Following this surprising, but not uncomfortable event, the individual gradually comes to the realisation that he must have died. Those who have held firm beliefs that physical death signified the end of everything, are astounded to discover that their personality has somehow remained intact and they are as alive as they ever were; much more so in fact—they have awareness, memory, (telepathic) hearing, and even the ability to see with an expanded 360 degree field of vision. Gradually, there is a dimly felt awareness of another spiritual presence, or presences, which seem to be radiating feelings of peace and love. These may be identified as a guide (it would seem that we all, without exception, possess a spiritual guide or guides) or a close relative, and these beings accompany or lead us away from the immediate earth plane.

However, if we have unfinished business, or feel it necessary to contact and comfort loved ones who may be grieving our loss, we have the opportunity to stay in the vicinity of the earth plane and attempt to get messages across to them indicating we are still very much alive and well. This may be accomplished in a number of ways, such as by influencing their thoughts, or manipulating their dreams. Time, on the other side, does not match that of Earth's linear time, and it matters little whether a day, a month or a year is spent in making contact with our still incarnate earth-bound fraternity before we move to the next stage. Truly, as they say, when God made time, He (or She?) made plenty of it!

Towards the Light

Following this, the spirit or soul passes, or is guided by the seen or sensed loving presences, out of the Earth's astral influence towards a point of light which grows steadily in size, and the soul emerges into a full, brightly lit, and vibrant pastoral landscape or a location with magnificent buildings. There he is met by his guide and often by deceased relatives and friends. He may even encounter individuals who are still living but who are temporarily travelling out of their bodies. These are indescribably joyous moments to the returning soul who now realises he has, once again, come home. From the continuous eternal existence of the spirit worlds, sojourns on Earth (or other planets) are recognised by the returning soul for what they are – temporary excursions into dense matter for the sole purpose of providing a learning experience which will contribute to the spiritual evolution of his soul. Earth, in this respect, is viewed as one of the most challenging environments to choose to be incarnated upon.

Guides

The so-called guide is a spiritual entity whose task is to keep an eye on us throughout our incarnation and assist us during the transition of death. Each of us appears to have at least one guide. The evidence for the presence of these spiritually advanced beings comes not only from life-between-life studies, but also from the world of the spiritualist medium. At death, we are often met by our guide and assisted through to the next phase. At this stage, preliminary discussions take place between soul and guide as to the success or otherwise of the completed incarnation. Such talks are carried out in a harmonious and understanding manner in comforting surroundings.

Guides appear to be associated with a given soul or soul group and are present with them through several incarnations. Defining who might be ROC's guide from all the beings he met is difficult, and it may be that more than one would be present to meet specific situations at the various stages of his life.

Healing

Where a life on earth has been extremely difficult, some restoration or healing of the soul's energy pattern is generally required, and this takes place in a special area bathed in healing light, and assisted by beings who have expertise in this function. If a soul has been particularly damaged through association with a body that had been dedicated to highly heinous practices while on Earth, and if this has been the pattern for that soul over a number of lives, the point will have been reached where normal healing will be insufficient, and the soul may eventually have to be restructured. Such souls may not reach even this stage for some time, as they are so overwhelmed by the guilt of their actions that they will prefer to linger "in the dark" in their own personal hell, refusing all spiritual help offered. Eventually, however, help will be sought or accepted, and the soul may then start to move on again. For the average soul (if there is such a thing), however, healing therapy will be administered to the degree demanded.

The soul and its continuing association with a physical body raises some interesting questions on good and evil. When the soul is first created, it arrives in the spiritual world afresh and is lovingly nursed until it is ready to join its first soul group. Its education then proceeds in its present environment and also on near-physical "playgrounds" where the new soul gets a feel of incarnation in an easy-going, physical-like environment. It may eventually accept incarnation (not necessarily on Earth, of course), choosing a likely body and conditions that it considers it will be comfortable with and which will provide the experiences it is seeking. If the novice soul incarnates in the body of a child on Earth, amnesia of its purpose sets in, and it is exposed to the influences, good and bad, of its chosen habitat. The brain of the child is programmed for survival, while the soul resides at a deeper level of consciousness, still with its noble purpose but submerged in a position of minimal but not insignificant influence.

Through the process of free-will, thoughts and actions for good and bad, positive or negative, will be pursued throughout its earth existence. It would seem to be immaterial whether the path leads upwards or downwards; negative behaviour is as important as positive behaviour, because without the presence of one, the other cannot be appreciated. Seemingly knowledge, or even belief, of what is right as seen from the soul's perspective is not enough; only by experiencing the negative directly can the positive be truly understood (and vice versa). Both sides of the coin are equally important.

The evolution of the soul, I envision, may be likened to a gigantic jig saw puzzle, with the centre piece the newly created novice soul to which are interlinked a series of concentric rings of pieces representing wisdom gained from successive lifetimes, extending ever outwards—a vast matrix of interlocking black and white sections. I suspect this evolutionary core resides at the very heart of even the most highly evolved souls. As described in his book *Destiny of Souls*, this idea is hinted at by one of Newton's more advanced souls—whose special attribute in the spiritual world is the nursery care of the newly created soul—when she indicates that while this new soul may be considered flawless, it will acquire "maturity'" through incarnation but overcoming the various obstacles in its path in the course of doing so will create adherent imperfections which "will never be totally erased" until some far future event occurs when all souls are joined together at the termination of the incarnation process.

It would seem then that while evil per se is inconsistent with the structure and operation of the spiritual realms, the evolving soul itself does, nonetheless, carry this propensity for good or evil into its succeeding incarnations. While the soul will have evaluated its choices carefully through study of possible future time lines within the upcoming incarnation to find a body and circumstances that will best lead to the experiences that will result in the rebalancing of particular weaknesses, the actions resulting from freewill, on all the participants' parts, can lead to unexpected situations that completely disrupt the original spiritual plan. As Burns would have said "The best laid schemes of mice and men, gang aft agley."

Council of Elders

Soon (if "soon" has any meaning in this spiritual arena) there is a progression to the next stage, and the refreshed soul will find itself in the centre of another special chamber where it will confront members of a special council of advanced souls generally described by subjects reverentially as the Council of Elders. Its purpose is to evaluate the life just completed, offer constructive criticism in an atmosphere of total love, understanding and compassion, and suggest areas of weakness that might be addressed in a forthcoming incarnation.

It is tempting to think of this council confrontation as analogous to a miscreant's court appearance here on Earth where the individual will be judged on the evidence presented and condemned and punished for his sins

R. Ogilvie Crombie

Return to the Soul Group

Following the encounter with the Elders, the soul moves on to again meet its own soul group which may vary in size from some three members to perhaps about twenty-five. The group is very close-knit and has evolved as a group over thousands of years, incarnating in various situations and in varying relationships with each another; a soul in one life may be associated with one of its group as a brother, or sister, and in another life, perhaps as a parent, aunt or uncle, and so on. Some of these relationships will have been harmonious, some abusive, but they nonetheless provide the necessary learning experiences which will contribute to the evolution of each soul.

Within the group, there will in general be one particular soul more closely associated with the returning soul and who will have incarnated with it over many lifetimes usually as its partner. Newton describes this as the primary soul mate. Gender changes between incarnations are common, although younger souls seem to have a preference for adopting one sexual identity more than the other. In the spiritual realms, souls appear to be genderless and only take on sexual differentiation to suit Earth-type incarnations.

In time, the constitution of the soul group may change as one soul may advance more rapidly than other members of its core group; not all souls evolve at the same rate and hence will move on to join a group more in keeping with its new-found status. Despite this, the bond with the original group remains intensely strong.

Rejoining the soul group, like the meeting with the Council of Elders, is a momentous occasion. Newton describes that the soul group cluster adopts either a semicircular stance around the returning member, or a chevron or arrow-head configuration, with the most important member in that soul's last life (usually the partner) stepping forward first in loving and joyous greeting. Other family members who may have been in incarnation as part of the family group, and who have perhaps given the returning soul a hard time while on Earth (perhaps even having somewhat over-played their designated part), may lurk almost invisibly in the background, coming forward almost apologetically at the end to proffer their welcome.

If, for example, primary soul mates have incarnated together as husband and wife, and one of these partners, say the husband, dies first, the wife will still be there in the spiritual realm to welcome him back. This is possible, because of soul division. At the point of incarnation, all souls divide into two (or more) parts, one becoming integrated with the body of the forming child, the other remaining independently active in the spiritual realm. This part that remains in the soul world becomes the "higher self" for the incarnate person. This may be a somewhat difficult concept to understand, but seemingly this modus operandi is fundamental to all souls without exception.

Soul Division and Integration

It is usually about this stage that the returning soul integrates with that part of its own soul energy which had been left behind in the spiritual realm. It would appear that only a portion of the soul's energy and presence, perhaps between 15 and 80 percent, is ever taken when embodiment in the mother's foetus takes place; the percentage depends much on the state of evolution of the soul and on how much may be needed to balance the likely personality influence from the child to the influence of the soul itself. It is crucial that one does not swamp the other. The portion of soul left in spirit, if of reasonable "size," can take part in normal spiritual learning activities, albeit at a reduced level. Not only can the soul divide in this manner, but on occasions one soul can be further split such that it is in existence in two bodies simultaneously. Whatever the case, it will nonetheless always have a portion remaining in the spiritual realm. It is stated that all these split-offs are in fact exact duplicates of the soul proper, having all its basic attributes but being less energy-concentrated. Analogies to the characteristics of holographic images have been made where despite the size of piece broken off the main photographic plate, the entire scene is still viewable in the fragment. Lawton in his book in fact titles one of his chapters "The Holographic Soul."

Life in the Spiritual Realms

Humour seems to be the hallmark not only of us incarnate humans but of souls and other beings in the subtle worlds as well. It is seen constantly in descriptions in the life-between-life and even the near-death-experiences.

In *Destiny of Souls*, Newton's case number 18 is hilarious and illustrates this very well from the point of view of the life-between-life scenario. Said case had been a preacher in his home town in the deep south of America who delighted in frightening the living daylights out of his parishioners with his vehement fire and brimstone sermons. Even the most trivial excursion from purity would incur the admonition that the perpetrator was "going to hell."

When the preacher died, he was met at the gateway by the figure of the Devil, complete with horns, fangs, and a reddish-green face, and was astounded that given his life of dedication, he himself should end up in hell. After suffering this anguish, he eventually realises that he is looking at his guide "in fancy dress costume." This realisation naturally earns his guide a rather vituperous response but eventually results in laughter all round.

Activities while in the soul realm are many and varied but taking high priority is the detailed examination of the previous life (and lives): mistakes made, cues missed, wrong paths taken, hurts inflicted by and on the soul. Reflection on these then shows what lessons and problems now need to be addressed in a future incarnation to achieve the necessary learning outcomes and to achieve the Karmic balance. This is initially carried out in a library environment where "records'" are consulted. This is considered in more detail below under "Next Life Planning."

Learning is highly important and classes are undertaken in vastly different topics and specialties. Many of those are centred on practice in the manipulation of cosmic energy which can bring into existence solid objects like rocks and, with advanced souls, even the assembling of life-forms. This can be both classroom based or accomplished during field study trips made to developing planets.

Parallel Incarnations – Aspects

In consideration of the topic of soul division mentioned above, it would appear that with very evolved souls much less soul-energy is required to be taken into incarnation (for example, the 15% level would be sufficient). This means that various aspects of the advanced soul could co-exist in a range of environments, each following its own course but fundamentally still linked to its other parts. At this percentage level, some four aspects could co-exist in incarnated form and still leave a meaningful 40% in the soul realm where it will be functioning as the "higher self."

Newton, in *Journey of Souls*, illustrates this process with a client who, in addition to an existence as an American male, is living a parallel existence as a woman in a poor community in rural Canada. This person also has the usual soul portion left in the spiritual realm—a three-way soul division. Advantages of parallel existences claimed by the soul are the speeding up of its evolution, with the side benefit that it then gives them extra time to reside in the harmonious spiritual realm to mull over the episodes in two lives instead of one life. While this parallel incarnation behaviour appears to be open for souls at all levels of development to pursue, the returns for younger souls may be diminished as they may find difficulty in coping with their physical lives, having energetically spread themselves too thinly.

Hybrid Souls – Extended Psychic Abilities

While the majority of Newton's many clients have reported that virtually all their incarnations have been on Earth, he reports on a particular type of soul who has been in incarnation initially on other planets, not necessarily of the very solid Earth-like density but in what Newton would describe as a mental or telepathic world, and who, for the sake of its further evolution, chooses to incarnate on a challenging planet like Earth. These souls Newton labels hybrid souls. He states that if these hybrid souls have been associated with planets with advanced technologies, such as those with abilities of space travel, they seem to be both older and smarter (in terms of soul evolution), and where they have had existence on telepathic worlds, they tend to have above normal psychic abilities in their Earth-based existence.

Next Life Planning, Predestination and Freewill

The incarnation (or re-incarnation) of the soul on Earth is no haphazard event. As mentioned already, following a previous life, the soul spends considerable time reviewing its past actions and attempting to understand how its actions have affected others and what alternatives could have been pursued for a more beneficial outcome. Virtually all subjects describe this activity as taking place in an extensive "library" where records of their lives are released to them for private study, often guided by "librarians" who are characterised as being advanced souls. The book images are three dimensional and can be viewed almost like a video, with the soul able to pause and go forward or backward as needed. Not only can these timelines be perused, but the soul can enter into the scene and experience the situation as it was. It can also elect to "live'" the alternatives as if they had made different choices and even experience firsthand the effect of their behaviour on a third party by temporarily becoming that third party.

This analysis then leads the soul to formulate some future life possibilities which will provide the necessary learning or balancing situations. While some planning of this nature takes place in the library environment, full examination of next life choices (as to parent, child, geographical location etc) are carried out in a special "theatre" with large screens, where the soul is presented with a number of possibilities from which he will choose one. The content displayed on the screen has been carefully selected by more advanced souls who are minutely aware of the life histories of the soul, and have researched suitable situations which will provide the required learning environment. Once again the soul can enter into the scene and experience it "live." This is perhaps one of the most amazing facets of soul world existence, where the (likely) future of suitable candidate bodies can be viewed from birth to death, with all major events in between (such as meeting with significant soul mates and the primary soul mate). While this time line is the most likely to occur, many alternative situations can alter this due to the general free-will of the participants, so outcomes are by no means a fait accompli.

The complexity of this projection into the future can only be wondered at, as not only the major actions of the soul itself have been worked out but also that of all the other significant players as well. The entire "cast" have to be satisfied with their new roles, intended to provide each and everyone with their own particular Karmic requirements. When a choice has been made, the "cast" are assembled and rehearse cues which will enable them to make the appropriate choices at major turning points in their Earth lives, recognising people, places, situations, etc., albeit subliminally. Sometimes several cues for the one event are employed to ensure the right choice is made or the correct course taken. However, there is many a slip between cup and lip, and alternative routes or branch lines may be followed. Most of these alternatives have also been pre-viewed and will contribute to soul evolution, though not as effectively as might have resulted if the main line had been followed.

Newton illustrates these branch line alternatives in a number of his cases, and one example will suffice here. In case 62 in *Destiny of Souls,* the subject is relating a previous life planning session where incarnation as a woman is chosen but who will die within two years of marriage for the benefit of the husband who requires to experience the loss of a much loved one as a balancing Karma from a previous life. During viewing of the timelines, this death is shown to take place within a fairly tight time span with the subject having the choice of dying quickly from a stray bullet from a gunfight between two drunken men (the geographical location was Texas!), by a fall from a horse or by drowning in a river. The subject naturally chooses the quick way. When asked by Newton if there was a chance that none of these events would take place and she would continue to live, the reply was that there was a slight one, but that would really have defeated the purpose of the exercise. The subject states that the manner of death was inconsequential, but the reason itself for dying was of over-riding importance.

Once the soul has selected and accepted its favoured choice, which may well be the opposite sex to the one it had in a preceding life, a further appearance with the Council of Elders may take place, and at the appointed time the soul will once again find itself travelling into the Earth plane to merge with its chosen body. The timing of this varies, some souls entering the foetus early, others much later, some even at the point of birth. A process of integration begins as the soul traces out the brain patterns of the child, and merges itself. Throughout the pregnancy, the soul may be absent for long periods but is always aware of the need to return should the child be in some distress, perhaps as a result of a stressful situation with the mother. These periods of absence decrease as the child grows, disappearing by around the fifth year of life.

By this time the amnesia blocks are firmly in place, and the child will now be unaware of its spiritual inhabitant or heritage. Freewill becomes the order of the day, save for the occurrence of the rehearsed cues for direction change at meaningful points along the timeline. In some ways there is a degree of predestination, at least in terms of the course preset by the soul for itself, and yet within that there still exists total freewill. If insufficient soul energy has been taken into incarnation, the physical component may depart massively from the plan. It would seem that some lives work out better than others. However, there is an eternity's worth of reruns until the goals are achieved. Some souls make it to the winning post faster than others, but it would appear that all will arrive there in the end.

Interestingly, these concepts of freewill are echoed in a number of messages received by ROC in 1966 and 1967, well before these later Newtonian observations. Peter and Eileen Caddy, mentioned in the extract, are the founders of the Findhorn Community in Morayshire in Scotland:

> 660824b. We on our side cannot interfere except within limits, but we can guide and help in many ways. There are however decisions that must be made on the human level in which freewill counts. Man must use his mind and intellect, carefully weighing up the facts known in any given case, and act according to his judgement, not forgetting the inspiration he can receive from within. Seek Divine Guidance, not to take the place of the human intellect but to help it to work to its fullest extent and arrive at the right answers. Man must not become a mechanical puppet, worked by the divine puppet master pulling the strings, but remain a thinking, acting, living individual, working in accordance with the Divine Will.

R. Ogilvie Crombie

661002a. I give you, and Peter [Caddy] through you, advice and directives when needed. This does not mean that it is to be immediately accepted, and followed blindly. Both of you are to turn inward and seek inner divine guidance as well, and Peter, whenever possible, is to get confirmation from Elixir [Eileen Caddy]. In this way, you can feel absolutely certain that you are following true advice.

At the same time, you must both avoid falling into the habit of only acting when there is guidance and directive. However true you believe them to be, you must also act on your own decisions. You are individuals with freewill, even if it is limited freewill, and you must use your mental abilities and your sense of judgement. Intuition is part of the mental equipment and is not necessarily always inspired from without. It is a function of the unconscious part of the mind and can operate entirely within the Self. Even when not inspired from outside, it can usually be trusted. Use all your mental gifts and faculties, stretch them to the limit, and then you will respond even better to guidance and directives coming from higher sources and even from the very highest.

670826. No human being can completely surrender his will to God, as God gave man freewill in the beginning. He can seek as far as possible to do what he believes to be God's will to the best of his ability, but he still remains a man with God-given freewill, and being a man, has human fallibility. The greatest saint can only do God's pure will at times, not all the time. To believe otherwise is a dangerous delusion and leads to presumption and possible inflation of the ego. One may make the surrender of the will to God and pray for Divine Grace to grant that, at times, one will indeed be doing the will of God. One may pray to be helped to lead a selfless life and hope to some extent it will be so, but to believe that one is infallible all the time, and can do no wrong, is the opposite of humility. True humility—not false humility, which is hypocrisy—is one of the great virtues.

The Near-Death Experience (NDE)

Detailed discourses on this phenomenon had never been reported in ROC's lifetime as he died in 1975 at about the same time as Raymond Moody's publication Life after Life first appeared containing in-depth descriptions of individuals who had been declared clinically dead but nonetheless returned to life to tell the tale. Now some thirty five years later, and with many thousands more NDE reports available for scrutiny, the experiences, containing much consistent and similar material, are challenging the stolid scientific belief that the physical world is all that there is.

Dr. Penny Sartori undertook a five year clinical study of NDEs in the Intensive Therapy Unit at Morriston Hospital in Swansea, Wales and reported the results in her 2008 book, *The Near-Death Experiences of Hospitalised Intensive Care Patients*. Her approach is solidly scientific, using the testimonies of those who clearly remembered their NDE and comparing them with a control group who had been in likewise near death situations but had no NDE. In her discussion she concludes on page 311:

> "However, as this clinical study in ITU has shown, our science can no longer ignore NDEs and other similar types of anomalous experience. Acknowledgement of this will therefore once again turn attention to the importance of religious / spiritual experiences."

Interestingly, she makes the salient point that it appears that many NDE experiences are likely to go completely unreported. Of her fifteen patients reporting an experience, only two—those who had the "deepest" NDE— mentioned it voluntarily. The remaining thirteen, who made up greater than 86% of the total sample, would not have reported their experience unless Dr. Sartori had specifically asked them. This implication must push the likelihood of total worldwide NDEs up to phenomenal levels. Given the high incidence of near death recovery due to improved levels of hospitalised emergency care, and the rapid increase in world population, the rate of NDE reporting is surely set to soar even further in the near future. This phenomenon will certainly not be going away! That many of us are now becoming aware of the ubiquitous nature of the NDE is in no small part due to the extensive communication facilities offered by the World Wide Web.

What follows then is a brief description of the salient features of the NDE. Not all aspects of the experience are the same, and not all the various stages will be encountered by the NDEer, and not necessarily in the same order. The generally accepted stepwise progression is somewhat as follows and is the same for infant, child, teenager, adult and aged alike, being roughly similar around the world but with differences in local detail dependant on cultural

Viewing the Scene

I have never had an NDE, and for that I must be thankful. I have nonetheless researched the subject in considerable detail and can to a large extent empathise with the unfortunate individual who has encountered a life threatening event, culminating in heart failure and cessation of brain activity, that is to say in biological and clinical death. This "flat lining" event results in the sudden precipitation—sometimes accompanied by an initial buzzing, ringing or even music—of the individual into a world never experienced before, one quite novel enough to take the breath away (assuming, of course, breath were still in evidence at all at this stage!).

Following this clinical death, many NDEers find themselves now viewing their physical body quite dispassionately from a somewhat elevated position nearby and seemingly with all their 'normal' faculties in place; they experience mental alertness, a unique 360 degree visual field (even if they are congenitally blind) and hearing abilities, all of which may seem even more acute than in the normal waking physical state. There is absolutely no sense of the situation being dream-like or hallucinatory. If in an operating theatre environment, an attempt may be made to communicate with the nurses and surgeons frantically trying to resuscitate the now lifeless body, exhorting them not to bother going to all that trouble as it feels just fine now in this out-of-body state where there is no pain and a deep peacefulness accompanied by an overwhelming sense of joy and freedom.

Alas, to their surprise, their protestations to the theatre staff go completely unheeded, with no one taking the slightest bit of notice. If the conclusion that they are now dead has not already dawned on them, it probably will do so at this stage. A sense of detachment prevails, even to the extent of feeling some disgust at the sight of "that body." If resuscitation is now successful, they will find themselves rapidly reincorporated with all the pain and anguish that goes with their present acute medical condition. However, the anguish arises not often so much from their substantial pain but from the feeling of loss engendered from having been yanked back so unceremoniously from that pleasant state of painless bliss. In a full-blown NDE trip, as described below, this anguish on return to life is often augmented by intense anger, occasioning much surprise on the part of the medical staff who might reasonably be expecting some praise and gratitude for their enormous efforts in restoring life rather than belligerent censure and abuse, which occasionally becomes physical!

Divine Encounter

If a return to body does not occur fairly quickly in the way described above, a point eventually arises when the individual, while still aware of his physical surroundings, becomes gradually cognisant of a further reality into which he feels himself inexorably drawn. He may be dimly aware of the presence of a friendly other or others whom he may or may not see and who might accompany and guide him on his journey. He can then find himself approaching the entrance to a dark tunnel into which he enters and moves steadily forwards. The tunnel, though dark, does not feel in any way threatening. In the distance a small point of light appears growing larger and brighter. On exit from the tunnel, a deceased relative, or a being of glowing radiance is often encountered who greets the new arrival and engages in non-verbalised conversation which, although clearly heard and unambiguously understood, appears to take place in a two-way telepathic manner. The light being is often equated with a heavenly figure such as Christ or Buddha and is usually of such radiance as to be described as blinding, although it causes some surprise that such an overpowering brilliance is not damaging to the eyesight in the manner it would be in the physical world. The principal feeling while in this presence is one of overwhelming unconditional love.

Life Review

In some cases a life review ensues, which can take various forms from a guided perusal of records in a "journal of life" through to a vivid high speed video-type playback of all the events of the individual's life to date encompassing the good, the bad, and the downright ugly. The detail extends to long forgotten episodes which, although extremely rapidly glimpsed, are nonetheless completely comprehended. Earth based linear time is completely missing here. As well as actions, even relevant thoughts that the NDEer has had during his life are made apparent.

This viewing is not a passive affair either. It takes a dualistic form in which the participant not only experiences his own positive and negative thoughts and actions at the time but also lives through the joy given or the hurt inflicted on the recipient. This third-party vicarious suffering experience is never allowed to become overwhelming. He does become aware, or is made aware, that had he perhaps taken a different approach, a happier outcome might have resulted. He is shown that the course of his actions resulted in not just one effect but that the ripples extended outwards, affecting situations distantly remote. Throughout the entire playback there is absolutely no feeling of condemnation, no accusations of guilt, no sense of rejection. The individual is continuously bathed in overwhelming feelings of unconditional love and acceptance.

Wonderland

When first arriving out of the tunnel, some may enter a harmonious landscape carpeted with beautiful flowers in eternal bloom, radiating the very essence of life itself which the individual clearly experiences. He or she is aware of the living qualities of the shallow streams flowing through this idyllic landscape, and of the very life of the trees and shrubs. They realise the almost incomprehensible interconnectedness of every living thing, down to the life, the cosmic essence if you will, in the atoms and molecules themselves, and realise that this extends to all realms, whether earth-based or otherwise. They may travel to or be taken to distant planets and galaxies. Their every question is answered and completely understood in the instant. There is no ambiguity. The meaning of life here and on earth becomes apparent, and there is an overwhelming realisation of just how simple it all is. There is the intrinsic feeling that they have known this all along. This is their true home. Birth on earth is shown to be for the betterment of the evolving soul, though in circumstances which will be anything but easy. They will understand that prior to birth, they have agreed to undertake a mutually agreed assignment and chosen parents and circumstances most likely to permit its achievement. Within the confines of this overall assignment, they can exercise complete freewill. The bottom line, of which virtually all NDEers are aware, is that there are only two major requirements desired of mankind – development of unconditional love and acquisition of knowledge. But the greater of these is love.

Choices—To Stay or Return

There's little wonder that when they are presented with the choice of returning to earth or continuing on in this blissful environment, most will plead to be allowed to remain. It is then pointed out that it is not their time, that they have arrived in the next world prematurely, that their earthly mission has not yet been accomplished, and therefore a return to earth is advised.

Nonetheless, they have a choice to either stay or return. They are aware, or made aware, that crossing a visible or invisible line or boundary such as a river, stream, or wall will mean that there will be no return to the body. An amusing interchange often ensues when the NDEer may attempt to bargain with the heavenly entity with whatever means he has at his disposal, or in the case of a child simply throw a tantrum; anything which will swing the balance in favour of being permitted to remain. This is greeted with bemused tolerance and a chuckle, but reasons for returning are proffered by the radiant being, such as the grief and hardship that would be caused to their loved ones if they did not return. If that does not sway them, then they are reminded of their duty to complete their mission which they had agreed to before birth, which, if not fulfilled will retard their spiritual progress and may necessitate another life or further lives until the mission is completed or the lessons are learned. Once a grudging admission and acceptance of the truth of all this has been made, they are immediately dispatched at high speed back to the physical body, which may even by this time be resting patiently in the morgue awaiting imminent disposal in the usual time honoured fashions.

After-effects

After returning to the physical body, the effect of the experience is to cause much mental anguish, in no small way aggravated by the physical state of ill-being at the time. Attitudes may range from heart-felt disappointment at the feeling of loss and separation from their divine "home," perhaps a feeling of rejection at being banished from heaven which might leave the person with a feeling of not having been good enough to remain, to frustration that much of the knowledge and understanding of the heavenly process and of the details of their clearly defined and understood personal mission have now been erased from their mind (many are informed during their NDE excursion that this memory blocking will occur). This latter feature is common to virtually all near death experiences, seemingly to ensure that the NDEer is once more forced back into a situation that will not infringe on making choices based on freewill.

Despite this, the NDEers return with a clear memory of the events firmly imprinted in their minds, so strongly that it remains with them, vividly alive, for the rest of their lives. For them the experience has been truly real, much more so than the reality of the physical world, and almost without exception it profoundly alters both their outlook on life and their approach to and handling of it. The experience is so transforming that many difficult years of adjustment are often required before the profound meaning can find full expression and be fully implemented in their daily lives. Many, in essence, perform a complete U-turn from their previous lifestyle, and this can impact powerfully on their relationships with parents, partner, children and friends, who bewilderingly now see a completely different person with views and attitudes entirely foreign and totally out of character. Occupations are affected likewise, where the usual quest for monetary gain and power now becomes a matter of less or even no importance. Within the NDE community there is therefore a very high incidence of divorce and perhaps several changes of employment, usually into positions such as those typified by the caring professions that offer the ability to help people.

Upon their return, NDEers have now no fear of death, many looking forward to it as a means of returning to the blissful state previously experienced. As with all of us, though, the dying process itself, for obvious reasons, is not looked forward to with any great relish!

Interestingly, despite the meeting with such divine figures as Buddha, Christ, and others who represent the godhead of specific religions, the NDEer returns with a more open and non-religion-specific outlook, realising that formal religion and its dogmas, creeds and practices are somehow unfulfilling; the often narrow and entrenched views and interpretations held by a typically highly orthodox clergy, of whatever religious denomination, fail to match the content and ethos of the direct confrontation that the NDEer has had with the Divine. It is recognised, however, that for mankind in general, such "normal" religious practices and observances do lead in an "upward" direction. The arrival point is the same; only the path differs.

Concomitant with the NDE, pronounced psychic abilities are now noticed by most NDEers. They can be aware of other people's or even animals' thoughts and be sensitive to their feelings. They can have a sense of future happenings in both their own lives and in the wider community. Additionally, some even report that their presence can result in interference with electrical equipment, causing light bulbs to blow, TV sets to switch on and off, and so forth. These effects may diminish with time but can be very disconcerting, not only for themselves but for unaware bystanders. Looks like Uri Geller may have company!

Feedback from many NDErs offers strong support that reincarnation does take place, and most tend to agree that at some point, presumably when all the required lessons of life and love have been learned, reincarnation, at least in an earth based context, ceases. One experiencer explained to Dr Ken Ring (author of Lessons from the Light: What We Can Learn from the Near-death

Experience) in a recorded interview in his audiotape archives that during the life review he saw things that had and had not been accomplished, not just in his present lifetime, but in past ones as well. He was emphatic that reincarnation is a modus operandi. Another account also in the same archives relates how the NDEer was puzzled why a number of light beings in her vicinity were, "kind of milling around here," and posed the question to them. Some of their number then approached her and explained that they were all waiting to be reincarnated.

Indeed, the NDE is in close agreement with the life-between-life (LBL) reports that reincarnation on both this planet and a multitude of others throughout the universe is the very cornerstone of soul evolution.

The Out-of-body Experience (OOB)

Out-of-body (OOB) experiences, unlike NDEs, are generally propitiated by procedures employed by those who deliberately wish to explore the inner worlds; the participants do not have to be ill and do not have to incur a near death event to accomplish this. OOBs can, under certain circumstances, also occur in a spontaneous and unexpected manner without any conscious effort on the part of the individual. Monroe, Buhlman, and Bruce provide details in their books on various procedures that may be used to bring about a successful OOB. It is usually best to predefine the desired outcome of the OOB such as meeting a deceased relative or friend, going to a specific place, or performing a particular task. With the return to the body, many of the resultant astral memories are conveyed to the brain and consciously remembered thereafter.

It would appear that there are a multitude of different levels or planes, extending all the way up from the lower astral to planes of ineffable and inexpressible wonder. The experiences and interactions with the inhabitants of these various worlds can range from the terrifying to the bizarre to the most loving and powerfully enlightening.

Lower Astral

There appears to be little difference between an OOB and the first stage of an NDE or LBL where the participant will be aware of himself or herself outside the body. The individual will have a fair degree of control of his movements (directed simply by thought or desire), and possess 360 degree vision and hearing. Where there is contact with other out-of-body entities or the denizens of these inner worlds, communication again takes place by telepathic means. Of the many planes or levels in the inner worlds, the lowest of these is often described as the lower astral plane. Here the OOBer will find himself in an environment which closely resembles the physical world. He will find that he can, however, pass through solid objects such as doors, windows and walls, though often with some difficulty, and he may be aware of the internal structure of these objects as he traverses them. He will be able to view people going about their daily lives in "real time" and objects will appear much as they are in the physical world, although a modern chair, for example, sitting in the corner of the dining room may take on an old-world appearance in the astral. The chair may not even be in the same relation to the room, but may occupy a mirror image position. This realm is still not an exact analogue of the physical world. Some experiments carried out by Buhlman and described in his book *Adventures Beyond the Body* showed that although a candle flame could be snuffed out in the astral, there was not a transfer of the event to the physical. The candle was still found to be burning when the OOBer returned from his wanderings.

Interaction of the OOBer with physical people can have some interesting and amusing properties. Monroe in his book *Journeys Out-of-the-Body* describes a situation where during an OOB he visited a Dr Bradshaw and conversed with him or rather with the consciousness in his astral body ("superconscious" is the term that Monroe has used). Dr Bradshaw continued about his business and remained totally unaware of Monroe's presence or the fact that he had engaged in a brief conversation with Monroe.

This raises some interesting points that in normal waking or sleeping life, our astral body may well be performing its own discourse with entities of the inner worlds, totally without our knowledge, while we are engrossed in the execution of our day to day or night-time routines. When asked, Dr Bradshaw had no memory of Monroe's OOB presence and certainly did not remember speaking to him. Yet that information must be recorded in the superconscious memory banks. The problem is then one of accessing these memories and achieving an effective superconscious memory-to-brain information transfer. This particular difficulty of communication affects us all, as during much of our sleeping time our astral body is out there, at least part of the time, up to something, but we will seldom be aware, or made aware, of its peregrinations. The fact that we are having this unconscious OOB is generally indicated in the accompanying dream sequence that almost all of us have experienced at one time or another of floating or flying.

Still on this lower astral level, Monroe goes on to describe an amusing incident where he visits a businesswoman who is engaged in actively chatting to her daughter and a friend. To make sure she remembers his visit, he decides to pinch her, with the immediate result that she leaps up. Interestingly, Monroe comments that she was able to show him the bruise resulting from his out-of-body pinch. It is generally accepted that the physical body possesses an etheric body which matches the general shape and contours of the physical body, and it would presumably be this etheric body that Monroe pinched.

This again raises some interesting points. Where psychic healing is practiced, either directly as in my own migraine case which I describe later or remotely, the effect would initially seem to be on this etheric body, although, on the basis of Professor John Hasted's work with psychic metal benders (which I describe later), perhaps it may also impinge directly on the physical body. In some way the etheric body may be considered to be changed by thought directed energy, and the resultant alteration to its structure then works its way through to manifest in the physical body which will then gradually start to reflect these changes that have been newly established in the etheric counterpart.

Higher Planes

While NDEs are in general transformative experiences, especially the deeper ones where contact with a divine figure has taken place, OOBs can also on occasions deliver a similar result. Monroe seems to reject the notion that there is a heaven as he has had his fair share of somewhat hellish OOBs, but despite this view he also describes in his book the sort of "heaven" that is immediately recognisable as being typical of the NDE or LBL accounts:

"Each of the three times I went there, I did not return voluntarily. I came back sadly, reluctantly. Someone helped me return. Each time after I returned, I suffered intense nostalgia and loneliness for days…, and something akin to homesickness. So great was it, that I have not tried to go There again. Was this heaven?"

Likewise in *The Secret of the Soul*, Buhlman records one of his respondent's OOBs where following the usual self-induction path, the lady in question finds herself in a place she feels is "the mind of God" and which she describes as "a place of endless, unconditional love pouring forth…"

ROC and OOB

Out-of-body work was the cornerstone of ROC's activities, occurring mainly during night hours but often also during the day. Much of this was in a fully conscious state with complete memory recall. For him, the act of consciously leaving the body did not appear to require any special procedures. He told me once that when he was required out-of-body, he would be helped out usually by some guiding entity stretching out a hand, grasping his etheric one, and gently pulling. Eventually even this method became unnecessary, and it was sufficient for the being to simply "call" him. He explained to me that he did not consciously attempt astral projection but waited to be summoned.

While the preceding information is interesting and valuable in its own right, it is meaningful to us because it describes the kind of "subtle environment" that plays such a prominent role in ROC's life. If we are to understand him, then we need to appreciate this environment for he was a master in navigating it and working within it. As we all are, ROC was a denizen of two worlds, the physical and the non-physical, but in his case, this "dual citizenship" was very conscious. In fact, the real meaning of ROC's life is that in him this duality became a unity, a citizenship of the planet as a whole blending its material and spiritual sides in a perfectly normal and organic manner. It was from this sense of unity that he learned to live his life and do his work. That is the story that now lies before us.

Fig. 1: Author and Ogilvie in October 1967 – Nervelstone, North Ayrshire

R. Ogilvie Crombie

Part II
Introduction

I first met Robert Ogilvie Crombie or ROC in July 1967 while I was still in the midst of my post graduate studies in metallurgy at Strathclyde University in Glasgow. At the time, I was 26 years old, Ogilvie 68. My wife and I had decided to pay a visit to the blossoming (literally and metaphorically) Findhorn Community on the shores of the Moray Firth in north east Scotland, and our visit coincided with one of Ogilvie's periodic stays there away from his normal domicile in Edinburgh. We hit if off fairly well right from the start as we had many similar interests in science (especially electronics), music and literature, and all aspects of the paranormal. Our close friendship extended from that day until his death in 1975, a seemingly brief but intensive eight years later.

When I completed my PhD studies the following year, I was fortunate in being offered employment as a materials engineer in Ferranti Ltd in Edinburgh and accordingly moved there with wife and family. As Ogilvie resided in Albany Street in Edinburgh's so-called "new town," and my route home from Ferranti virtually took me past his door, it was convenient for me to call in most days.

Chapter 1
The Ages of Man

Ogilvie, standing almost six feet tall, was a person with a presence. He was not difficult to pick out in a crowd. Passing him in the street would convey an impression of a somewhat serious looking gentleman but with kindly eyes and a purposeful and directed gait.

He was well built, though by no means overweight, clean-shaven, and with neatly trimmed hair. In public places he was always well dressed, even when the occasion was relatively informal, generally sporting a hat— especially in cold weather—tweed sports jacket, and the obligatory shirt, collar and tie. Where weather demanded it, this apparel would be supplemented by a light rain coat or full length overcoat. His alert grey-blue eyes showed a remarkable depth and stillness and conveyed an impression of an inner wisdom and trustworthiness. He was courteous and reliable, in every respect a real gentleman.

Fig. 2: Ogilvie during a visit to the Blackhills Gardens (~1969)

R. Ogilvie Crombie

Fig. 3: Ogilvie at Nervelstone - 1968

In conversation he listened more than he spoke and in answering would carefully weigh up his words beforehand. His knowledge on topics such as music and the arts and ancient and modern literature (fiction and non-fiction) was staggering, and his memory was seemingly up to remembering the vast bulk of it. His knowledge of the esoteric was unsurpassed. As an avid reader and book collector, his library eventually burgeoned to some 5,500 books.

He was an accomplished pianist and organist and would regularly give recitals for his guests. On many occasions, we would have a stab at playing duets, but his musical abilities were far in advance of mine, and where possible I would choose the easier parts. Great fun nonetheless!

Ogilvie was born with a serious heart condition which was to dominate the pattern and direction of his entire life. In retrospect, however, this handicap can be viewed as a blessing in disguise, allowing him a more contemplative life and providing time to develop a close contact with nature and the nature kingdoms.

In the following sections, I have outlined the major external events in Ogilvie's life from cradle to grave. Information available from his earlier years is unfortunately rather scant and is taken from assorted memorabilia. This is in stark contrast to the extensive, almost daily accounts available for his latter years.

The Occult Diaries of

Braid Crescent, Edinburgh

School Years

Robert Ogilvie Crombie was born on Wednesday, 17 May 1899 in Edinburgh, Scotland. His father, John Crombie, married Anna Tannoch Ross at St. Cuthbert's Parish Church in Edinburgh in 1884, and the couple had already taken up residence at 14 Braid Crescent in that city by the time that ROC was born. ROC had two older sisters, Catherine ("Katie'"), some thirteen years older than himself, and Margaret ("Mattie") who had tragically died the year before ROC's birth before she had even reached her twelfth birthday.

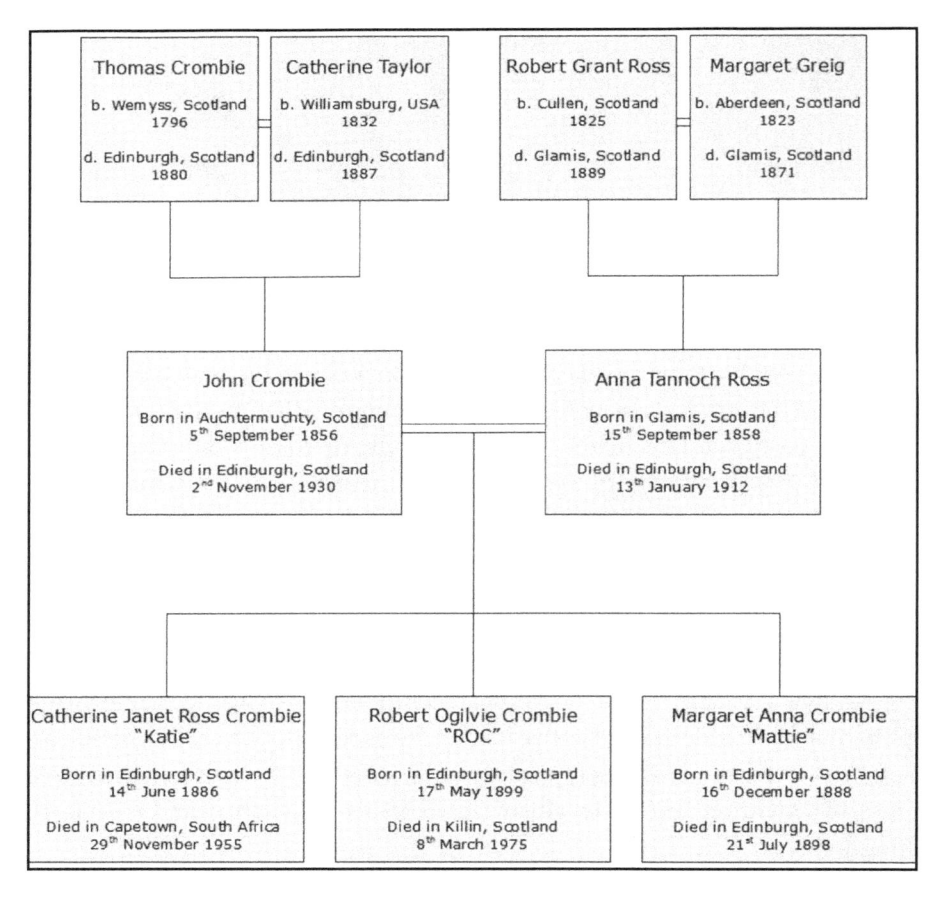

Thomas Crombie	Catherine Taylor	Robert Grant Ross	Margaret Greig
b. Wemyss, Scotland 1796	b. Williamsburg, USA 1832	b. Cullen, Scotland 1825	b. Aberdeen, Scotland 1823
d. Edinburgh, Scotland 1880	d. Edinburgh, Scotland 1887	d. Glamis, Scotland 1889	d. Glamis, Scotland 1871

John Crombie	Anna Tannoch Ross
Born in Auchtermuchty, Scotland 5th September 1856	Born in Glamis, Scotland 15th September 1858
Died in Edinburgh, Scotland 2nd November 1930	Died in Edinburgh, Scotland 13th January 1912

Catherine Janet Ross Crombie "Katie"	Robert Ogilvie Crombie "ROC"	Margaret Anna Crombie "Mattie"
Born in Edinburgh, Scotland 14th June 1886	Born in Edinburgh, Scotland 17th May 1899	Born in Edinburgh, Scotland 16th December 1888
Died in Capetown, South Africa 29th November 1955	Died in Killin, Scotland 8th March 1975	Died in Edinburgh, Scotland 21st July 1898

Fig. 4: Ogilvie Crombie genealogy

Katie and ROC were raised in a household both musical and intellectual. In addition, there was a strong church connection through ROC's father who

R. Ogilvie Crombie

was an elder of St. Mathew's Church. ROC's mother, Anna, died in January 1912 at age 53 (she was a relatively mature forty years old when she gave birth to ROC), leaving the main influence to be his father, very much the traditional Victorian gentleman with traditional Victorian outlook and values. His early relationship with his father was by his own admission, "difficult," but grew more harmonious as the years wore on as they grew to understand each other better and accept their differences.

Before the age of ten, ROC was already experiencing the debilitating effects of his congenital heart condition, brought on largely by his school gymnastics exercises. Following medical advice he was excused from further participation in such activities.

His schooling was thorough and rounded. After attending the select, boys-only, Merchant Company School, Daniel Stewart's College in Edinburgh (now Stewart's Melville College), he emerged in 1916 with certificates in English, Mathematics, French, Science and Drawing.

The home at Braid Crescent, which was to see itself turned to many functions through the following years, was put to good use in its earlier days when a teenaged ROC set up a science lab, experimenting with various chemical reactions, especially those designed to end in a pyrotechnic display; he loved fireworks and devising and building ingenious devices with an electrical slant. At school he was nicknamed "The Professor," but more often he was called "ROC," which were his initials but which also carried an association with the stories of Sinbad—the Roc being the fabulous bird that carried Sinbad off to the valley of diamonds which were guarded by serpents.

He was an avid follower of *The Exploits of Elaine*, a serial film produced in 1914 and was intrigued by all manner of detective stories. In fact, at this stage he envisioned a career as a scientific expert at Scotland Yard!

War Effort

Following the outbreak of the First World War and fresh out of school, ROC embarked in 1917 on a radiotelegraphy course and gained first class proficiency working on, amongst other things, a 1.5kW Marconi Standard Apparatus transmitter. These were spark transmitters, as the valve, old hat now, had not reached the stage where it could be incorporated in communications equipment. Messages were transmitted and received in Morse code as voice communication by spark transmission was impossible. Following the course, he was assigned to *HMS Teviot* as their radio officer, the ship plying between the UK and France on war work.

Fig. 5: Ogilvie, radio officer on HMS 'Teviot' (1918)

R. Ogilvie Crombie

His French identity card showed there were a total of eight visits by *Teviot* in 1918 to the French ports of Cherbourg, Boulogne or Dieppe, but his itinerary also covered many of the UK and Irish ports, including London, Bristol, Belfast, and Glasgow. The crew of the *Teviot* were drawn largely from the Scottish islands of Barra and Jura and created quite an impression on the young ROC. He very much enjoyed his time at sea, and it improved his health, despite concerns arising from the general hazards of wartime and especially of the ever lurking presence of U-boats. On board, he also had the company of his wind-up gramophone and many "78" records.

However, his relationship with the first mate was strained to say the least, and ROC's quick sarcasm on one occasion nearly earned him his first swimming lesson. The first mate, a man of quick temper and clearly substantial physique, in response to this particular barbed aside, grabbed his not inconsequential 5'11" tall radio officer, swung him horizontal, raised him bodily in the air, and advanced to the rail of the ship with the clear intention of launching him overboard into the surging sea far below. I imagine a quick climb-down on ROC's part managed to avert this life-threatening disaster. With friends like that, who needs the enemy!

University and Science

With the cessation of hostilities in late 1918 (at least on the continent, if not on board ship), ROC returned to Edinburgh and in October of that year commenced a three year Bachelor of Science course at the University of Edinburgh in his life-long interest in pure science.

With his abiding interest in drama, he also created the Golden Eagle Dramatic Society in 1919, and via the auspices of his home in 14 Braid Crescent, set up the 'Bijou Theatre' where performances of various plays could be given to small groups. Later, these productions graduated to more public venues, such as Morningside Church Hall. Charles Henderson, a boyhood friend who lived only a couple of doors away from him and who shared his interests in radio, photography, music, and drama, joined with ROC in these enterprises, and the aspiring Ogilvie Crombie-Charles Henderson duo was always at the heart of the shows.

During these study years at University, ROC was also granted a permit by the GPO in 1920 to experiment with wireless telegraphy at Braid Crescent, a natural continuation from his position and experience aboard *HMS Teviot* during the war years. What with rehearsals and performances of the various plays and the experimentation with radio, the home must have been a hive of activity.

However, the intervening war years had done nothing to improve his heart condition. This was further aggravated when a young lady with whom he was passionately in love decided to marry another, leaving ROC totally devastated and feeling there was now little purpose left in life. Acting on medical advice, therefore, in 1921 he reluctantly abandoned his science course in its final year before he had the opportunity to sit the final exams.

Radio Consultancy

In spite of his health problems, ROC's radio pursuits continued apace with the construction of various pieces of an amateur radio kit. A photograph from August 1922 (the date carried by the prominently displayed Wireless World magazine) illustrates the installation of some then state-of-the-art equipment at his home in Braid Crescent.

Fig. 6: Ogilvie's home built radio apparatus in Braid Crescent, Edinburgh (1922)

In addition to this avid interest in radio communications, ROC was also a keen photographer and did all his own developing and printing in a makeshift darkroom. This photograph is one example of his handiwork.

R. Ogilvie Crombie

ROC clearly had visions of a career in radio telegraphy. He decided to relocate to Manchester in June of 1924, setting up a consultancy business along with Charles Henderson at premises called 'Kenilworth' in Whalley Range. Unfortunately, although proving highly popular, the business venture failed to bring in a meaningful wage for the pair as at that point in history radio was still in its infancy, with its dedicatees mainly enthusiastic, if impoverished, amateurs. Both men eventually returned to Edinburgh.

University and Music

While Charles now changed career to disciplines of speech and elocution, eventually becoming an examiner, ROC, for the second time, entered the portals of Edinburgh University in October of 1926, this time embarking on a course in music with emphasis on theory, practice, and composition. His mentor for some of the studies was the renowned Sir Donald Francis Tovey, the appointee to the Chair of the Reid School of Music, a position he had taken up in 1914. In addition, he took organ lessons and passed several relevant music examinations.

ROC had come across works by various modern composers including those of Leo Ornstein, an American born in the Ukraine. Ornstein's compositions were regarded as highly avant-garde at the time, although nowadays they would not seem the least unusual. At this stage in his life a career in music clearly appealed, and the first step was taken in 1928 when he approached the BBC in London and offered to play Ornstein's works. He received a letter from K. A. Wright, Assistant Musical Director of Programmes, inviting him for an audition. A date was duly arranged for Thursday, June 28th at 3 p.m. in the London studios, but, alas, Mr. Wright was unable to attend the audition himself, having gone on holiday. He nonetheless responded to ROC on 18th July:

> "I am sorry that your visit coincided with my absence on holiday, as I wanted to hear some of your Ornstein music.
> I honestly do not see where we are going to use it at present; it is not the sort of music which broadcasts very effectively judging from what I have seen and heard of it."

Well, so much for that anticipated career move!

On leaving the University in June of 1929, ROC accepted a position as organist and then choirmaster of an Edinburgh church and gave piano recitals to the Terpander Club in April and December of 1929 and March of 1930.

In November of that year his father, who had much distinguished himself by attaining the rank of Sub Inspector of Schools for Scotland, died at the age of 74. This event precipitated ROC's move in the same year to a rented first floor flat at 28 Albany Street.

Albany Street, Edinburgh

Exploring Life

Once established in the new flat and having settled all the necessary family affairs, ROC invested in a Bechstein grand piano and later betook himself to Paris to visit the Exposition Coloniale Internationale, which opened in May 1931.

The drama activities continued with ROC appearing with Christine Orr in a play entitled 'Muckle-Mou'ed Meg', staged in St. Columba's Hall, Edinburgh in 1933. ROC was also responsible for production. One newspaper had this to say:

> 'The scene in the dungeon, with Meg (Christine Orr) and Will (R. Ogilvie Crombie) was carried through with admirable verve and convincing effect. One felt that if the episode was not historically true, it ought to be true. ….. Charles W. Henderson looked the part of the harper, and sang with pleasing effect'

The Crombie-Henderson team clearly had interests and abilities that extended far beyond their ham radio enterprises!

Christine Orr went on to found the Makars in 1933-34 and wrote a play *Pan Pipes*, performed in 1934 and in which ROC again appears. This began a theatrical association that lasted for several years.

For example, the following year, ROC played the part of Damian in *Flodden*, the play produced on this occasion by Christine Orr and performed at the Little Theatre. Yet another year on, in 1936, ROC appeared in the Makar's production of *Twelfth Night* at the Belford Studio, and in Anatole France's *The Man who married a Dumb Wife*, presented at the Division Final of the Scottish Community Drama Festival in the Festival Theatre, Elm Row. The adjudicator, Robert Young, offered praise indeed, as he considered ROC's performance the "finest individual performance of the festival."

ROC had himself written a three act play, entitled *Let's be Romantic,* and this was performed by The Makars in April 1937 at the Dean Studios. The

R. Ogilvie Crombie

play was produced by his friend Edward Shanley. ROC did not appear in the play. In its review, *The Scotsman* response was lukewarm, but another newspaper described ROC as "a well-known personality in Edinburgh dramatic circles."

Both the listening to and the performance of music continued to be a major influence in ROC's life. A photograph from this period taken in the Albany Street flat shows ROC seated at the keyboard of his elegant Bechstein Grand playing with studied seriousness!

Fig. 7: Ogilvie seated at his Bechstein piano in the flat in Edinburgh (ca 1935)

His heart condition continued to plague him, and he suffered a heart attack in 1933. A subsequent medical diagnosis indicated a problem associated with thickening of the coronary artery and neuritis from the swelling of the nerves around the heart. His doctor obviously considered the problem severe enough to comment that he should consider himself retired. Not perhaps the most sanguine advice for an aspiring thirty four year old man.

By 1935-36, he was suffering regular attacks of angina, and by 1939 his heart condition had become so severe as to virtually confine him to the flat. With the onset of the Second World War (Britain declared war on Germany in September, 1939), ROC, to avoid the physical stress resulting from air raids, was advised to make a "move to the country." He duly found temporary accommodation with friends who lived in the county of Angus at Glenisla, not far from Blairgowrie.

Cowford Cottage, Stanley

Fig. 8: Cowford Cottage as it was in the 1940's when occupied by Ogilvie

Close to Nature

The quest for a more permanent country abode was soon realised in the form of an ex-gamekeeper's cottage, "Cowford Cottage," in Stanley in Perthshire, obtained for the princely rent of twelve pounds per annum plus a further one pound, fourteen shillings and tuppence to cover the annual rates bill. This des res he moved into, lock stock and barrel, on 28th May, 1940. Although the grand piano was not moved with him at this time, he did have an upright piano and his entire book collection. The premises were totally without any modern conveniences, but clearly ROC found the place utterly enchanting nonetheless, a dream come true. He made one return visit to the cottage with friends on 10th May, 1973, finding the cottage much the same as it had been when he lived there, although the surrounding young trees, which were being planted when he left, had grown considerably in the intervening thirty odd years. Fig. 8 provides a view of the cottage as it was in the 1940s.

He reflects in his writings how he first came by the cottage and describes his life there:

> 730623. My friend, Edward [Shanley], on impulse asked a colleague who had been an estate agent as to where there was an empty cottage available. He was told yes, an ex-gamekeeper cottage, but possibly too isolated. He went to see it, again on impulse, on his way to paying me a visit. I was staying in Comrie at the time. When he told me about it, I knew at once it was the right place and took it without even seeing it. When I got there a few weeks later, I felt I had come home. That house welcomed me.
>
> I soon got used to what many people would call the drawbacks—coal fire; cooking by one stove; lamps and candles for light; no water, as it all had to be carried in buckets from the spring at the foot of the hillock across the stream and, of course, the outside toilet closet. There were two sheds, one old with two small windows, the other a new washhouse with only one window in which I kept the bath. I used to shave in the scullery which had a shelf below the window. These things didn't matter. All mod cons, etc. don't necessarily make for good living. I loved that cottage. The rooms were big enough not to be cramping; it was dry and draught-free, protected by its own wood. It was snug in winter, and there was plenty of timber from fallen branches to burn and from old tree trunks discarded when the woods opposite had been cut and sawn up into logs. And the winter wind roaring through the bare branches of the trees. It was always lovely at any time of the year.
>
> I do remember, however, the very bad local flood nearby, when the cloudburst in Little Glenshee broke down the reservoir wall, and of the burn at the cottage rising quite surprisingly in flood and turning brown.
>
> I shall also never forget the one long winter when the snow

lasted from the beginning of December until the end of March, the heaviest fall of all being in the middle of March, and it never lost its dazzling whiteness. The branches of the trees and the barks were coated with frost, shimmering like jewels in the sunlight. It was an enchanted place.

Of course, I was considered mad by most of my friends to go there on my own with a serious heart condition, subject to frequent severe attacks of angina, with no possibility of getting help if needed—the nearest house was out of sight over half a mile away. But it was right, as I knew at the time. I practically never left the cottage all that time except to go down very occasionally to the nearby farm, and once to the farm over the hill opposite. I had no means of transport, and I could not walk too far, of course, because of my heart condition, though I did cover a radius of about a mile from the cottage.

I lived alone except for occasional weekend visitors. I never felt lonely. There was always plenty to do, and I had books and music, lots of time for study and thought and contemplation. After the first three years, Edward was transferred to Perth and came to live at the cottage. He was away most of the day, and quite often returned to Edinburgh at the weekend. I did a vast amount of study and reading. Drama for instance from the plays of Sophocles, Seneca, Plautinus and on through to medieval mystery plays, Greek and Spanish plays of the Golden Age of literature. Shakespeare's entire works in more of less chronological order, on to restoration plays and after, poetry and study of the sonnets of early authors, Dante, Cavalcante, Michelangelo, Petrarch, many Spanish sonnets; the English sonnets to Shakespeare, then the early Spanish novels, through to Defoe, Smollett, and Swift; a reread of the works of Aldous Huxley, one of my favourite writers, in chronological order; Dorothy Richardson, D.H. Lawrence, Proust, and so on. No, I was never bored or lonely with all the great minds within reach, though I have to admit, I had moments of depression at times, but I always felt it was the right place for me.

The last two or three years were a happy and contented time. Edward was transferred to Droitwich, so I was entirely on my own again for the last eight months.

R. Ogilvie Crombie

Towards the end of his stay at Cowford, there was much activity associated with tree planting in the region of the cottage, and ROC decided that as he was no longer afforded the same degree of privacy, it probably indicated that perhaps the time had come to make a move. ROC felt that the cottage "had served its purpose."

Albany Street, Edinburgh

The Flat

The move from Cowford Cottage back to Edinburgh took place on 17th October, 1949. ROC, still in relatively poor health, was faced with the not inconsequential task of rehabilitating his burgeoning book collection and taking up his life again in Edinburgh society.

The flat in many ways reflected the Spartan existence of his Cowford Cottage days, consisting of two main rooms, one of which, the "front room," faced onto Albany Street, and the other, the "back room," had windows facing onto the back gardens and rear of the houses in the street below, which was Barony Street. These two main rooms were separated by a small hall with an alcove piled high with old Times Literary Supplements, magazines, the old wind up gramophone for "78" records that he had had with him on *HMS Teviot* during his war service, and even pieces of string, the entire stack being neatly concealed behind a full length curtain. With the austerity of the war years, as was common practice, nothing that had any potential use was ever thrown out. Photographs of front and back rooms, taken in 1975, show some of the 5,500 books, the grand piano, and general room furnishings.

Leading off the back room was a small kitchen, which was furnished with only an ancient gas cooker and a white ceramic sink with a single tap (that only provided cold water) fed by a sagging lead pipe which snaked along the wall.

The kitchen itself doubled as a primitive washroom, with an improvised shower comprising a suspended aluminium pail with a rubber pipe leading out of it and terminating in a home-made shower head. This was surrounded by a waterproof curtain, the water draining into a movable shower base which in this case was a body length galvanised metal bath. Aficionados of Dudley Watkin's *The Broons*, a well-known comic strip published in the Scottish newspaper *The Sunday Post*, will no doubt have seen Paw Broon carrying out his Friday night ablutions in such a tub in front of the fire. This aerial shower pail had itself to be filled manually by transporting smaller buckets of water up steps and emptying them into the shower pail. On completion of the showering activity, the bath had then to be emptied by raising it to the level of the sink, using a low table as a pivotal surface, and emptied carefully into it. ROC accepted this practice willingly as a piece of daily ritual, although I am sure it would not be everybody's idea of heaven.

Fig. 9: The kitchen in the flat in Edinburgh (1975)

On very chilly occasions a warm shower was taken, but this required the additional procedure of boiling a kettle of water first and emptying it into the overhead shower pail, already half filled with cold water. Eventually I managed to persuade him to let me incorporate a kettle heating element in the shower pail and to connect a detachable filling hose to the tap, with an electronic device in the shower pail to indicate water level which could be displayed on a meter above the sink. This, and a general view of the kitchen, is shown in Fig. 9. Nonetheless, he still used this automatic heating function sparingly, much preferring the cold alternative.

Even more seriously, there was no toilet in the flat, the nearest "convenience" being located two floors below adjacent the back door to a drying green in the basement. It was somewhat akin to an outside toilet but with no actual need to leave the building to get to it. The stairs, of course, were common property to the flat above, and "paying a call" meant running the gauntlet of the omni-present spirit of the stairs, the garrulous female occupant of the top flat and her matching pair of ribbon-bedecked cairn terriers. Avoidance of this threat became paramount, and it was to be hoped that the escalating "need to go" would never reach the point of forcing the issue, only to be further exacerbated by a verbal and lengthy harangue on the way down. Being the gentleman he was, ROC politely listened to the daily outpourings, surreptitiously crossing his legs no doubt. Surprising indeed that he did not develop urinary-related problems in addition to his heart condition!

Despite the humble surroundings, ROC, like the true scholar, spent any funds he acquired on books and music. His grand piano, which took pride of place in the front room, was tuned and played very regularly. By now he was an accomplished pianist, and throughout his life was delighted to entertain his visitors to musical episodes, with gradual introductions to the more "difficult" music of Bartok and Stravinsky, his favoured composers, via the "easier" Debussy, Ravel, and Scriabin. Despite the emphasis on new age composers, the "traditional" like Beethoven and his contemporaries were not ignored in the repertoire.

Fig. 10: Part of the library in the front room of the flat in Edinburgh (1975)

The books were arranged around the walls of both the front and back rooms, and he was able to lay his hands on any desired book at will as their location had been firmly imprinted in memory. The majority of the bookshelves he had himself constructed from scrap wood from old tea chests (not the modern plywood versions but from ½" thick aromatic pine grown in some remote corner of the Empire). While some of these home-made bookshelves were stand-alone, the same wood was used to link those with an assortment of other bookcases to form continuous walls of shelves. Despite the mixture of types, when populated with books, the dominant appearance was one of homogeneity and attractiveness. The photograph in Fig. 10, taken in 1975, provides a view of the piano and some of the bookcases.

Literature, Drama and Poetry

Much of ROC's time was devoted to the arts of drama, poetry and music and to avidly collecting and studying books of every persuasion. Given his drive to acquire knowledge, it was fortunate indeed that he was blessed with a prodigious memory which served him amazingly well until the end of his days. Of the multitude of books collected, he claimed that he had read the vast majority of them and in addition could still clearly remember their contents. This capacity to remember as well as his extensive acting experience served him well in the many talks and lectures which he gave throughout this latter period of his life.

He became interim editor of the *New Athenian Broadsheet* in 1951—a publication devoted to modern poetry—and corresponded with Hugh MacDiarmid, a talented and prominent Scottish literary and political figure, about inclusion of his poem, "The Glen of Silence" in an issue of the "Broadsheet."

He resumed his involvement with the Makars, producing Love in Albania for them at the Little Theatre in the Pleasance, Edinburgh, in January 1952. This comedy, a play in three acts by Eric Linklater, received excellent newspaper reviews calling it an "unfaltering production."

In October of 1954, he went on to play the part of Gayev in Chekhov's *The Cherry Orchard* and again received warm praise by the press for his performance: "Mr Crombie merits unstinted praise for his portrayal of one of the less lucid characters in the production."

In May of the following year, he dons the part of the king's private secretary in the Makar's production of *The Apple Cart* by George Bernard Shaw, hosted at the Gateway Theatre, and this again was well received by the press.

In November of 1959, the Makars presented Noel Coward's play *Relative Values* at the Little Theatre with ROC as the producer. The following year he

R. Ogilvie Crombie

also produced with them Ionesco's plays, *The Chairs,* and *The Lesson,* which were staged in March at the Duke Street Clubrooms. ROC earns further praise from the *Evening Dispatch* for his "skill" and "ingenuity."

1961 was a particularly busy year for ROC as thespian and producer in his continuing association with the Makars. In February, this company put on Brecht's *The Good Woman of Setzuan* at the Duke Street Clubrooms, ROC taking the part of the "Third God." This is followed the following month with ROC in the title role in a production at the Gateway Theatre of *The Woodcarver*. With perfection ever ROC's aim, *The Scotsman* reviewer echoes his aspirations in this comforting accolade: "As the woodcarver, Ogilvie Crombie puts over his longing for achieving the ultimate expression of his craft." Later in June, he produces Peter Ustinov's *Romanoff and Juliet* at the Gateway, earning the following statement from the local press: "Producer Ogilvie Crombie and his cast of 13 do not disappoint."

The following year, building on his successes, ROC produced a version of Beckett's *Waiting for Godot* at the YMCA in South Saint Andrew Street, his efforts being rewarded with the comment that "Ogilvie Crombie keeps a tight grip on the production."

By 1963, his stage days were moving more towards appearances in TV and film, his closing stage performance being with the Makars in their adaptation of Mayakovsky's satirical play, *The Bedbug*, at the Traverse Theatre in February.

TV and Films

After successfully auditioning for the BBC, ROC appeared in several TV series, notable among which was *Dr Findlay's Casebook* (where he doubled, as necessary, for Dr Cameron), the series running from 1962 until 1971. In November of 1965, he has a part as an extra in the Vital Spark series in episodes entitled "A Drop O' the Real Stuff" and "Salvage." In February, 1966, he plays the part of Professor Stewart Watson in the BBC's series *This Man Craig*. 1967 also saw him as an extra in *Random Sample* and *The North Side of Ben Vorlich*.

This television activity became somewhat of a financial lifeline for ROC, as did his appearances in minor roles in film (for example, as a pedestrian in the delightful *The Battle of the Sexes*, the 1959 version with Peter Sellers and Constance Cummings). However, this intermittent work provided little consistent income, and his life then and in the future would be somewhat of a hand to mouth existence. It never apparently caused him great concern—at least he never made it obvious—as he believed that his basic needs would always be met.

Talks and Lectures

Throughout this later period of his life, ROC was also much involved in giving lectures on matters of an esoteric nature. Many of these were at Attingham Park, an adult education college near Shrewsbury administered by Sir George Trevelyan. Over the course of two years from 1969 to 1971, he gave a series of lectures at conferences which were generally held over weekends. A list of the titles shows the range of topics he addressed as he began to bring some of the fruits of his esoteric work and thought to the general public.

His most popular lecture was "The Reality of the Elemental World," first presented at a weekend course in October of 1969 on "The Frontiers of Reality"; three months later under the banner of "Youth Questing," a similar lecture was presented at Attingham, as the previous one had clearly made quite an impact on both Sir George and the audience. Then in June he returned to that college to present both "A New Vision of the Elemental World" and "Modern Music in the New Age." Finally, in 1971, the Attingham lectures continued with "The Doors of Perception" and "The Development of Awareness."

ROC was a popular lecturer. He could speak on esoteric subjects such as the subtle worlds and the inner kingdoms of nature with authority from personal experience, and his stage training allowed him to give his presentations an eloquence and drama that captivated audiences. At the same time, his essential humility and grandfatherly appearance deflected any glamour that might otherwise have attached to him. He made the extraordinary seem ordinary, and audiences loved him.

For this reason, as well as for the personal friendship that had grown up between ROC and Sir George Trevelyan, when the latter retired from Attingham College in 1971 and set up the Wrekin Trust to continue offering conferences on spiritual and esoteric themes, he made sure to invite ROC to continue his lecturing. The Wrekin Trust organised large annual gatherings, and from 1972 until 1974, ROC appeared at each one, giving the following lectures: "Man's Relationship with the Nature Kingdoms," "The Heightening of Sensitivity" and finally "The Elemental Worlds of Nature." After 1974, the deterioration of his health due to heart problems prevented any further participation in these yearly conferences.

Most of ROC's public talks, however, were given at the Findhorn community in Morayshire, Scotland, a place to which ROC often resorted. His numerous talks there covered a range of topics in music, art, and spirituality. Some of these have been published by Findhorn Press, in particular in a book titled *The Gentleman and the Faun*, later published in North America as *Meeting Fairies*.

Health

During the latter part of 1974, ROC's heart problems resurfaced and began to impede his activities. As he records:

> 741012. Jocelyn [Ross] brought me to Killin on Saturday. The activities at Findhorn had been so intense that I was really glad to get away. Very good journey back, visiting Randolph's Leap on the way. The autumn colourings were beautiful. We did not reach Killin until after dark.
>
> I suppose it was reaction from the busy fortnight that I felt unusually tired, and my heart was racing badly. I did not sleep well, the pounding heart being accompanied by severe breathlessness. I had to sit up a good part of the night. All Sunday, my heart continued to race, and through Sunday night.

ROC returned to the Edinburgh flat from Killin six days later. His heart condition continued to worsen over the coming months. Because of this, and worries about having perhaps to find somewhere else to live (the renting agency wanted to carry out redevelopment of the property at Albany Street, and had people in measuring up the flat in December), he decided to accept the invitation of Peggy Balfour to spend some time at her home in St. Boswells, located in the Scottish Borders. He therefore moved there on 9th January, 1975. His health, however, did not improve, and his daily diary entries showed a progressive decline taking place. As can be seen from the following entry, death clearly held no fears for him:

> 750116. Very bad night. Sat in chair until 2am, but was sick until 1am. Went to bed, but had to get up. Heart behaving very strangely. Sat up in the dark until 3am, then in chair. Lay down again. Very strange dreams which I cannot remember, but which had some meaning. A strong feeling I might die before morning. Not important—ready to go when my time is up.

He requested a visit from a retired female doctor friend from Edinburgh, and I collected her on 23rd February and ran her down to St. Boswells. She seemed to show little professional interest in ROC's condition and apparently made no examination of him at all, although by this time he was showing very obvious signs of oedema which had caused swelling of his legs and feet. ROC, to say the least, was extremely disappointed at her cursory approach. She said she did not have her instruments with her for carrying out tests and simply prescribed Librium and iron pills, the latter making ROC violently sick.

He considered that he might receive better medical help at Killin, as Jocelyn Ross had two friends living nearby who were qualified in both conventional and homeopathic medicine. Jocelyn accordingly collected ROC from St. Boswells on 26th February.

Despite ceaseless attention from all three at all times of the day and night, his situation continued to worsen and reached its climax on the 5th March. By the following day, however, ROC appeared to have recovered considerably and was very cheerful. Despite some vomiting of blood, his outlook appeared much improved.

On Saturday, 8th March, his caregivers had been with him until 2.30 am. Before retiring, Jocelyn said: "If there's anything you want, just ring the bell," to which ROC replied, "Yes, I'll toll the bell'. Jokingly but prophetically, Jocelyn answered, "For whom the bell tolls."

ROC passed over some three and half hours later peacefully in his sleep at approximately 6 am in the morning. Jocelyn reported that his death was followed by some freak weather conditions: a fall of snow, followed by driving rain and then brilliant sunshine—all in rapid succession.

It appears that ROC's psychic friend, Maisie, had had a vision or dream around the 5th March, some three days before ROC's death, in which she saw a framed picture of him drop from the wall, with the glass shattering when it hit the floor but the frame remaining intact. The meaning of that particular dream is certainly not obscure.

Funeral arrangements were made, and the following obituary appeared in *The Scotsman* on 10th March.

> At High Creagan, Killin, on Saturday March 8th 1975, after a short illness, Robert Ogilvie Crombie of 28 Albany Street, Edinburgh. Funeral service at Mortonhall Crematorium (Pentland Chapel) on Tuesday 11th March at 12.15.

It was suggested that ROC's friend from Attingham and the Wrekin Trust,

R. Ogilvie Crombie

Sir George Trevelyan, might be an appropriate choice for taking the funeral service. Sir George was famous for his erudition and lyrical eloquence as a speaker. When approached, he was delighted to accept the role. Clearly, given ROC's unusual life, the traditional religious presenter would undoubtedly have been a bit out of place!

The service went off without a hitch, and Sir George delivered one of his usual stunning speeches, one of thanksgiving for a life well spent. He quoted extensively from sections of Tolkein's *Lord of the Rings,* with ROC portrayed as the Gandalf figure, and from Bunyan's *Pilgrims Progress*:

> Then said he, "I am going to my Father's; and though with great difficulty I have got hither, yet now I do not repent me of all the troubles I have been at, to arrive where I am. My sword I give to him that shall succeed me in my pilgrimage, and my courage and skill to him that can get it. My marks and scars I carry with me, to be a witness for me that I have fought his battles, who now will be my rewarder."
>
> When the day that he must go hence was come, many accompanied him to the river-side, into which, as he went, he said: "Death, where is thy sting?" and as he went down deeper, he said, "Grave, where is thy victory?"
>
> So he passed over, and all the trumpets sounded for him on the other side.

The Occult Diaries of

Chapter 2
Jungian Dream Sequences

ROC had an abundance of meaningful dreams and visions over many years and recorded almost 900 of them which would, on their own, fill an entire book. At present, the vast bulk of these records remain untranscribed in ROC's nearly indecipherable handwriting. Many of these dreams, especially the early ones, illustrated the Jungian process of integration, the coming to terms with the shadow, and the interaction with the various archetypes of the unconscious. (Should my reader wish to further his knowledge in this area, Jung's fascinating book, *Memories, Dreams and Reflections* makes an excellent and readable introduction to the subject).

ROC was, like you and I, a human being who displayed all the very normal characteristics and emotions of the physical ego and who was subject to all its varieties of temptations. He often felt that he was quite unworthy of the inner work that he believed he was called upon to do. Throughout his life, the progress of coming to terms with the self was mirrored in many of his dreams, as shown below, and this path to integration, a term Jung uses to describe the process, can clearly be discerned. These illustrations are valuable to us and perhaps emphasise the importance we should pay to our dreams and to seeking the meaning concealed within them.

The following dream embodies many of the elements of Jungian symbolism and represents the inter-relationship between the conscious ego and the unconscious.

> 640403. I am in a strangely shaped room, an irregular octagon about twenty feet across. The ceiling, too, is a series of planes at odd angles. The walls and ceilings are brownish grey. It has one window; this room is in a very strangely shaped house. It is very high—six or seven stories high, and one mass of odd accretions and turrets. Somehow I know this in the dream as I am familiar with it. From the window I can see a higher storey to the side of the house with a lighthouse-like room. This room has a dome-shaped roof and many windows. It is festooned inside with yellow electric bulbs which are lit, though it is daylight. There is a woman with me in the room I am in. I cannot see her or describe her, but I sense her presence, either in the room itself or in the house. She is worried, the lights in the turret room must remain lit at all costs and she is afraid of a power cut.

Outside the window there is a curious lead covered projection—not quite a dome, as it is flat on top. A voice says — "No, there really is no need for a railing; after all it isn't very far to the ground." I crawl out of the window onto the lead covered platform and look over the edge. The ground is far below but I have no sense of giddiness. I see more of the odd shape of the house—all bulges, domes, turrets and oddly projecting windows. I crawl back into the room.

Sources: The strange shaped house may be due to reading about Jung's curious house at Bolingen; fear of lights going out, to a threatened "work to rule" at the Portobello power station which might lead to power cuts; lead covered domes etc, a memory of Braid Crescent with the lead covered roof projection outside my study window and the curious lead or zinc domes over the drawing-room windows, opposite. Crawling out onto the roof I had frequently done when fixing radio aerials.

Interpretation: A highly significant dream. The strange odd shaped house is my whole self, the domes, turrets etc being various accretions of knowledge and experience I have gathered in my life time. The octagonal room is my conscious self (ego). From it I can sense and see the rest of the building. The high lighthouse-like room is the spiritual or higher self, radiating golden light. (cf. The Secret of the Golden Flower, translated by Richard Wilhelm, commentary by Jung). The light is kept burning by the activity of the whole Self, and it is of the highest importance that the light be kept burning. The unseen but sensed woman is the Anima. The crawling out onto the roof and looking down to the ground and the lower storeys without giddiness, and the voice saying there is really no need of a railing, I take to mean that I can safely try to establish contact with the unconscious in the lower depths right down to the ground.

While the above is a clear example of a dream, the following illustrates a combined vision/dream sequence. It begins with a vision in which the world is viewed at an early stage in its evolution, portraying it prior to the emergence of life.

The vision moves into a dream with 20th Century elements but finally reverts to a vision. As above, ROC proceeds to analyse this vision / dream.

R. Ogilvie Crombie

640407. I am in a very strange place unlike anything I have ever seen and difficult to describe. It is a sea shore though the sea is some distance away. There is a beach of sand and many rocks, none of which are very big. It is of vast extent, and the line of the sea is straight. The colouring which is very striking and intense is mainly in shades of brown, from sand colour to a dark reddish brown of some of the rocks. There is no sign of vegetation of any kind. The sea is dark and the sky overcast. Yet, in spite of an apparent utter desolation, there is a feeling of complete serenity. I have the feeling that this is the world before any life appeared on it - calm, serene, timeless. The sense of timelessness is very strong. I am naked, which seems right as clothes would be an anachronism, but I am hardly aware of my body. I seem to be both myself and not myself. In other words I am aware that my conscious self is only a part of something much greater which lies behind material reality. I feel very conscious of this whole Self and am aware also of being part of the Mind behind the whole of creation. The stillness and timelessness give this extraordinary feeling of serenity and peace.

I am now aware of an immense pillar of rock—reddish brown, which has risen from the ground some distance in front of me. It is a phallus, slightly curved and almost an exact replica of a penis [c.f. Jung's description of a similar vision that he had]. As I watch, it becomes perfectly straight, and the shape changes from round to square, and then two arms appear, turning it into a cross. At the same moment, the sky clears and glows with a dazzling orange light behind the cross. The sea turns a brilliant blue, and the whole landscape glows with light that is almost blinding. I have never seen light and colours like this in a dream before that I can remember. The cross rises into the air and rapidly moves away from me into the glowing sky and vanishes.

The landscape begins to change. The sea disappears and mountains spring up all around, but still leaving a vast sandy plain in the centre. The sky remains an orange-yellow and very bright. In the centre of the sandy plain—which although a desert, still radiates serenity—there appears a vast trilithon (two standing pillars of stone with a third across the top) built from reddish-brown blocks of stone of vast size. Though this is now evidence of mankind, there are no signs of life. The trilithon slowly changes shape and turns into a perfect ring of stone. The mountains grow higher, and I seem to rise above them into the sky so that I am looking down on a vast awe-inspiring landscape of mountains and valleys. I find myself on top of one of the mountains looking down into a deep valley. The predominant colours remain shades of brown and the feeling of serenity and timelessness persists.

The landscape begins to fade and I become aware of music. It is a Salvation Army band, and I find myself in the drawing room of the old house at Braid Crescent. I go to the window but can see no sign of the band, though the music continues. The street outside is like Albany Street, not Braid Crescent. The music changes to modern dance music, and I think some people opposite must be having a party. I look across the street and can see people dancing in a room further to the left. The window is open, and two people, a man and a girl, are sitting at either side of the window with their backs to it. I think it is time for me to go upstairs (Braid Crescent again). I leave the room and go into the adjoining bathroom to wash my hands. This washing seems to be a ritual. A voice said "The power of the phallus can never die." I go upstairs to my study and look out of the window (at Braid Crescent). I can see over the roof tops opposite, and I seem to rise into the air as I can see over the entire city.

As I watch, the scene melts into the one I saw at the beginning of the dream. I am once more aware of the serenity and timelessness, in spite of the apparent desolation of the scene, and aware of my complete Self—this seems to be ever-present.

The dream is so vivid that it will never fade and be forgotten.

ROC's comments: Very significant and more of vision than a dream. The landscape is completely strange and unknown, and I am sure is based on nothing I have ever seen. The serenity and the timelessness are significant and the feeling of being more than my conscious self. This might suggest a further degree of integration of the personality, as does the feeling of a link with the divine ground.

The nudity suggests the interesting speculation that this was an out-of-the-body experience and a vision. Occult teaching tells us that to find oneself naked in a dream may mean astral projection. The phallus is probably the most fundamental archetypal symbol of creation and therefore of God himself.

There is a suggestion of early creation in the first part of the dream. As the cross originally may have developed out of such a symbol, the transformation is what might have been expected. The orange glow, and the exaltation of the cross are further evidence of the divinity behind the symbols. The change in the landscape is suggestive of the evolution of the earth—the formation of the mountains and so on. The barrenness of the landscapes, which yet had serenity, might be to show that divinity is there behind the most forbidding scene. The trilithon is another religious symbol of very great age, and it turns into the unending circle, the fundamental symbol for eternity—the snake swallowing its own tail.

After the trip over the mountains and valleys comes the sudden intrusion of the twentieth century with the Salvation Army band. This associates with Braid Crescent and the drawing room of the old house, as I remember an occasion when I was extremely annoyed by such a band which struck up, complete with big drum, side drum and tambourines, just outside the house, as I was listening to a broadcast of a piece of contemporary music I was most anxious to hear, completely spoiling it. The dance music and the street outside being Albany Street, belong to the present. The students in a flat opposite often have dances and keep the windows open.

Going up to the top flat, and seeing right over the town, must have deep significance. It parallels the seeing over the mountainous landscape.

The main pattern that is already emerging from my dreams is that now and then amongst the less significant dreams which seem to be synthesised from a large variety of past experiences, there is the significant dream—or more probably, vision—which is undoubtedly significant. It may be symbolical with a definite communication from the universal unconscious, or it may be coming from "outside" (what Aldous Huxley calls "Given").

I am undoubtedly meeting personified Jungian archetypal figures in my dreams. I believe this study to be important as bringing about a further stage in the integration of my personality.

The Occult Diaries of

On the basis of the following dream and vision, the integration of the archetypal "shadow" discussed above is now seen to be complete. The symbolism is somewhat easier to understand here:

> 640426. I am walking along a shore somewhat similar to the one in the previous dream (7th April). The colouring is much the same and there is no sign of life. There is the same serenity and sense of timelessness. I am naked. I am now on the top of a mountain with a wonderful panorama of mountain ranges and valleys.
>
> I am back on the shore but this time I have a companion—the dark haired young man who keeps appearing in my dreams and who I now know to be the "shadow." He puts his arm round my shoulder as we walk along the shore. We stop walking, and he turns towards me, and with his other hand pulls me round to face him. He looks right into my eyes and says "We really do understand each other now." He smiles and we walk on.
>
> Suddenly he melts into me and we become one person.
>
> ROC's comments: This seems to belong to the type of depth dream that is or borders on a vision. I was awake when this "dream" started. I was vividly aware of the shore belonging to a different plane of existence. At the same time I was aware of lying in my bed in my room, as if the other plane was being superimposed on the physical plane. I became less and less aware of the physical plane as I entered more fully into the other one. Sea shores and heights seem to be recurrent themes in my dreams. Here again I find myself naked in a dream—possible suggestion of out-of-the-body travel. Nudity in this way never seems to be out of place or embarrassing but is perfectly natural and right. It is important, as it suggests one is one's natural self, unadorned and uncontaminated by clothes which are artificial and belong to the physical material world.
>
> I have no doubt at all that the companion is my "Shadow" and that the merging into one person after his significant words indicates that I have come to terms with him and am now completely integrated. I doubt if he will continue to appear in my dreams except occasionally but certainly no longer as the enemy. In my waking life there has been no trace recently of my projecting the shadow on to other people, which is most satisfactory.

R. Ogilvie Crombie

The following is the last dream sequence I would like to present and rounds off the Jungian integration theme. To accept our visions (or dreams) literally will generally be totally unacceptable, but it would seem that they may well embody some meaningful underlying message. Interpretation of the symbolism then becomes all-important:

640501. I am by the sea, not the sea of my previous dreams, but a rocky coast. The sea is very dark. There is an island opposite and I know that I have to get to it. There is someone with me—an elderly man. A very flimsy boat is brought into the shore.

My companion objects to it. "We can't go in that," he says, "because of the crocodiles." To which I reply "Nonsense, there is only one crocodile and he is harmless; he is much too lazy to attack anybody." I am about to get into the boat when the distance between the shore and the island begins to lessen. The shore seems to be floating over towards the island until the boat is left almost on dry land bridging what is left of the water between. I cross it and am helped up the fairly steep shore of the island by a dark haired young man. The elderly man seems to have gone. The island is hilly and is not very large. We climb up by a path rounding a hillock and come into a slight depression overlooking the open sea. My new companion sits down and indicates to me to do the same. I look at the ground. It is very damp so I refuse to sit. The young man looks at me with a grin. "Of course, if you're afraid of the damp." He shrugs his shoulders, rises and we walk on.

Comments: I am planning to go to Dirleton [near North Berwick] today and this may be an anticipation. The island could be Fidra or one of the other nearby islands. There is also a memory of the *Kidnapped* B.B.C. episode at Oban. The flimsy boat is the one we had to get into there, which was a crossing from an island to the mainland. The crocodile is a mystery, though recently in some B.B.C. programme someone said something about crocodiles being lazy. The shore and island approaching each other is the sort of thing that does happen in dreams. The dark young man is almost certainly again the shadow and as he is helping me, this is another indication of the reconciliation that has taken place. The closing in of the island and the shore could symbolise the much greater ease in making contact with the unconscious. (Meditation on this dream has brought out that the shore was a floating island whereas the island was the peak of an underwater mountain growing up from the earth). So this must be the case, especially with the shadow there to help. His sitting on the damp ground and wanting me to do so too, indicates that he may still want to do things I would not want to do. But his good natured acceptance of my refusal indicates the degree of liaison now existing between us. It is interesting that the upward climbing motive is present.

R. Ogilvie Crombie

Chapter 3
Supranormal Abilities

The Psychic Element

As can be seen from the following examples, ROC possessed many of the abilities usually associated with gifted psychics. Some of these incidents involved others and some myself and my family. The sketches are mainly anecdotal, of course, but taken together they are fairly convincing, especially when it happens to oneself.

Migraine

This particular event I am never likely to forget. My work as a materials engineer in Ferranti involved a considerable amount of microscopic examination which often triggered a migraine attack. At that particular period of my life, these migraines were recurring every three or four days; one would just be clearing up when the next one arrived.

My migraines were, I thought, a wee bit special. They would start with the optical effects that many sufferers experience of coloured flashing "jaggies" at the periphery of the visual field. In addition to this, I would find that anything I looked at directly was immediately greyed out, although the peripheral vision seemed clear enough. The natural tendency was therefore to swing my gaze to these clear areas, but as soon as they came into my line of sight, they were likewise occluded. A little after the onset of the visual effects, I would then get a band of numbness starting in the left hand. It would progressively work its way up the left arm and shoulder, across the mouth (a most strange sensation), and then carry on down the right shoulder and arm, ending in the right hand. These effects would gradually subside and give way to the traditional nauseating headache.

As I have mentioned earlier, my route home in the evening from work passed by ROC's abode, and as usual I called in. I now cannot remember the exact date, but the year would be about 1970. After chatting for a while, I rose to continue my journey home, only to find the migraine effects beginning. As it is impossible to drive safely in this condition, I asked ROC if I could sit for a while longer until the "opticals" had passed.

At this point he said that although he believed it was not his function in life to be a healer, if I was willing, he would "see what he could do." I remonstrated that I had tried all the usual remedies and really thought he was wasting his time. Undaunted, he stood behind where I was sitting and placed his hands over but not in contact with my head. I was still objecting and pointing out that he was wasting his time. He politely told me to stop resisting, cease arguing, keep quiet, and sit still. After a few moments he said, "I am aware of a sort of knot in your brain which appears as though it may be causing the problem. I will see if I can undo it." In spite of his apparent confidence, I was still mentally arguing the point with myself as fundamentally I sincerely doubted if he could accomplish anything positive.

By this time the numbness had just reached my mouth with the next expected stage that of moving onto and down my right arm. But incredibly, the numbness not only stopped in its tracks but started to dissipate. This really did put a dent in my belief system, or perhaps I should say, my unbelief. But still, ever the scientist, I thought, yes, this is all very well, just a bit of serendipity, but give it another couple of days, and the migraine will be back with a vengeance, no doubt with strength redoubled.

But that was it. Gone. I never had another migraine attack for a further twenty five years. After that, I did get, and still do get, the very occasional one maybe every five or six months, but while these are accompanied by some of the visual effects, no numbness conditions have ever reappeared.

Strangely, ROC did not seem the least bit surprised at his cure or made anything of his ability to do so. It is not even hinted at in his notes. I often wondered afterwards that if he claimed that his earthly mission was not as a healer, how much more effective he might be at what he did consider to be his "mission." I concluded after this that this person could indeed have hidden depths.

Illustrious Doctors

While the above happened directly to me, and the effect was undeniable and remarkable in its immediacy, ROC's influence was also apparent on other members of my family. In 1970, my wife, Jean, was in hospital awaiting the birth of our second child, David. There were complications, as said child, by now a chunky nine pounds weight, seemed very reluctant to make his way into the world. In addition he was in the awkward 'breach' position. There was still no baby appearance in the next few days, and we were becoming increasingly concerned at the prolonged non-event. I asked ROC if he could do anything to help the situation on a psychic level, and the following day when I visited Jean, she said, "A funny thing happened last night. I was lying in a somewhat dreamy state, but definitely not asleep, and gradually became

R. Ogilvie Crombie

aware of four figures standing round me and looking intently at me. I was a bit startled, to say the least, but nonetheless didn't feel afraid. I actually felt very comforted and reassured in their presence, and I somehow got the feeling that they were doctors. But," she said, "they were not dressed in up-to-date doctor's apparel, but were wearing suits and ties and appeared old." She did not have the feeling that this was a dream. The net outcome was that David was born without further mishap a few days later.

Interestingly, Jean has never been aware of spirit presences either before or after that event. As described below (through a channelling from the medium Albert Best), it was indicated to ROC that although he might not be aware of it, he was engaged during out-of-body travel in healing missions with a small team of other-world doctors. Were these Jean's suit- and tie-wearing apparitions?

Dreams and Precognition

ROC had this dream in late 1965. At this time, my wife and I were resident in Glasgow and had not yet moved to the Nervelstone farm steading in North Ayrshire. We had not even considered moving at that stage nor, in fact, had I ever met ROC at that point.

Fig. 11: The pool at Nervelstone

When we did eventually take up residence there in February 1967, I soon discovered a pool near our new home which had a waterfall cascading into it. I bathed in this pool almost daily.

ROC attempts to find some meaning for the dream at that time, but only later on re-reading it in 1971 does he suspect the significance and that the dream might have been a precognitive one.

> 651207. I am in an odd kind of stone built house. It seems to be part of a ruin. There are a number of people about.
>
> In the basement is a pool; it is irregular in shape—an outdoor rock pool, about twenty five feet across, with not very high cliffs with trees on top and a waterfall pouring down into it. Young man—unknown to me—is swimming in it.
>
> I am now in it myself; it takes me almost up to the neck. The water is pleasantly warm and brownish in colour. There are odd objects barely discernible on the bottom.
>
> Comment: I was talking to someone recently about how dirty the river Almond is, and yet boys were bathing in it last time I was there. There may be a mix up here of this river, and the old Roman fort on its bank near the falls. There could also be a memory of the River Isla in spate and its brown colour. In the dream there was no thought of the water being dirty, rather the brown peaty colour of highland rivers. Possibly the "pool" symbolises the unconscious and the objects in it, dimly discerned, things in the depths of the unconscious.
>
> Note: (March 1972). About a year ago on re-reading this dream I suddenly realised it could have been a pre-cognitive one. The pool in the dream was very like the pool in the river at Nervelstone, where Gordon and Jean Lindsay were living at the time I met them. (October 21st, 1967). I think it probable that the young man in the pool was Gordon.

The pool was of such a depth that it did in fact come up to about neck height, and "objects, barely discernible" there certainly were, as it was strewn with large stones and boulders which were largely obscured from view by the intensity of colour of the brown water. In summer the water did become pleasantly warm. The size he gives and the presence of the surrounding cliffs topped by trees are also accurate.

R. Ogilvie Crombie

Crocuses

One further unusual experience I think is worth recording here, as again I was involved and can vouch for the truth of it. The Nervelstone house where we lived for a time was the steading portion of the main complex. It was a two storey building comprising in the downstairs section a kitchen, bathroom and living room, with two bedrooms upstairs, one used for ourselves, the other for visitors. The steading was sandwiched between, on one side, a large byre (unused, as there were now no farming activities of that nature being carried on), and, on the other, the "Big House" where the owners of the property lived.

On occasions, ROC had visited and stayed with us in our country abode, occupying the upstairs visitor's bedroom. On this occasion he had arrived on Friday 15th March, 1968. Both bedrooms overlooked the manicured lawns of the adjoining "Big House" and thence over contiguous fields. I was idly gazing out of the bedroom windows and noticed hosts of crocuses on the grass. I was surprised because there had been no sign of them days before. I mentioned this to ROC, and we both stood at the window, commenting how nice they looked. They really graced the lawn:

> 680320. Nervelstone. Vision of crocuses seen by Gordon and myself round tree in field opposite. Later found not to be there. These were seen from the bedroom I was using after Gordon returned from Kilbirnie 9.20am. I saw them clearly—clumps of purple and white crocuses the same as those in the lawn of the house (next door). I did have a fleeting thought that it might be an illusion due to small flakes of snow, but there was no snow on the ground within sight, except a thin line under the hedge at the far side of the field to the left. The purple colour was very strong, and I could see the stems and leaves of the flowers so I felt certain they were really there.

I thought no more about it for a couple of days and then decided it would be well worth recording the crocuses before they all withered. I put some 35mm film in the camera and went outside to record the spectacular display in the lawn of the house next door and round the tree in the adjacent field. However, there were absolutely no crocuses to be seen anywhere, in lawn or field. In fact, there was not the slightest indication, such as withered stems, that they had ever been there at all. I was really puzzled:

> 680322. Nervelstone. Gordon went to see if the crocuses in the field were photographical and found there were none there! I felt certain I had seen clumps of crocuses, and so had he. The illusion was very real indeed, and I believe this was a kind of vision, quite probably given to Gordon to show that he could "see" things that were not really there. He was convinced he had seen real flowers and yet was doubting.

Truly, I had been complaining that I had no sensitivity to the "finer" worlds. Alas, this still remains the situation, and I feel rooted in an all too-physical world.

Card Tricks

This instance relates to a card "guessing" experiment, the result being that ROC already knew the card that would be drawn in advance of it happening:

> 631230. Robin and I arranged a spoof E.S.P. experiment for tonight. He was to get one of his friends to draw a card and then phone me. By means of a prearranged code, Robin, who rang the number, gave me the card which I named to his friend David.
> About 8.30, before the card was even drawn, I had a persistent feeling that it was going to be the ten of hearts. At 8.45 I wrote it down and, in order to have a witness, I phoned Nell at 9.10 and gave her the name of the card—ten of hearts. At about 9.20 Robin phoned, and, to my complete astonishment, the code gave the ten of hearts, so I asked David to phone Nell immediately he rang off and to ask what the card was, giving him her phone number. This was either pure chance 52 to 1 or E.S.P. in truth stepping in to confound us. I got the card before it was drawn, so if not pure chance, it must have been precognition or psycho-kinesis—my mind in some way exerting an influence on the drawer of the card.

Dowsing

A further example I would like to present is one surrounding the ability to dowse using rods or a pendulum for finding the position and depth of underground pipes, springs and water courses. The technique is also equally applicable to discovering the nature, position, and depth of minerals below ground. This facility is possessed by a number of individuals, and interesting claims have also been made that by simply holding a pendulum over a map of the area of interest, the pendulum will start swinging or rotating when it is over the relevant area. These examples are brief. Given the copious notes on just about everything else, one comes away with the feeling that ROC treats the topic as of being of minor importance: sort of "Dowsing, hmmm, no big deal." I have tried dowsing on a few occasions and completely lack any ability whatsoever!

> 670917. Findhorn. At lunch time, Ross Stewart talked about, and demonstrated dowsing. Found I could do it both with a whalebone rod and with two right angle bent wires. Could get approximate depth by tapping foot, each tap representing one foot.

> 691104. Findhorn. Peter came to tell me that the foreman of a gang working on the road is a dowser, and has rods with him—would I like to try? Leonard had started talking to the man and somehow the conversation got on to finding pipes, and dowsing, and the man said he used rods and produced them; a couple of 1/8 inch brass rods inside metal pipes, that are an easy fit. They can be held easily in the closed fists, parallel to each other, one slightly higher than the other. Walking slowly and steadily, the rods swing in over a pipe. I tried it, and they swung over two pipes which both the foreman and Leonard had found before I joined them.

> 700111. London. Later tried dowsing with Karl's pendulum in the garden for a spring they believe is there. Found a spot in the centre of the garden; traced the course of the stream diagonally across the garden from left, by the corner of the house, to right.

Train

Another instance of "prompting" occurred when ROC was making a trip by train to Attingham from Edinburgh's Waverley station to deliver a lecture there on "The Reality of the Elemental World." He knew that two of his friends, Armine and Lizzie, would also be on the train, but due to the timing of their connecting train, he would not have been able to meet them:

> 691229. Edinburgh. Arrived at Waverley station by 10.15. There was already a queue for entrance to the platform, so it was fairly obvious that the train was going to be very full. For a moment, I regretted that I had not booked a seat. However, I walked down the platform to the New Street end of the train, then turned and walked straight back to a carriage and into a compartment second from the front end. There was an empty, corridor side, corner seat, facing the engine, but the window side was reserved. A clergyman was sitting in the opposite one. Armine and Lizzie's train was not due until 10.20, therefore it would be difficult to meet them. Then I suddenly knew the reserved seats were for them. I went and looked at the tickets and saw that they were both for Crewe and had been booked from Aberdeen, so I was certain. About 5 minutes before leaving, they arrived and were astonished and pleased to find me in their compartment. I changed seats with the man next me. The carriage was absolutely full.

Chapter 4
Who was ROC?

Spiritual "Paternity"

By posing this question, I suppose I am really asking "Who is ROC?" Not the man by the name of Ogilvie Crombie whom we have previously met, but the eternal part of him: his soul identity or higher self. As ROC is no longer with us, there is no way we can use the standard procedures that Newton and others apply to LBL investigations by having him hypnotised and simply asking what his eternal name is, what soul colour does he sport (which would show his degree of spiritual evolution), and who was he historically in previous incarnation, information apparently easily elicited from you and me when under deep hypnosis. In the space of a mere half an hour or so, we could have all the answers we need. Knowing ROC as I do, I seriously doubt if he would have subjected himself to hypnosis anyway. In any case, he really would not need to, as he already had a pretty sound inside track furnishing most of the clues.

These clues came to him as a result of his high degree of psychic sensitivity to the finer worlds. While he was interested and intrigued with the beings appearing to him, he remained coolly analytical of what he was seeing and hearing. Interestingly, he was not inquisitive. He did not pursue contacts; they came to him, and in surprising guises and numbers.

One of these contacts, the one pertinent to the question we have posed, "arrived" with Peter Caddy, the founder of the Findhorn Community, when he visited ROC in the closing days of 1965. In ROC's words:

> 651229. Peter Caddy arrived at 5.50. During his visit, sitting in the front room here, I was aware of a tall figure in a long cloak standing slightly to the left hand side of Peter who was sitting in the armchair with its back to the window. The curtains were drawn and the lights on as it was dark. I had no idea who this being was and could get no communication, though there was a strong feeling of familiarity. In some way or other I knew this man well. At one point in our talk, Peter mentioned Saint Germain who he said over-lighted himself and Findhorn. As he did so the figure pointed to himself and bowed.
>
> Since then this Being has been present in the flat quite often. I see him as a fairly tall, roundish faced man dressed in 18th

century clothes—black knee breeches, black stockings and shoes with silver buckles on them. He wears an ornate green brocade pointed waistcoat with yellow and black designs; a skirted jacket of purple with gold and black patterns. On his head is a light grey wig with side curls and a little pigtail at the back tied with a black bow. As a rule, but not always, he wears a long black cloak lined with red hanging from his shoulders and carries a black three-cornered hat.

I know very little about Monsieur le Comte de Saint Germain. I have come across references to him from time to time in my reading, often derogatory, dismissing him as a charlatan which somehow seemed wrong to me. I had also heard about a movement called "I AM" which was started in America and spread to this country, which had a connection with him. A friend of mine in Edinburgh belonged to it. I had not been impressed by what he told me about it.

Peter had told me that Saint Germain was one of what was called the "Hierarchy"—the Cosmic Masters. He was also known as the Master R. (Prince Rakoczi). He was the Master of the Seventh Ray—whatever that is! I have not read much of Madame Blavatsky, in spite of my theosophical friends, nor of Alice Bailey. I must find out more about my mysterious visitor. Why this strong feeling of familiarity? Who is this Being and why show himself to me? In what way am I linked with him?

While St. Germain's arrival was co-incident with that of Peter's, his departure was certainly not. Throughout the coming weeks and months, his closeness to ROC increased. ROC, however, still challenged his identity and the authenticity of the messages that were being channelled through him. During a visit to Findhorn almost nine months later, St. Germain was clearly getting a little impatient with ROC's continued doubts:

> 660824a. Surely you were satisfied that I had proved my identity on the shore on Monday, just as I tested your suitability as a channel to take over and work through. Of course it is right for you to continually question the authenticity of the material you receive, but do not hinder it from coming through; set up no barriers. Question afterwards, if you feel you must and not while it is coming through as you were trying to do tonight. I

am St. Germain [underlined in hand written script], of that you must have no doubt. There may well be times such as yesterday when what I have to say must come through with conviction. You must accept it, however strange, however at variance with your own ideas and convictions. In fact, while acting as a channel, you must have no ideas and convictions. These must be totally suspended for the time being so as to allow a free flow of what I am giving you. Opinions of people and feelings for people must also go for the time being. The personality must abdicate. This is much to ask, and you must be certain that I am the one I claim to be before you can submit so utterly. But it is required of you in order to fulfil the role you are called upon to play. You cannot turn back now. I know you believe in me, and I rely on you to comply exactly with your directions.

A month later ROC's acceptance level of St. Germain had clearly been sufficiently raised:

660926b. One of the very necessary things was to build up your complete and absolute faith in my identity. This I now know to have been achieved. Not a shred of doubt remains.

Over these last nine months, ROC has gradually become aware that St. Germain bears a close relationship to himself. He is aware that this presence overlights him as he does Peter Caddy. But ROC also is realising that St. Germain may in fact be his higher self. Less than a year later, a communication through ROC from a group referring to itself as "The Hierarchy" [perhaps the Elders that the LBL investigators mention?] offers further confirmation that St. Germain is ROC's higher self. At this time, St. Germain is presented as a discrete figure apart from ROC acting in an overlighting role but with the capacity to integrate more fully when necessary:

670711a. You are being used in out-of-the-body travel in your etheric body which is the counterpart of your physical one, as a representative human being. The one who overlights you—St. Germain—and who takes you over at times is not doing so or making himself known to the beings you are contacting until they have accepted you as you are.

In a later script still, almost three years later, St. Germain comments on the ongoing process of integration, and ROC subsequently finds random memories of St. Germain's life beginning to surface:

> 700812. Findhorn. At morning session, St. Germain, standing behind me, placed his hands on my shoulders and said I must not dodge the responsibility of who I am. False modesty is out of place. There is no fear of feeling self important. We are one; he is me, and I am him. I will be less aware of him outside of myself—he is within. This is identification. I was aware of great power and of his presence within me.
>
> I felt very strange when I returned to the caravan and began to have brief memories, very elusive and difficult to grasp, of Paris in the time of Louis 14th, of events during the life of Louis 15th, and Madame de Pompadour; of Marie Antoinette and the French revolution; a feeling of Vienna and also of Catherine the Great in Russia; then awareness of being Auriolis playing Hamlet. This is producing strange physical feelings.

And a few days later:

> 700815. Findhorn. Still very much aware of St. Germain and of that aspect or part of him which is, I presume, my higher self. A much higher degree of integration and stabilisation [is occurring]. The memories are not so running into each other as they were, but are still fleeting or elusive. I have a desire to take snuff. St. Germain must have been a very fastidious person.

In the library area in the buildings of the Findhorn Foundation, there hangs a picture of St. Germain, housed in an oval frame (shown in Fig. 12). The origin of the painting, its arrival in Findhorn, and the dual importance to both Peter Caddy, the early founder of the community, and ROC himself is fascinating.

R. Ogilvie Crombie

Fig. 12: Painting in the Findhorn Foundation of St Germain

In his early days of spiritual seeking, Peter developed connections with the Rosicrucians, in particular with a group called the "Rosicrucian Order

The Occult Diaries of

Crotona Fellowship" set up and led by one George Alexander Sullivan (1890-1942) in Liverpool. In 1936 the group moved to premises in Christchurch. Peter became a disciple of Sullivan, known to his followers as "Auriolis," and in his sanctuary at Christchurch there hung this portrait of St. Germain. Peter obtained this painting in the 1970s, the frame was restored, and it was prominently displayed at Findhorn. It would certainly not be accorded the honour of being considered the best portrait study in the world, but when ROC first saw it in April 1972, there was an immediate rapport and identification. In ROC's words:

> 720418. I returned to the caravan. I then went to The Park and into its sanctuary where the St. Germain picture is, putting on the red light outside the door so as not to be disturbed. The room is done in cream with a natural stone fireplace opposite the door. There are two large magenta Findhorn candles on the mantelpiece, a brown cord carpet. The picture frame is round, faded gold. The picture as a painting is bad, but that does not matter. It is a symbol and radiates power. Standing in front of it, I was communing with my higher self. The flat painting seemed to come to life. The eyes chuckled with wit and a degree of mischief, and the lips smiled. I went through the oddest experience of looking at and speaking to myself. There is no doubt that St. Germain not only overlights me but is my higher self, and is in part incarnate in me. He greeted me with much affection. At last I was in this room with the picture. It would not have been right to have come sooner. Now was the time. The picture kept fluctuating from the flat picture to a living smiling being, and the power kept building up. "This is a bad picture" he said, "a poor copy of the original which was not in my case a good likeness. I have never worn such a badly made wig. I would not have been seen dead in such a one. My nose is wrong. But it will serve." I sat down facing the picture (there are four chairs similar to the sanctuary chairs) looking at the picture with which I felt an identification. It still kept coming to life.

From all these extracts, we may reasonably reach the conclusion that ROC was the embodiment of St. Germain. St. Germain is his soul or higher self. In Newton's terms, ROC would be incarnated with a portion of that soul that is an exact if less energetic part of it. What soul proportion ROC took into incarnation will never be known, of course, but for such an evolved soul as St. Germain appears to be, that percentage would be relatively small. This then leaves "spare capacity" for other parallel incarnations, as we shall see later.

As regards the painting, the only person in a position to comment authoritatively on it and its origins would, of course, be St. Germain himself, and he indicates to ROC that it is a copy of a poor original. Thus we may take this as being a fair probability of the likeness to the historical St. Germain. The appearance shows some resemblance to an engraving by Nicolas Thomas, done in 1783 and held in the Louvre in Paris.

If St. Germain's image from his painting is fairly clear, his life turns out to be anything but.

Historically, St. Germain (the "St." is a familial name, not a title) lived from 1712 until 1784, but both dates may be called into serious question. His ancestry falls into a similar category, where he was variously attributed to be the son of a Prince of Transylvania, Francis II, the son of Maria Anna of Pfalz-Neubure who was married to Charles II of Spain, a Sephardic Jew of humble birth, and so forth. From the 1740s onwards, he was generally attributed the title of the Count of St. Germain. The confusion is not helped here by St. Germain adopting other names in other countries at other times. The waters are further muddied by characters like Casanova pretending on occasion to be St. Germain.

In December of 1745, Horace Walpole in correspondence notes that "The Provost of Edinburgh is in custody of a messenger; and the other day they seized an, odd man, who goes by the name of Count St. Germain. He has been here these two years, and will not tell who he is, or whence, but professes that he does not go by his right name. He sings, plays on the violin wonderfully, composes...."

He is quickly released, and following the two year sojourn in Edinburgh, we find some of his music published and performed in London (two of his compositions from 1745 and 1760 reside in the British Museum). He was by all accounts also a skilled linguist (speaking Swedish, Portugese, French, Italian, German, Russian, and, of course, English), possessed an astounding historical knowledge, and is recorded as always having been a young looking man in his middle forties. This latter may well account for his fabled longevity, extending well beyond the 1712 to 1784 timeline. Among his known and available publications is *The Most Holy Trinosophia*.

There is an interesting allusion to St Germain having visited Cluny Hill (near Findhorn) in ROC's notes. The year of 1750 is given, and this date would accord with St Germain's alleged presence in Britain around this time:

The Occult Diaries of

> 680615. Findhorn. St G was with me and said he had been on Cluny Hill. I tried to get when from him. He was evasive at first, and said one time he was in this country. Later, I suddenly was given the date—1750

His next appearance is in France where he acquires accommodation in the Chateau de Chambord, and during his brief two years there (1758-1760), he is a regular acquaintance of Louis XVth and Madame de Pompadour. During this time, under the king's auspices, he inaugurates laboratories and carries out experiments with dye making.

In 1762 he is in Russia at the time Catherine the Great ascends to the throne on the death of her husband, Peter III. Taking various other names, he makes appearances in Belgium and Germany in later years.

Throughout his life, he is recorded as having the alchemical ability to produce diamonds, repair flawed ones, and transmute metals. He was certainly a unique man, well capable of making inroads into famous households.

On esoteric fronts, we have accounts by the theosophist Helena Blavatsky who described the St. Germain who appeared to her as one of the highly evolved humans she called the "Masters of Wisdom" In similar fashion, C. W. Leadbetter claims to have met him in Rome in 1926. In the theosophical tradition—and particularly in the writings of Alice Bailey—he is also considered to be the "Lord of Civilisation," a master magician, a sponsor, if not the actual source, of the Rosicrucian Society, and generally the primary overseer of the Western magical and esoteric tradition.

That St. Germain was ROC's higher self no longer seems in much doubt. But we find we are on shakier ground when we try to elucidate details of the historical St. Germain himself. That he lived is well enough attested, but his name-changing and continual country-hopping during his lifetime blurs the picture, giving rise to much legend. As to his esoteric powers and reputation, they also vary depending on different esoteric traditions.

However, if, as with ROC, he preferred to do his inner work secretly and out of the public gaze, then we are yet one step further back from discovering the true esoteric side of the historical St. Germain. In his appearance throughout ROC's writings, he almost revels in communicating in both enigmatic and paradoxical terms; his *Trinosophia* is a veritable set of enigma variations in itself.

If St. Germain is an "ascended master" as some have claimed, there is clearly little way of proving it if we look only at his general lifestyle in the 18th century.

R. Ogilvie Crombie

Spiritual "Fraternity"

> "When incarnate as three separate beings, the soul is not a third of the whole, but a complete soul and yet is a part of the one; an "entity" can manifest as "an aspect" of itself which is at the same time the whole; it can manifest in several aspects at the same time in different places, but each aspect is the whole."

This quotation could have been lifted directly from the writings of the life-between-life pioneers when describing parallel incarnations, as I described in Part I. But it was not. Remarkably, this was a statement from St. Germain made through ROC in 1968 well before the observations of parallel incarnations had ever been publicly (or privately) aired. This concept remained a mystery, and the inner beings who were ROC's spiritual mentors did not appear to wish to attempt further explanations. Taken from the same quotation as the above, St. Germain adds that the concept is "almost impossible for us to understand ... but gradually [it] will become clearer as mankind evolves on mental and spiritual levels".

Some half century later than this statement, our dawn of understanding does indeed seem to have arrived, and the concept of soul division or aspects is beginning to be understood as a result of the studies of the life-between-life pioneers.

As I mentioned in Part I, Newton explains that even relatively "young" spiritual souls sometimes embark on parallel incarnations, leaving part of their soul energy in the soul world and taking a proportion of it into its incarnations. This concept, so novel to many of us, is a key to understanding many of the entries in ROC's diaries as he himself struggled to sort it all out and come to an understanding of one of the great mysteries of incarnation. At the risk of repetition, we can benefit from a further explanation of the process involved.

As St. Germain points out, the divided soul is not a part of the higher self, like a slice taken from a pie, but a complete pie in itself, albeit of smaller size (less energetic, as Newton would put it). Lawton and others liken this to the properties exhibited by a holographic image. Due to the lower "soul" concentration of young souls, the number of "pies" that can be got from the main soul-pie is limited (about three seems to be the maximum for the average mortal). This leaves the parent soul-pie much diminished, and its activity in the soul-world then becomes minimal. With more evolved souls with a much greater energy concentration, correspondingly more "pies"—more aspects—can be produced without seriously affecting the size and activity of the "parent-pie" or higher self. It would seem that ROC was part of a pie of many slices.

Viewed from the bottom up, then, St. Germain would be ROC's higher self. Viewed from the top down, ROC would be considered an "aspect" of that higher self, the St. Germain entity. For most people, there would in general be but one aspect, that is, one soul to one incarnation, as souls choosing parallel lives tend to be in the minority. But was this the case with the St. Germain entity? Was there or is there more than one aspect?

This topic comes up time and again in ROC's writings, and there are frequent mentions of other aspects. On the basis of Newton's life-between-life research, there are no barriers to those aspects being distributed literally across both time and space; some on Earth may still be in existence, some will have already outrun their lifespan here (as in ROC's case), and some may yet have to be born. Indeed, if we follow Newton's observations, this situation will also likewise pertain on other planets and mental worlds both in and out of our own solar system.

I appreciate that coming upon these concepts for the first time will be mind-boggling. We are so accustomed to viewing everything from our limited Earth-bound perspective. With these new concepts, we have to view things from a more remote point, somewhere "out there." It seems that we should no longer consider that "the world's our oyster," but that the universe is our oyster!

Many of the beings making contact with ROC have truly mythological connections. All beings, including ourselves, are protean in nature in the finer worlds but can and do take on appearances that permit the human viewer a means of identification of the ethereal entity. Many of these forms have been imposed on them over the aeons by the projection of humanity's conceptions and beliefs, and these ethereal presences have therefore adopted and appear in these expected or "traditional" forms.

Merlin Aspect

In this respect, the following communication from Apollo (and mentioning also both Hermes and the great god Pan), gives both a reinforcement of the conclusion we have already arrived at of St. Germain being ROC's higher self, but now introduces another "aspect": the Merlin aspect. Merlin, the magician, needs little introduction, although in fact we know even less about this historical gentleman than we do of St. Germain—and that is very little.

R. Ogilvie Crombie

710418. Edinburgh. While still in bed this morning, sitting up listening to the radio, the door suddenly swung open (it does this sometimes with wind if the front room window is open). This time Apollo walked into the room, crossed to in front of the window, turned, and looked at me. He appeared as a radiantly beautiful naked young man with golden hair, about human size. He smiled at me and faded out. Though I have seen him several times on the beach at Findhorn, this is the first time he has made himself known here in the flat.

After I had been sitting in meditation for a while (afternoon), I was again aware of Apollo, who greeted me.

A. Hail, fortunate mortal!

ROC. Why fortunate, great Apollo?

A. Because you have been chosen for the work you are doing. Because you have been invested with power very few human beings are allowed to use.

ROC. Is this a test? Are you trying to produce ego inflation?

A. No, that will not happen with you—that is why you were chosen.

ROC. What powers I have, if any, are not due to me, but are given to me by God's grace. I always try to hold it in my mind that I am no more than a channel.

A. You are much more than that, and you must not belittle yourself or you will fail in the work you have to do.

ROC. I seem to be faced with the choice between self importance, leading to ego inflation, or failing in my work.

A. That is not so. In your case, the ego and the higher self have reached a state of integration which makes ego inflation, as you call it, impossible. It is true that on the physical level, your brain, your intelligence, belong to the material person Ogilvie Crombie, but you know who your higher self is. Never mind whether that higher self incarnated at your conception, or birth, or took over later in your life—that is unimportant. The fact remains that your higher self is now the great Master—the Compte de St. Germain. You may consider that part of that great being not only overlights you but is actually incarnate within you, and you are well aware that the integration has increased since you are aware of him within you and not outside yourself any longer.

This we know you will not tell to anyone (Gordon is a possible exception, because of the link between you). The true master makes no claims. A very few have and will recognise you for what you are. Some will possibly pick up the over-lighting, but very few the actual incarnation. This is as it should be. The true master works quietly behind the scenes. The part of St. Germain incarnate in you is the part who was Merlin, so you are in effect a reincarnation of Merlin. Though many question the physical fact of Merlin's existence, he was a real being, though perhaps not entirely physical. You understand what I mean.

ROC. Yes

A. You are a magician, whether you like the fact or not. You have been invested with the full powers of Merlin, and behind him, as you know, are the power of Solomon and Moses. There are others, too, and I will now reveal to you that I endow you with much of my own powers. I too, am a magician. You have been trusted with this infinite potentiality because of the integration between the two selves. You, the lower ego, will never use the power given unless inspired and directed by St. Germain, who obeys the will of God. You have the humility that will keep you on the true path, but beware of false modesty. You must be constantly aware of who you are and of the potential powers you have, otherwise you may not be aware of your full responsibility, and that could be much more dangerous.

The magician works alone, and the work that you, Merlin, have to accomplish on this earth before you leave it will mainly be in secret and silence. Gordon, who is your heir as you have always known and have recently symbolised on the material level, has much to learn. He is at the moment somewhat overpowered by his material commitments, and because of a sense of inferiority that overcomes him at times, is apt to become negative and open himself to influences from the dark. As you know, there is very powerful opposition to your work, though your identity is not known as yet. You are under very powerful protection—very powerful indeed, but there are times, as you already know, when certain conditions favour the dark. For the time being, I and my brother Hermes, whom you know and love, will be with you. You are not alone though you may seem to be. Pan and many of your elemental friends are frequently with you.

> There may be many things that you have to do physically alone, but there will also be many you will do with Gordon who is also under our powerful protection. He is used in many ways that he is at the moment unaware of. Certain energies can only be channelled when he is present. His link with you is very important as he is a main channel in helping to preserve your health and protection. Both you alone and you with Gordon are needed. The work is becoming more and more vital as the struggle between the light and the dark increases. Doubting Thomas must have patience. The work you do together is much more effective as it is. Were Gordon to be having visions and paranormal experiences, it could not be done so well. He is a necessary anchor if only he could recognise it. We will stop now.

As can be seen from the previous message, I was sometimes the topic of conversation between ROC and his inner contacts. I always had the feeling that I could better appreciate and contribute to what was going on in ROC's supranormal environment if I could but view what he was viewing and experience what he was experiencing. Such abilities might also have made considerable positive inroads into lessening my "doubting Thomas" status. As the old adage goes, "Seeing is believing." Apparently, though, wiser heads thought otherwise. As it was, without such paranormal abilities, I was forced back onto relying on simple logic, which in retrospect is perhaps no bad thing.

Saturnian Aspect

This entity, associated with Saturn, our ringed gas giant, also appears repeatedly in ROC's notes. In line with the already mentioned protean characteristics of ethereal entities, the Saturnian can at need appear in the expected space gear or as a thirty foot high individual in blue and silver robes. ROC eventually discovers his name is Cafron. He plays an important part in association with Merlin in support of ROC's role in creating shells of protection against the dark forces both around individuals and around places such as the Findhorn community. This being also acts as the link with the "flying saucer" appearances on the beach at Findhorn discussed in a later chapter. In the following extract, ROC appears as his space suited Saturnian aspect in assisting some earth bound spirits who had lost their lives in the last war during a flying sortie.

The Occult Diaries of

670920. Findhorn. As soon as I went to bed, I left my body and was by the Nissan hut as my Saturn aspect, this time of normal height like myself and dressed in a blue and silver spaceman's outfit, complete with helmet.

Walked about on the moor for a bit, and then approached the other Nissan hut that had been an alternative choice but was rejected because of the strange disquieting atmosphere. As I (Saturn aspect, of course) approached, I called on any earth bound spirits or entities to reveal themselves as I came to them with love and the desire to help. On the third repetition, the door of the hut opened, and a young man in RAF uniform came slowly and warily out, followed by two others, similarly dressed. Another two came up from behind me. They seemed frightened and yet prepared to be belligerent.

"Who are you?" one of them asked.

"A friend. I come to help you if I can."

"You can see us?"

"Of course."

"And talk to us?"

"Yes."

"You are wearing a strange uniform," one of them said, referring to the space suit. "Are you a German?"

"No."

"Is the war still going on, or has it been won?"

"The war you mean is over. Germany and Japan lost it."

"We did not know." They exchanged uneasy glances.

"Somehow we do not seem able to make contacts." The speaker looked worried. "We are all that seems to be left of the crew of a bomber. We –" He broke off, and the others looked very frightened.

"I don't think you should speak of that," one of the others said quickly. "It's better not to remember."

"You do not need to remember." I said. "I understand."

I knew that the plane had been destroyed and this part of the crew, at least, killed. These five young men, all about the same age, probably early twenties but of very different types, were earth bound spirits who must be freed if possible. Sudden death, especially in the young, can bring this about where there is disbelief in an afterlife or lack of spiritual knowledge. I (or

R. Ogilvie Crombie

rather my Saturnian aspect) must try to free them.

"Will you answer some questions if I ask them? Remember, I am your friend. I come to you in brotherly love, with the desire to help."

I held my hand out to one of them – the one who had come out of the hut first. He shrank back, and then with a very sad look, stretched out his hand and took hold of mine. He gave a sudden cry, and laughed.

"At last!" he said. "Someone I can feel." He grasped my hand with both his and felt it. "I can feel it." He turned to the others. "I can feel it!"

As disembodied spirits, they would not have been able to feel or touch living beings, but in my etheric body and Saturn aspect, they could.

"You have been aware of human beings round you but have not been able to make any contact. They cannot see you, nor hear you speak."

"That's right."

"You have seen no one you could make contact with?"

"No, it has been terrible."

I knew then that no discarnate beings had been near them. For some reason or other, they had been isolated. The speaker told me his name was Joe, and named the others, Alec, Tom, Jimmy and Harry. As he named them, each one shook hands with me. They were surprised and delighted, and had lost all suspicion.

They told me they were doing a ceaseless round of activities, but could not tell me what they were. This distressed them, and I told them to leave it. In a vague way, they realised they were dead and living in some other conditions, though they knew it was still on earth. One of them, Tom, had been brought up a Christian, but the war had undermined his faith, and he had come to curse God for allowing it.

At this point ROC's entry ceases, so we are left without knowing exactly how this encounter resolved itself. One wishes to assume that contact having been made at last, this invoked the help which the lost airmen needed, enabling them to move on from their earth-bound condition. But we find no confirmation of this or further reference to this event in other diary entries.

It's important to realise that in writing his diaries, ROC wasn't attempting to compose narratives. He was reporting as accurately as he could on his actual experiences which did not always resolve nicely into a dramatic arc of beginnings, middles and endings. Life can be untidy as we encounter it, and that seems to be as true of the spirit realms as of the physical world we know.

Peter Caddy Aspect

Yet another aspect, in the form of Peter Caddy of the Findhorn Foundation, may be added to our growing list. In a script from St. Germain—and he ought to know the true state of affairs, as he is the common factor of all these aspects—this relationship is voiced. *The Trinosophia*, a book attributed to St. Germain as its author, is also mentioned:

> 660926a. You are now beginning to see the pattern gradually building up, and things given to you in earlier scripts which did not seem to have much meaning at the time are now fitting into place as part of the pattern and are taking on meaning. It was right that my *Trinosophia* should come into your hands now. Reading it, you remembered and knew that you had experienced it. I should perhaps say our *Trinosophia,* for we are one. I can so completely take you over that we become one, as we were in the past. There is mystery here which you cannot understand. I am not reincarnated in you as you understand reincarnation, and yet it is as if I were. We are one. You are me and I am you.
>
> In the same way, I become Peter, and Peter becomes me. You and Peter are one in that both of you are me, and yet you are each individual human beings. Simply accept this mysterious fact. Do not worry about it and offer no resistance. You have both much work to do, some of it as your individual selves, some of it as me. Often this will be together, working as one and yet in different aspects, but sometimes it will be alone. Through you as channel, I will help and direct as much as I am able. You now know that what is coming through is the truth even if it occasionally carries accretions from your own unconscious. You have the intuitive discrimination to sift out the truth.

So now we have the host St. Germain soul acting as the higher self still resident and active in the spiritual realms, but with four (or more) "aspects" split off from it in various past and present configurations: discarnates Merlin

R. Ogilvie Crombie

and Cafron, the Saturnian, and mortals ROC and Peter Caddy. However, the inter-relationship of aspects and higher self is clearly somewhat complex, and we will need, I suspect, simply have to be content with 2 and 2 making 5 in the meantime!

This other-worldliness of ROC seen as aspect or perhaps as higher self is spotted by a psychic friend, Maisie, during a visit ROC made to her home in Fife in 1969:

> 690401. Abernethy. During the visit to the "gnomes," Maisie received some strange things. She said that every time I visited them, she was strongly aware of the presence of a great being. She said she did not know who he was, but she saw me as a great master of ceremonies. Curious how with their awareness of St. Germain—though it may be mainly as Prince Rakoczi (Master R)—they fail to recognise the truth. Maisie is evidently prevented from doing so, no doubt for a good reason.
>
> She saw me performing a ritual wearing long robes of light blue, which glistened, and a strange round hat.
>
> She asked me why I was on Earth as there was no need for me to incarnate at all. I must have come here for a special purpose.
>
> How near she has got to the truth! I suppose that what she is allowed to know will be given to her.

In Summary

Trying to match ROC into the pattern discovered by Newton seems to place him into the category of an advanced hybrid soul or sage. The most advanced souls that Newton came across he placed in category VI, but clearly the range will extend well above this, as, in cosmic terms, it is highly unlikely that we would be the most evolved souls in the Universe! If, on this basis, ROC is "off the scale," then our knowledge and understanding of such a soul's capabilities will be, at present, very restricted, but it seems reasonable to conclude that such a soul would be capable of multiple parallel existences or aspects which could be simultaneously in existence in a variety of settings, including physical worlds like the Earth, mental or telepathic worlds such as the subtle realms around Saturn and Venus, and soul worlds. ROC himself remained puzzled as to the exact nature of his aspects. During a session at Findhorn, this personal communication was received by ROC which is fairly unambiguous in defining his higher self as that of St. Germain (since this information is conveyed by none other than St. Germain himself!):

> 680914. At the session this morning during the meditation, so much happened that I doubt if I can remember it all. It was for myself alone and not to be shared. The important things were … St. Germain placing his cloak round my shoulders and handing me a red rose and saying "You are me, and I am you; we are one. Part of me is incarnate in you."

From another being, the following was received, this time when ROC was staying with us at Nervelstone in Ayrshire. This reaffirms the identity of the higher self and that ROC has more than one aspect:

> 680318. In the non-physical realms you are in a way one with St. Germain and have other aspects which are also one with him. You—in the all-including sense—represent the spirit of Saturn, the ruler of this new Aquarian age, but in incarnation, you are a human being.

R. Ogilvie Crombie

Chapter 5
Spiritual Teachers

All ROC's spiritual teachers were from the superconscious worlds, and, like their physical counterparts here on Earth, their purpose was similar in providing knowledge, wisdom and counselling. He would have been about thirty four years of age when he first became aware of these transcendental presences, and they were to remain with him for the rest of his life, surfacing as necessary to meet present and future esoteric needs.

ROC's teachers are introduced as much as possible in the chronological order that they first appeared to him. However, as the years pass, this distinction blurs as they all make their entrances in random manner.

The Veiled One

Prior to ROC's move from his Edinburgh flat at 28 Albany Street to Cowford Cottage in Perthshire in 1940, and also while there, he had become aware of a veiled figure whom he felt strongly was imparting teaching:

> 631011a. I should perhaps mention here that for many years, from 1934 to 1939, I had been aware of a presence who came through the back room door and stood at the foot of my bed almost every night. This presence was a being clad in voluminous long robes of either black or very dark blue. There was a hood over his head and his face was veiled, though I could faintly make out features through this covering. He used to spread out the outer cloak he wore over the bottom of the bed. I always had a feeling of protection when he did this. I knew that he was my "teacher" and that I was being given knowledge while I slept. I also knew that if I saw his face unveiled I would die.
>
> When I went to Cowford cottage in 1940, this being only visited me very rarely during the ten years I stayed there. I know now that he had completed his teaching and had given me all I was to be given then. Living at Cowford was living very close to nature, and I now know that it was the nature forces who took over my teaching and that very close links were forged during these years, though I was unaware of any actual presences. The foundations of my present work were being very completely laid.

The identity of the veiled one became clear some years later during a visit to Findhorn, when ROC had the following vision:

> 670424. [I was] sitting quietly in the caravan having been directed to do so. I had a series of vivid colour visions rather like those of the previous morning. A large being in black robes with a small black hat, a rounded face radiating great love, came into the caravan. The name Koot Hoomi occurred to me.
>
> Later, I described the being to Eileen and Peter [Caddy] separately. Both immediately recognised him as Koot Hoomi.
>
> In the afternoon, I went to the beach by the moor, though it was very dull and looked like rain. Koot Hoomi was soon walking beside me. He said he wanted me to describe him as I had done so as to give me confirmation of his identity. Some time later, when entering the wood, he asked me if I did not recognise him. I said "No," and he put his hand up to his face and he appeared veiled. I immediately recognised him with surprise as my veiled teacher of many years ago. I reminded him that I had also felt that if I ever saw his face, I should die. He told me that if I had seen his face then, I would have seen the Divine Light in strength, a thing I was not then ready for. Later, when I told Peter, he expressed surprise that Koot Hoomi had been my master.

Three days later, on another excursion to the beach at Findhorn, Koot Hoomi appeared, followed a short time later by Saint Germain:

> 670427. Shortly after starting to cross the moor to the beach, I was joined by Koot Hoomi who walked on my left.
>
> K.H. Isn't it strange that some people think I was not the right master for you. Yet I assure you, you couldn't have had a better one. You were one of my favourite pupils and yet you showed considerable astonishment when I revealed the identity of your teacher. Do you think all these years were wasted?
>
> ROC. Certainly not. I am quite sure you were the right master for me otherwise you would not have come to me.
>
> K.H. Good. Then let's have no more of this nonsense.
>
> ROC. Why did you stop coming to me. Was it because I had been taught all that was right for that time or was there some other reason?

K.H. when it was decided that my most sophisticated and elegant colleague here was going to take you over, I withdrew — gracefully.

St. Germain had joined us and was walking on my left. Koot Hoomi, on referring to him, bowed to him a little clumsily from his bulk (true alas, but worth it) [K.H. has just added]. The elegant St. Germain (also true) gave a beautiful bow in return.

ROC. Now you have made yourself visible to me and given the identity of the veiled teacher, is there a reason?

K.H. I still have a paternal interest in my erstwhile pupil and (with a look at St. Germain) it is necessary to keep an eye on the afore-mentioned colleague in case he tries any tricks. He needs very careful watching. He is a wily man.

[To St. G.] Do you remember that time when you....? Koot Hoomi burst into a great guffaw of laughter, and I did not hear the story as St. Germain wagged his finger at him saying, "Now, now, that's enough."

Then St. Germain came up to me and laid his hands on my shoulder and looking very serious, said:

St.G. Do you think I would trick you?

ROC. No. I do not. After all, it would be tricking part of yourself, wouldn't it?

St. Germain smiled and Koot Hoomi said: "Well, that's that. You see you belong to both of us."

He linked his arm with mine, and St. Germain did the same on my other side, and we walked on.

A little later, K.H. said that apart from being a musician, he was also a celebrated cook and loved preparing his own meals. Did I not realise that my own love for cooking and baking came from him. "We'll prepare some great meals together yet."

A little later they left me (No, we did not – it was simply that you ceased to see us; we were still there).

Golu

Abbreviated simply to "G" in his diaries and records, this teacher took the appearance of a young Indian. ROC, unaware of his name at the time, first meets him in late September of 1963. In his records of the event written a short time later, he explains entering a hyperaesthetic state and thereafter becoming aware of the presence of Golu. As with many of these contacts, ROC questions the encounter and wonders if the whole thing is not just a figment of his own imagination:

> 631007. For the last fortnight I have been aware of the presence of a being in the flat—this differs from my frequent awareness of astral or other worldly beings in that the new presence is in the flat while the others are outside of it. That is, I am functioning with other higher senses on a higher plane and sense the other beings there. The new presence is an Indian—young, milk-chocolate coloured, clean shaven, and with black longish hair and very dark brown eyes. I sense rather than see him. He is often here sitting in the lotus position on the divan which is in the back room. He sometimes wears a loincloth and sometimes is completely naked. I feel he may have come to be my teacher possibly in answer to a query or a wish.
> About twelve noon I had a strong degree of hyperesthesia with the usual heightening of the physical senses, deepening intensity of colours and shapes—more significance, greater awareness of sound—at the same time accompanied by a paradoxical fading out. It is impossible to express this state in words; it has to be experienced to be understood, presumably a shifting of the senses from the physical to a higher plane. There is a sense of unreality—also usual—the walls of the room seem to vibrate and shimmer as if one was becoming aware of the active atoms making them up and of the spaces between. There is a strong sense of expectation of something about to happen together with a certain feeling of excitement; a slight degree of breathlessness. Possibly all these are explainable in physiological terms as due to a condition of cholinergia. But if so, what is the precipitating cause?
> I was suddenly aware of a presence behind me but felt no impulse to turn round—in fact I doubt if I could have turned. A strong voice suddenly said "I am He." No doubt subjective but it made me jump. The voice went on "go into the front room and sit in the armchair with the back to the light. Take a pen and a pad of paper and relax." I felt I was to try automatic writing again (I had not done so since the early 1920s) and did as commanded. There was no feeling of tingling as in the previous attempts but

the pen—a ballpoint—moved. Only unintelligible scribbles so far, but occasional letters could be made out.

With memories of previous encounters with evil or at least undesirable entities, I began by asking God's blessing and later asked for a cross to be made. This was instantly done.

I shall try again from time to time and see what results. The Indian is sitting in the armchair opposite me and seems to be pleased.

On the question of an Indian presence. Since the early twenties I have been interested in Indian religion, mythology and philosophy. There has been an Indian music and an Indian Exhibition at the recent Edinburgh festival. And I have just finished reading the *Autobiography of a Yogi* by Paramhamsa Yogananda, a fascinating book which I much enjoyed, feeling strongly drawn to the personality of the writer. The Indian presence is not Yogananda, although I think the presence who spoke behind me might have been. The words "I am he" have great significance here. My aroused interest may have made some form of contact or possibly the whole thing is subliminal and imaginary. The Indian smiles and shakes his head.

Two nights later, on the evening of 9th October 1963, a further encounter with Yogananda took place in the front room during another period of acute hyperesthesia and heightened awareness. ROC states: "Yogananda appeared to me with great clarity, confirming that he was Monday's presence. There was a period of silent communion after I had greeted him, then, after blessing me, he turned and walked through the wall seeming to me to walk away into the distance."

On the next evening, the following verbal script was obtained. After this, there were further attempts at automatic writing, but these were again largely unsuccessful:

631008. Sit quiet and relax while thoughts flow between us. There is a deep communication to your unconscious mind. I am giving you knowledge and information most of which is not intended for use on this earth but is all part of the preparation for a higher plane. It is my function to add further knowledge to that you already have. Some of this knowledge may be used here, and it will come up into your consciousness as needed.

The Occult Diaries of

When this happens you will KNOW that the truth is there. I can communicate with you in this way as can others. In the meantime my name does not matter; it may be revealed later. Accept me as your guru and friend and have faith. That is all. Greetings and Blessings.

A couple of days later, a further dramatic event occurs as Golu brings about a closer integration between ROC's conscious and unconscious mind through stimulating the opening of what is usually termed the "Third Eye":

631010. Golu told me that the integration process of my real self had been taken as far as it could unaided. The division wall between my conscious mind (the ego) and my unconscious self was very thin. He said, "We are going to break through that wall, forming a doorway through which a freer two-way communication will be possible." He said this would bring about a further stage in the integration of personality and would also enable me to make use of some of the knowledge which is stored in the unconscious mind. He warned me that the immediate consequences would be alarming but that "they" knew what they were doing, and if I had trust and faith, everything would be well. He asked if I trusted him. I said I did. He told me to stand quite still and relax.

I was conscious of a bright blue flash and a sudden jolt in my head almost as if an explosion had occurred in my head. Then followed the most frightening experience I have ever gone through. As if a dam had burst, an uncontrollable flood of images—some terrifying—thoughts and ideas rose into my mind, producing the feeling that my head was going to burst or of the onset of acute insanity. It was impossible to make any sense out of this surging turmoil. Gradually it began to calm down.

I could hear Golu urging relaxation and reassuring me, and my mind slowly returned to more or less normal. Since then there has been a continuous flow of ideas. Whatever subject I think about, a vast amount of knowledge immediately starts coming. I feel slightly like someone who has bought an encyclopaedia and keeps eagerly turning the pages to search out information on a large variety of subjects. I must control this impulse. It is quite impossible to write down all the information on such subjects as "matter," "astral matter," "flying saucers," "materialisation," "illusory world," etc., etc., that I have already acquired. Certain of this matter must remain in my mind, but the knowledge is there and no doubt will be available when needed.

I feel a vastly different person since this experience. Communication with Golu is becoming much more easy.

On the following day during the morning and afternoon, more communications on a range of topics took place between ROC and Golu. Particularly interesting is the explanation of why Golu appeared to ROC as an Indian. This, I feel, is an extremely important point, as it helps explain why a number of sensitives will see the same entity in completely different ways. Spiritual beings are fundamentally protean in nature and can at will take on whatever form they choose to suit the occasion. This has echoes in the NDE, as the divine figure that the experiencer meets, although believed to be the same Christ figure, for example, may be seen completely differently depending on cultural background and the individual's personal belief structure:

> 631011b. I asked Golu if he could materialise and become visible to my physical sight. He said not without great difficulty, as he was using a body of much finer material than the etheric body. It would require a medium and the building up of this body. He thought this unnecessary as I had accepted him and could see and hear him with my non-physical senses.
>
> I asked him how, if his body was made of such fine material, he could sit on a physical chair without falling through it? He laughed and said that he was not sitting on a physical chair but on its non-physical counterpart that he had mentally created. He only appeared to me to be sitting on the physical chair. He said the mechanism of this was difficult to explain to human beings, that it was in reality simple, but in the meantime I would have to leave it at that.
>
> He said he appeared to me in human form because it was the simplest way and made my acceptance of him easy and communication natural. He had been incarnated as an Indian, so he took on the form he had then had at its best. There was great and profound truth in Indian religion and philosophy as I knew. The recent Indian Exhibition and music and Yogananda's

Autobiography, together with the Chinese Philosophy I have also been studying recently, partly brought it about (Golu's appearance and what followed), plus my expressed desire for further teaching. The visit of Yogananda had been due to my deep interest in his book.

From the time of my return to Edinburgh in 1949 until now [October 1963], I had been unaware of any beings in the flat, except from a rare visit from the veiled one. There was continued interest in psi phenomena and related subjects, but it was only recently that I had wondered if I would ever have another "teacher" and expressed a strong wish that I might. The almost immediate response was the appearance of the young Indian whom I refer to now as "G."

Golu tells me I shall not be able to distinguish completely between the knowledge he gives me and that which rises from my unconscious, unless where he replies directly to my questions. He gave a long explanation and warning about the "contamination" question where any kind of psi communication is concerned. It is always liable to occur where a human being (channel) is involved. The more egotistical the person, the more likely the falsification. The knowledge given to me by my previous mentor (the veiled one) is pure and true in my unconscious mind, as is also that which I am getting from Golu, but in the process of emerging into consciousness and in either writing or talking about it, there is a possibility of modification. I must always be aware of this. My conscious mind also will go on working on ideas and develop them. This is natural and right but could lead to misconceptions if the logic is false.

In this dictated script, Golu now makes some interesting distinctions between the methods of communication that can be used between the physical and non-physical worlds; in one case, the perception is via the paraphysical senses of sight and hearing; in the other, it is through the detection of and communication with a more dense, nearly physical etheric body while in a hyperaesthetic state.

631222. On the question in your mind earlier this evening, we do communicate mainly by telepathy but there are times when you hear my voice speaking to you by means of your higher (non-physical) sense of hearing just as you see me with your non-physical sense of sight. This is a different phenomenon from hearing with the physical sense in a state of hyperesthesia or heightened awareness. Could I use an etheric body and make it sufficiently dense in the manner I told you about, you would be able to see me and hear me physically.

You do not need to see me or hear me with your physical senses as you believe in my existence. As I am personal to you alone it does not matter whether anyone else believes or not.

You know I exist and the bond between us is now very close and firmly established. You are right in thinking that you must seek out knowledge for yourself and work things out. My purpose is to help and guide you to this end. There is much I can and will teach you, but it must be gradual.

Why am I communicating with you by this means [i.e. dictated directly] since telepathic means are so well developed? Because you wanted it. It does give a record which is otherwise missing unless you note down at the time what I say. Sometimes I do not wish you to do that, as the information is for you alone.

In this extract, Golu demonstrates his more light hearted side:

631012. The other evening he appeared at the Hazells while I was there, much to my amusement. He was capering about round the room, turning cartwheels and making faces at me trying to make me laugh. It was perhaps as well they could not see him, as he had left his loincloth behind.

In the train today on my way to Glasgow to a TV engagement, Golu appeared sitting on the opposite seat. He pretended to be hurt because I didn't buy him a coffee though I explained it would look strange if I ordered two as he was presumably invisible to all but myself. I then said to him, "How nice for you being able to travel without a ticket." He leant his elbows on the table, grinned at me and said: "Don't you wish you could?"

I like G's exuberance and boyishness. It forms a nice contrast to his intense seriousness when giving me knowledge, and I do not think it detracts from his authority as a teacher.

On this later occasion, Yogananda is mentioned as having been present earlier in the day, and ROC is told by Golu that he, Yogananda, will provide spiritual teachings. As always, ROC continues to question the reality of his experiences:

> 640131. I asked the question of Golu: "Were you connected with Yogananda?"
> Answer — Yes. There was a connection in life, and it still exists; he was with you this morning. You will feel his influence and be aware of his presence.
> Q. Why is he here?
> A. Because he can teach you things that will advance you further in your search for wisdom, self-realization and spiritual enlightenment. You are ready for such teaching.
> Q. Will you still be with me?
> A. Of course. I shall always be with you. You know that I am part of your life now. Yogananda is smiling and nodding. He is glad that you realise my reality and accept me. I am not —I repeat—not a creation of your imagination. I know you have accepted me as real, as your friend and guide, but there are times when you doubt it, though those times are few. You must try to accept me completely, as it gives me more power to help you.

Third party evidence for Golu is provided on a visit by ROC to the "Gnomes," Annie, Maisie and William, three friends who lived in Abernethy. They were affectionately nicknamed thus because when ROC first encountered them in their garden, all three were wearing woolly pixie hats! The following information came through Annie:

> 660410. She [Annie] then said there was a young Indian standing beside me who looked about sixteen, was very vivacious, and full of energy. He was wearing a cream satin tunic, light trousers, a white turban with an osprey, and a large sapphire in front, and I think a blue sash. I was a bit startled, as she was obviously describing Golu, though he is not sixteen but often looks it. He was standing behind me. He leant forward and whispered in my ear, "You see, I have put on my Sunday best to do you honour." I had certainly never seen him dressed like this before. Annie could, I suppose, have picked him up from my subconscious, but the fact that he was dressed so differently

from his usual loin cloth or total nudity was impressive. I have wondered sometimes if a clairvoyant would see him and how he would be dressed. I am sure now that he would be wearing his gala rig-out, as he reveals himself only to me. Annie said he looked like an Indian Prince which she felt he had been. I am fairly certain I had not mentioned Golu to them, and it is unlikely that the Walkers had. They have only met recently, and there has not been the opportunity. Annie said Golu was with me a great deal, and when he was, I usually felt very young and vital, which is true.

[On the following day] as I was sitting reading, Golu came into the room (back room) still wearing the Indian Prince outfit. I asked him where he was going as he was all dressed up. He said he had forgotten how nice he looked in this rig-out, and seemed to preen himself in front of the mirror. He said "It does suit me, doesn't it?" I answered him it did, and he burst into peals of laughter and capered about the room.

Chinese Sage

While being one of ROC's teachers, his appearances throughout ROC's writings are relatively few. As most of the teachings given to ROC seem to be during periods of sleep, it might be easy to underestimate the overall influence of the Chinese Sage simply because he was not clairvoyantly visible and communicating during waking hours.

Tio

Tio is first experienced through a dream-vision ROC has on 23rd March, 1965, where he encounters him in a mountain-side cave setting in the presence of another being of whose identity ROC is unaware. As revealed in later scripts, Tio continues to be recognised as Polynesian and throughout the coming years attends to ROC's physical health and energy via Huna treatment applied to the etheric body which then gradually manifests in the physical counterpart. The second excerpt is also a dream-vision of the 28th May, 1965, and illustrates the Huna practice. However, in the vast bulk of encounters with Tio, he appears to ROC in his normal awake state and not in dream, and the "massage" is applied in full waking consciousness.

650323. A brief dream in which I again visit the cave. I could look through the opening and see the valley below and the opposite mountains, but I am still unable to describe this room in the rock. The Being is sitting in a carved wooden chair—I think he was in the previous dream, but I was unaware of the chair. Also I think as before, I am sitting cross legged before him and I am again naked. There is no definite feeling of communication or further instruction, just great peace and contentment. The native is there, standing opposite the opening. I am now sure he is Polynesian though rather dark skinned. He is not very tall, rather stocky, but finely proportioned. As before, he is naked.

Comments: I wonder if I shall be visiting this cave often. This may he the beginning of further instruction. The nudity is definitely significant. One cannot take any material things into this place so clothes must be left behind. The naked self is there, nothing must he hidden. If I am here in my etheric body I suppose I could clothe myself by thinking of clothes, but in this dream I didn't. I never thought about it as the nudity seemed right. I do not know if the "native" is an attendant on the Being or a pupil like myself, nor can be certain that he is the unseen being who gave me the previous massage treatments.

650528. Dream Vision. At the end of a massage treatment given me by the Polynesian whose name I now know to be Tio, in which I am lying on my back on some kind of divan. Tio places the forefinger of his right hand on the top of my head. He then draws it down to the centre of my forehead, where he pauses. Then continuing the movement he draws his forefinger down the front of my face and stops at the throat. He goes on tracing a line down the front of my body, pausing at the other major Chakras. I immediately feel a strong clockwise force forming a whirling helix round my body and producing a direct force along the length of my body (induced by the whirl?) which begins to circulate up the spine to the head and then showering down through the body (Huna, mana or fundamental cosmic energy).

Comments: These massage dreams seem to come periodically, sometimes when I am not feeling well or am tired. They invariably increase my energy which is, I believe, due to the tapping of cosmic energy. It is highly significant that after the [massage] treatment Tio traced this line down the front of my body, pausing at the places where the chakras are situated.

Many further meetings with Tio take place, the example following again being an out-of-body experience, and shows the indescribable joy that results from contacts such as this occurring in the etheric:

> 670625a. Very clear out-of-the-body experiences. I find myself standing on a sea shore. It is a semi-circular sandy bay with clear fine sand sloping gently towards a very blue calm sea. There are rocky promontories at each end of the bay. The rocks are mainly dark brown and red and in places massive. Behind the bay is a forest mainly, I think, of beech, birch, and sycamore and elm trees. There is lush grass under the trees. The colours are very intense and meaningful as they so often are in these experiences. I stand at the edge of the wood looking towards the sea. I am naked, and my body seems very solid and real. Someone comes round the corner of the bay and starts running towards me. It is Tio, very stalky and solid with a grin all over his attractively ugly face. He too is naked. He stops in front of me, laughs and then embraces me. He says it is quite a time since our last meeting as I have evidently been too busy to think of him. I tell him that is not so, as he is often in my mind but that I have been unusually busy, being used for so much at Findhorn. He laughs again and says he knows about it and that he was frequently with me even if I did not see him, and that I did not need him.
>
> We walk over the sand towards the sea and I tell him we will always be very close as we are brothers, apart from that fact that he is the appointed guardian of my physical well being. We walk on round into a neighbouring bay which stretches for some distance. There is a gentle warm breeze. Tio puts his arm round my shoulder and I feel we are really one. There is a unity and closeness of contact in the etheric regions and out of the physical body that is unknowable and cannot be understood by the material mind. This unity is not physical and is something very wonderful. I count myself very lucky indeed to be able to experience it in this life and gain some understanding, however slight, of what it means and how it reflects and foreshadows union with the Divine.

The Occult Diaries of

After walking for a time, Tio gives me an extended Huna treatment which I am in need of after the strenuous Findhorn experiences. I feel filled with energy and reactivated and this is carried over to my physical vehicle.

Chapter 6
The Channelled Message

While many of us have had unusual occurrences at some time in our lives, for example a bit of déjà vu, we tend to remark on it at the time, wonder for a moment, then later dismiss it as perhaps a bit of coincidence or even imagination. When, as in ROC's case, there is in addition contact with some internalised source that conveys messages or impressions, or is even visible to the inner eye, we start to rightly question the source of such impressions. Are they from our active imagination, or do they come from some external individuated source in the unseen worlds? These same questions constantly assailed ROC, and he was always at pains to discern the difference.

In the following extract, he is reflecting on the differences between the creative imagination, dreams, visions, and what ROC termed "aware of" personalities. The approach here, totally representative of his earlier and later thinking, shows a healthy scientific questioning as to what is actually occurring and an awareness of the alternative possibilities and possible delusional qualities.

> 650707. I think that the creative imagination is a part of the unconscious mind that is rather like a very intricate computer. It can be programmed by the conscious mind with, say, certain details for plot, situation setting and characters for a fictional work—story, novel, play, etc. Every writer knows the manner in which the unconscious can work out details and produce the whole thing ready to be set down and create characters on slight hints supplied by the conscious mind. This is the normal process of creative writing.
>
> I believe the creative imagination can also be programmed by the unconscious to produce the material for dreams and fantasies. The unconscious may be inspired by the universal unconscious or by influences or entities existing at other levels or planes than this material one. People in dreams may be suggested by real people or be a synthesis of several different individuals, or they may be completely non-existent in the physical world. Some dreams are undoubtedly wish fulfilments, or expressions of suppressed desires, sexual or otherwise, as Freud maintains; some may be an expression of the lust for power, according to Adler, or personifications of archetypal symbols as Jung suggests.

But Freud was wrong in insisting that all dreams have a sexual basis.

From my own extensive study of my own dreams I am sure that many of them have no deep symbolical significance but are quite superficial and are, in fact, the unconscious mind amusing itself by telling stories. Of course they are in symbols as the unconscious cannot use words. Apart from these, there are the depth dreams which are deeply significant. Some of these may well be visions—i.e. coming from outside the mind. These dreams are usually brilliantly coloured and have a timeless feel about them.

This hypothesis might suggest the possibility that Golu, Tio and Numa [a non-physical lion that ROC saw clairvoyantly and which acted as his protector in the etheric realms] are therefore creations of my own creative imagination but programmed from the unconscious, since I had no conscious idea of them until they appeared. They could equally well be separate entities from other planes. I keep an open mind about it. Golu has never appeared in a dream—he is entirely an "aware of" being. So is Numa, unless I regard a dream last year in which a lion cub appeared as his first appearance. If so he must have grown up very quickly. Tio was, at first, too nebulous to register in a dream, though I was aware of a presence and felt his touch. Then he gradually appeared as a definite being in a dream and now does so both as a dream being and an "aware of" one in [my] waking state. He appears only in what I call depth dreams. One of his main functions is to look after my health as he frequently gives me what appears to be some kind of Polynesian huna treatment with massage. In some ways he is a personification of a primitive cosmic energy.

Any communication from an "aware of" personality must ideally be channelled into consciousness without a loss of meaning. In this following script, Golu emphasises the importance of being constantly aware of the possibility of colouration and distortion arising during the transmission of information from entities in the superconscious realms. This applies equally to ROC and other sensitives.

Golu explains the mechanism by which these communications take place, points out how distortion can arise, and how it may be recognised and minimised. He also indicates that some communicating sources, such as an entity from the planes of illusion, may give rise to completely erroneous and false "truths." The planes of illusion usually infer the lower astral levels closest to our Earth vibrations which are most easily accessed by psychics. These planes have their fair share of mischievous and even evil spirits, and hence the quality of the channelled messages can be highly dubious. This topic is discussed more fully in the later chapter on ROC's space connection.

An important distinction needs to be made here. In the life-between-life worlds that the soul inhabits when not in Earth incarnation, the "scenery" there may also be illusory in that it can be created at will by the thought processes of the soul. The soul, in its "home state," is well aware of the temporary nature of these creations which dissolve when no longer needed. This does not however infer that communications from this source are also themselves illusory or fundamentally impure.

However, superconscious entities "in high places" apparently do not wish to spoon-feed us with answers to all our questions. This would arguably infringe our capacities for freewill and self discovery. Confusingly, messages may be deliberately enigmatic, leaving us in the position where we are forced to form our own conclusions. It was once stated, "knock, and the door will be opened to you." However, the particular door was never specified, nor was the length of time one had to knock. Seems at times that a battering ram might have been a more effective solution than a door knocker! Indeed, patience is a virtue.

> 630609. As has been said before, and can never be sufficiently emphasised, all communications coming through a "channel" are liable to contamination. There is no such thing as a perfectly pure channel, though many people think there is and are prepared to accept as profound truth every word that comes through.
>
> Communications come in the form mainly of images and symbols and are translated into word by the channel's unconscious mind. The word may seem to be heard directly inside the head, but the translation is still taking place. There will usually be a different kind of thought from the channel, but the words used will be taken from the channel's vocabulary, though some of them may not be in frequent use. Some may have only been heard or read once or twice, so unusual words can appear.
>
> Most communications are terse and to the point, so long-windedness may usually be put down to the channel's desire to

pad out the information given. If the channel is a long-winded person, this will be quite normal. There is also wishful thinking on the part of the channel which may colour the script unconsciously. There are associations which tend to be added, and there is often a tendency to give the script a twist which will take it in a way conforming to the channel's manner of thinking and ideas. The totally unexpected may be a sign of true communication. Be on guard all the time, and try to separate out the truth from the accretions. This applies to what you are getting now and have received at other times.

Do not question the truth of what is coming through at the time of receiving it, as this would raise a barrier which would impede the message. Receive it uncritically, keeping the mind as blank as possible. Criticise afterwards, and question the truth as much as you like.

You ask if there are long winded entities which might explain wordy scripts. 0f course there are, but they are usually on a low vibration level which should be easily detectable. This present script is being given to keep you critical. The warning will be repeated from time to time.

You have already been told of the planes of illusion. Many sensitives tune into them and bring through false material. The planes of illusion are not necessarily bad or evil. They are just not in accord with the higher facets of truth and thus out of harmony with God's will. They are necessary for some people who would be unable to face the difficulties of their earth lives without their beliefs. The planes of illusion must ultimately be dispersed, but this will take place in the course of spiritual evolution. It is not wise to set out to destroy a person's beliefs coming from such planes. This can cause great trouble and suffering. The realisation of false beliefs must come about gradually and naturally.

Further aspects of communication come from another one of the many beings that ROC was in contact with, in this case from an Egyptian entity who discussed ideas of auric and telepathic communication. ROC was initially given the message verbally, but was sufficiently impressed with it to ask that it be dictated.

651030. "Yes, I will give you what I said in writing. I asked you why you were wearing clothes, because it helps communication when you are naked since, as well as what you call telepathic means, a second path is provided through the interaction of the auras and the various rays produced by the different bodies which reinforce the communication and make it more certain. In your case, as you have a physical body, you also have a physical aura. This aura is stopped by clothes and is only visible round the head and hands in a distorted and contaminated way. People who are able to see it seem not to realise this distortion. The result of wearing clothes is to pull the whole aura out of shape. That is one reason why you are happier without clothes because you are unconsciously aware of the auric distortion which causes you mild discomfort.

"You suggested that it is only the physical aura that is suppressed by clothes, since what you call clairvoyants can see what must be an astral one. This is true, but the astral aura, as you call it, is also distorted and contaminated to some extent by the suppression of the physical aura which leads to misjudgements on the part of the sensitive. In my case, as I have no physical aura having no physical body, it is the interaction with your non-physical aura that matters. It must not be contaminated, so a much freer and truer flow of thought takes place when you are naked. We can of course communicate, as we are doing at the moment, by what you call telepathic means.

"You also asked how I came to talk good English. I don't. It is your own brain that provides the illusion that I do so. While you have a physical body, you have a physical brain which has been trained to use and understand your native language—in your case English. What you call your unconscious mind does not use words. It uses or "thinks" in images and symbols. Telepathy is a function of the unconscious with living people, therefore the word message being exchanged must be translated into the unconscious mind's terms—images and symbols. It is transmitted in this form. As I have no physical brain, it is my normal form of thought. Images and symbols are to a great extent universal. What I want to convey to you is transmitted to your unconscious in this form as images and symbols. It is transformed by your mind (unconscious and conscious) and brain into your own language. When you think you hear me talking to you, the sound of my voice is in your own mind. This does not mean that it is artificial, for your brain is producing the exact equivalent in English of my physical voice, when I had a body, speaking in my own language.

"Your brain at the moment, aided by your unconscious mind, is transforming the images and symbols received from me by your unconscious into words in English which you are writing down. The writing is your own handwriting, possibly modified by an influence coming from me. Any "automatic writing" you get will probably be the same: your own hand slightly modified. Neither Golu nor I are trying to move your hand or control your muscles. We work through your mind. When you relax and try to make your mind as blank as possible, this can be done.

"Of course, you can never be certain how much is coming from the entities we claim to be and how much from your own mind. You must either accept or reject. You are right to have reasonable doubts, but we feel now that you are fairly certain that we are real. Belief makes things easier. It delights me that you can see me. I have a deep affection for you because of the bond between us. Blessings."

Note: the handwriting original of the above document (30th October) is distinctly different from the script of two night's previous. The above one is narrow and spidery compared to the smaller rounded appearance of the 28th October.

A further script, source unnamed but likely to be from St. Germain, received almost three years later, again reiterates the warnings regarding channelled messages and how to discern their truthfulness and authenticity:

660620a. The planes of illusion are easily tapped, and continual watch must be kept, just as it must against conditioning by dogma and prejudice. The truth in any case is many faceted and elusive and must be constantly sought. It does not matter where it comes from, as long as it is recognised for what it is. Trust your intuition and instinct. Messages like this get repeated to drive home the importance of the content. Many messages tend to get repeated over and over again, with little variation, because they are there, and can be tuned into. It is like playing the same bit of tape over and over again. All these bits of repetition have to be cut out of the message in order to get the new and original. Many channels get this repetition and very little new. They then pad out the repetitions with words, many of which sound impressive but have little contribution to make to the meaning.

Many caveats on channels and channelled information are voiced to ROC (again, likely coming from St. Germain but not directly stated). This one is given almost a year later from the previous one. In fact, these warnings are a very common theme throughout all the years that ROC himself was receiving messages and emphasise that there is really no such thing as a 100% pure channel. Even if the source is genuine—and recognising that is a major challenge in itself—no two channels, supplied with the same message, will express it in the same words:

> 670520a. You will be used to discern the true from the false. A very high percentage of the messages coming through various channels at the present moment are either false—coming from the planes of illusion, or from undesirable entities who wish to give wrong information and deceive—or coloured by the channel's mind by his desires and wishes. These are often unconscious, and may even come from secondary personalities.
>
> It is not an easy task to sift the true from the false without guidance. Look for tricks of speech belonging to the channel—though these do not necessarily mean false, rather colouration. Masters and entities communicate in direct and simple ideas and concepts as a rule, though there are some long winded entities, but this is usually channel colouration. Look out for flowing language or pseudo archaism. Beware of praise of the channel. This is sometimes given when well merited but is usually the channel praising himself and trying to make it appear it is from someone outside himself. Criticism sometimes received is more convincing, though again, this could be the conscience giving colouration and due to self condemnation. Look for imitation—one channel getting much the same as another—though here you must distinguish between the truth coming through two or more different channels and thus giving confirmation, and one emulating another because of acceptance or praise. It is usually possible to distinguish between what has a fairly obvious human origin and what could only be from a spiritual source.

The greatest care must be taken over material received through a channel and whenever possible confirmation sought.

And in a script from St. Germain, the emphasis is on what has happened, not what was written about it:

> 670207a. It is what happens that matters, not what is written about it. An account can very rarely relate exactly what happened. To begin with, it will only consist of the events and details that have registered in your mind—the things that have caught your attention. It can never be complete, however careful and observant you may be. It is likely to be modified or coloured by your own outlook and ideas. It may well convey a totally different picture to other people who hear or read it, according to their own outlook and ideas. You can never be sure that another pictures what you saw and experienced. At the same time, it may help others to learn about your experiences, and in any case it is as well to write them down even if you show them to no-one. Re-reading such accounts later will bring them back to memory—though the important ones you should never forget. Always write an account as soon after the experience as you possibly can; this will minimise any colouration.

Chapter 7
Nature Kingdoms

Arguably ROC's most important work and esoteric contribution was a result of the contacts which he established with the nature kingdoms. As pointed out in the following script given from "The Hierarchy," this role was to be carried out in ROC's capacity as a human being and not as his higher self, as it was crucially important that this contact be totally representative of "Anyman." For similar reasons, it was important that Pan was accepted in the form of the goat-foot god as this was the image that human beings had imposed on him.

> 670711b. Many of the [elemental] beings you are now contacting and forming the closest of links with dislike the human race because of the thoughtless harm it has done and is doing to the earth's surface, the waters of the earth and the atmosphere, to say nothing of the depths of the earth itself where many of them dwell. They think that the only word the human race knows the meaning of is
>
> "hate"—it does not know the meaning of "love." Some of them would like to see the whole of humanity wiped out as not fit to live. You must show them that at least some human beings do know and understand the meaning of love and can love greatly and unselfishly. You must tell them about these beings. You yourself have developed greatly in your capacity to love and you are finding that when it is real and true it can be limitless—there is enough and more than enough for every being on earth and in heaven. The beings you are meeting know that your love for them is true and real and deep, for they can read your heart—you cannot deceive them.
>
> Not only do they need love, but they must be shown that a human being is capable of it and knows what it means. They must be brought to realise that there are humans who have great qualities and only wish to serve God and mankind and all kingdoms, and to carry out His will, and that they are increasing in numbers as we enter this new age, and that because of them the human race is worth helping and saving in spite of the black sheep, however numerous they are, and however predominant the greed and lust for destruction and possession may be.

This is your main task, and it must be carried out as your human self, though you will receive inspiration, guidance and help. It is man who has abused nature and turned from God, and man who has alienated the nature spirits and beings of all the kingdoms by disbelief and distortion and stupidity. It is through man that this must be put right and reconciliation brought about. You are one of those chosen, trained and prepared to do this. May your work prosper!

While ROC's early experiences with nature spirits, leading to his first encounter with Pan on the Mound in Edinburgh on Saturday 23rd April, 1966, are already recounted in various previous publications, they differ in important detail from his diary entries. This was principally because ROC wished to keep them closely focussed for the general audience new to the subject but especially because there were certain sections of dialogue which might seem to be placing ROC himself on a spiritual pedestal. In his typically humble manner, therefore, these sections were omitted and appear only in his written notes reproduced here.

The sheer diversity in the range of elementals that ROC encountered is staggering, and while the following sections perhaps appear to go over the top a bit in terms of details, it nonetheless represents only a small fraction of ROC's almost daily interactions with nature spirits, among whom the unusual was commonplace!

Kurmos (and Numa)

As was often his wont, ROC paid a visit to the Botanic Gardens in Edinburgh on 19th March, 1966, and on this occasion had his first encounter with an elemental. It was a faun, the goat-footed, horned humanoid from classical Greek mythology, a somewhat miniature version of the Great God Pan whom ROC would have occasion to meet soon after.

That day ROC entered the Gardens feeling tired and depressed, concerned for the health of a close friend and reacting to his strenuous TV acting schedule on the *This Man Craig* set. As he sat under a tree in the vicinity of Inverleith House, he gradually felt the heavy atmosphere lifting from him. He started to sense the life of the tree against which he was leaning and the rising of its sap. In this changed and heightened atmosphere he gradually became aware of a faun gambolling around a tree. Eventually the faun approached ROC and stood staring at him. When greeted by ROC, the faun reacted in a startled fashion and asked if ROC could really see him. On assurance that he could, the faun performed a few antics and asked ROC to describe what he was doing. ROC's description apparently satisfied him. ROC then learned the name of the faun is Kurmos.

The immediately following amusing episode involving the encounter of Kurmos with ROC's etheric lion Numa is not included in the various published accounts—I think for fairly obvious reasons—but I cannot resist including it here. It did happen, after all!

> Numa was with me in the gardens and came up. The faun looked at him, and then at me.
> F. Is that your lion?
> ROC. He is my friend and protector. His name is Numa.
> The faun went up to him, and spoke in his ear. Numa rubbed his face against him. The faun jumped on to his back and Numa loped off. Presently they came back, and the faun jumped off and came and sat beside me on the seat, and Numa lay down with his paws stretched out. I thought how sad it was that none of the staid strollers in the gardens could see what I was seeing - or perhaps it was just as well they didn't.

The dialogue between ROC and Kurmos continued as Kurmos attempted to get an explanation of why human beings wore clothes, why they lived in houses, why they dashed around in boxes with wheels, and so forth. ROC tries to offer explanations as best he can. His diary continues:

> It is necessary to explain that the interchange between us took place by thought transference—i.e. largely in images and symbols and not in words. But to make it intelligible, I have to translate it into words. By doing so, I inevitably personify the faun, and make him seem more human than he was. He is not human but is an elemental nature spirit. He does not think or reason as humans do, but I have to put words into his mouth, which to some extent falsifies the meeting. I had the impression that he had infinite nature wisdom, but in many ways, to me he showed the naivety of a young boy.

Kurmos intimated that he assisted in the growth of the plants in the Botanic Gardens but said regretfully that nature spirits had now lost interest in the human race because their contribution was neither seen nor appreciated. He indicated that withdrawal of their support would be bad news indeed for the well-being of the planet and its inhabitants.

Kurmos showed interest in furthering contact with ROC who invited him to visit the flat if he so wished. Having reassured himself that ROC had a genuine liking for him and nature spirits in general, this offer he immediately accepted, and the pair made their way back to Albany Street. As ROC comments:

> What a lovely thought of the sensation it would have caused, if he could have been seen. Numa, too, was loping along ahead of us.

Back in the flat, Kurmos was curious as to the large number of books and their purpose. He wondered why they were needed at all. Could not knowledge simply be obtained for the asking, as in his kingdom? Once more ROC set about attempting an explanation.

Kurmos remained for some time and a close harmony developed between the two. When he eventually announced that he would have to return to the Botanic Gardens, ROC opened the front door for him. He didn't need to, of course, but Kurmos appeared so physical to ROC that it was an automatic reaction.

Thus ended one of the most memorable and touching moments in ROC's life, but it was to mark the start of intense involvement with the elemental kingdoms that lasted unbroken until his death.

A short note on Numa might not be out of place here. Whilst Tio was charged with maintaining ROC's health, Numa, a lion, was assigned to his protection, principally for periods when ROC might be astral travelling out of his body. It is also indicated that Numa might well assist during unwanted physical encounters, but understandably ROC was reluctant to expose himself to situations where this might have to be put to the test! Numa appeared almost two years before the encounter with Kurmos.

> 641109. Sometime in June, 1964, coming up the stairs to this flat, I caught a glimpse of a shape like a very large dog, which passed me, stopped for a moment on the landing, turned and looked at me, and then continued up the stairs and into the passage way. Then it stopped again and turned. It was a large and very beautiful lion. I took the keys from my pocket, opened

the door of the flat and, turning to the lion, I said. "You are welcome. Are you coming in?" It looked at me and then loped past me into the flat. It looked in at the door of the front room, went right round it, then crossed the lobby into the back room, went round that, had a look into the kitchen, and then stretched out like a cat on the hearth rug. (Golu appeared, grinning all over his face, and asked me how I liked my bodyguard. I said "Very much; please explain."

He said that in future I might be exploring more deeply into the astral plane and, as there were parts of it that are frightening and possibly dangerous, it was thought best that I should have a bodyguard to protect me. He told me the name of the lion was Numa, after Numa Pompilius, and that he was a king in his own domain and could summon helpers if needed. [Interestingly, there was a lion named Numa in Gay's Lion Farm in El Monte, California in the 1920s].

Golu said something to Numa who raised his head and growled—a deep rumbling sound. Immediately six other lions came trotting into the room, circled round it and went out again.

Numa rose, stretched and loped after them, leaving me not believing what I had just seen.

Golu told me that if I was ever alarmed by anything, to call Numa and he would be there. I asked if Numa would be able to help me in this physical world; suppose, for instance, I was attacked by toughs. Golu said "Certainly." I asked how he could help, to which Golu replied, "By appearing as himself to them, they would soon scatter." It's very nice to have this feeling of protection, and somehow I have a strong belief that it would work, though I hope I shall never have to put it to the test.

A day or so after this experience I was walking along Princes Street when I saw Numa trotting along at my side. It caused me much amusement wondering what would happen if he became visible to the passersby.

First Meeting with Pan

The account of ROC's momentous meeting with Pan is well documented in other publications, so I will make do with a précis here.

The Occult Diaries of

ROC was returning on foot from a visit to friends on the south side of Edinburgh on Saturday 23rd April, 1966, and as he walked through "The Meadows," he initially became aware of the presence of many nature spirits around him. As he continued homeward along George IVth bridge, he entered what he describes as a denser than air atmosphere. Crossing into and going down "The Mound," he was suddenly confronted by a large faun, taller than himself, whom he at first took to be Kurmos in grown up form. He quickly realised that this could not be the case. The pair moved on in silence for a bit, and the faun then turned towards ROC, looked at him, and demanded to know if he felt afraid of him. ROC replied that he did not, as he sensed no evil in him. The faun then asked ROC if he knew who he was, and at that moment ROC knew intuitively that this was the Great God Pan.

On providing this answer, Pan then retorted that ROC ought therefore be afraid of him; the word "panic," after all, was derived from the legendary frightening effect Pan's presence had on man. ROC explained that he had no fear as he had much love for Pan's subjects. Pan then challenged ROC again that if this were the case, did he therefore love him? On giving an affirmative response, Pan then remarked that ROC had just said he loved the Devil (the early Christian church considered this to be the case, as with all such elemental beings). Again ROC responded that he felt no evil from him; he was the god of the woodlands and all that dwelt in them; Scandinavians called him Vidor, the god of the woods, and that he even had a picture of him hanging in the front room of his flat.

As they walked on and crossed Princes Street, Pan continued to probe for negative reactions from ROC by enquiring if he thought he looked ugly and smelt rank like a goat. On the contrary, replied ROC, saying he was aware of a pleasant musk like smell, like the fur of a healthy cat, of the smell of wet leaves, and of pinewoods. Looking for further signs of fear, Pan put his arm around ROC's shoulder, but ROC still registered no fear.

On enquiring if Pan had pan-pipes, he obligingly produced them and started to play a curious melody which ROC had difficulty remembering. By this time they had reached the flat in Albany Street, and although Pan had now disappeared, ROC was still aware of his presence.

The published accounts of this meeting with Pan stop here, but Pan once again made his presence felt as ROC was preparing to go to bed that night. For reasons of humility, ROC never made this episode public. This extract is from his diary entries:

> 660423. It was not until I had undressed and was coming

through to the front room, as I usually do last thing at night, to gauge the power building up, that Pan suddenly confronted me. He was looking very fierce. He drew himself up to his full height, and said "You know who I am. Kneel down and worship me."

ROC. Oh no. There is only one true God who is above all the Creator. He created you as well as me. You owe him allegiance as well as I do.

P. You know who I am.

I drew myself up to my full height, and said "But, do you know who I am?"

At that moment my higher self took over. Pan took a step back: "Now I understand why you are not afraid of me." He bowed to me.

I returned the bow, and said "Now we respect each other."

P. Let us embrace as brothers. I and my subjects will help you when you need us." He stepped forward and embraced me, and vanished. I was left with the scent of pinewoods and damp leaves, turned earth, woodland flowers, and the faint musk-like animal scent. It lingered for quite a while.

During a further visit to the Botanic Gardens the following day, ROC was still aware of the presence of elementals. His thoughts regarding a rather tubby-looking nature spirit were clearly not appreciated:

660424. Edinburgh. Quite a nice day. Aware of Kurmos and certain brown-clad earth spirits. I was thinking that they looked like rather fat infants. One of them, looking very annoyed, came up to me and said, "I'm not fat."

Pan – Christ Reconciliation

During a visit to Findhorn the following month, ROC, in the company of Peter Caddy and the psychic Kathy Sparks, climbs up to the mound on the top of Cluny Hill near Findhorn. Standing on the power point there (see later in this book for a description of power points), ROC is once again acutely aware of Pan standing as an immense figure behind him, but also of the Christ presence in front of him. These two figures then link through ROC—with ROC once again apparently acting as a representative of humankind—in a ceremony of reconciliation, bringing together once more the elemental kingdoms, which had been outcast by the early Christian church, and the Christ spirit. ROC records the following in Peter's journal, *The Unpremeditated Pilgrimage*:

> 660512. I felt a tremendous power running through me coming up from the ground, and then later on coming down from the sky, and I had a feeling that some tremendous power, a great being, completely took me over and seemed to be functioning through me. I saw at one time rings of elemental spirits of all sorts dancing joyously around the Mound, and I was aware of the figure of Pan standing behind me and felt his hands on my shoulders at one time. Opposite me, behind Kathy, I saw a radiant figure of Christ, who seemed to raise His hands in blessing, and I felt this extraordinary bond that existed between the Christ figure and Pan.

Testing times

The next meeting with Pan took place in the afternoon, again in the Botanic Gardens where he had first met the faun, Kurmos. Once more Pan attempts to elicit feelings of fear in ROC. The dialogue continues:

> 660607. Edinburgh. In the afternoon, I felt compelled to go down to the Botanic Gardens. At the gate, Pan joined me and walked by my side. Partly into the Garden, I crossed to a seat under a tree and sat. Pan sat beside me, very close to me, and put his arm round my shoulder.
> P. Still not afraid?
> ROC. No.
> P. Not even the slightest little tremor?
> ROC. No.
> P. A human being who does not shrink from Pan?
> ROC. You know why.
> P. Yes, but you are incarnate in a physical body. Doesn't that shrink from me the least little bit?
> ROC. No.
> He was watching me very closely and had his back almost touching mine. He was radiating an immense power, but it was pleasant and not overpowering. I was conscious of the same

pine wood, faintly animal scent which I had smelt on the first meeting.

P. But, of course, like all foolish human beings, you have clothes on. Perhaps if you had none it would be different—you might then shrink from my touch!

I reminded him that on that first occasion when he confronted me in the flat at the end of the meeting, it was after I had undressed and was naked. When he embraced me, I had felt his body against mine with nothing between.

P. Yes, but you had been taken over by your Higher Self then.

ROC. You think that made a difference?

P. Of course.

ROC. Well, I can't take my clothes off here to prove to you that I am neither afraid nor would shrink from your touch.

P. Some time I will test that statement when the Higher One is absent.

ROC. Why do you want to do that?

P. I must be certain that human beings as represented by you, through whom the great reconciliation has been brought about, are no longer afraid of me. In the inner and higher life we are brothers and in a way one, but in the material plane it is different.

ROC. I don't think I shall fail in any test you apply to me as I have no fear. I have only love for you.

P. And you cannot deceive me since I can read your thoughts.

He suddenly stood up, and turning, stood opposite me.

P. Tell me. Am I not ugly?

I looked at him.

ROC. No, Pan, you are not ugly. You are beautiful.

This is true. Only conceited humans who judge all other beings against themselves as the ideal, would think otherwise.

Pan smiled.

P. I know you believe that and I am glad. I must be accepted as I am in this aspect if I am to help mankind.

A further encounter with Pan was again intended to test ROC's fear reactions. The sequel, involving the entrance of a large snake, was certainly not anticipated by ROC!:

> 660610. Edinburgh. This morning after having a shower, I was just finishing drying myself when Pan walked in. "Now is the time," he said. "You are naked, and the Higher Self is absent." He came up behind me, and putting his arms round me held me close against his body.
>
> P. No fear? No shrinking?
>
> Again I felt the wonderful scent of pinewoods and earth and the faint musk like smell. He radiated power, and I could feel energy flowing from him into me. There was a feeling of security and peace; not the least trace of fear. He asked me if I was not repulsed by the feel of his hairy legs against mine. I said "No." The hair was fine and silky, and the contact warm and pleasant. He felt my body all over with his hands, watching closely for the slightest sign of fear or repulsion. I felt none. I felt a strong sense of being one with him, a feeling of both surging energy and peace. I could rest in his arms for ever, enveloped in this sense of security and the scent of pinewoods. He turned me round and held me tightly against himself, his hands stroking my back. Again the sense of warmth, surging energy, and at the same time, peace and security. I asked him if he was satisfied now that there was neither fear nor any shrinking from his touch on my part. He smiled and said yes, he was satisfied. I had passed the test well but would be further tested. He disappeared.
>
> I began to wonder if I would be visited by some grotesque or repulsive entity as the script above had hinted. What happened was very different from what I expected. A large serpent came crawling rapidly into the room. It was a huge cobra. I knew what was going to happen, but after a slight tremor, I felt no fear. The snake reached my feet, and rearing up, wound itself round my body in a clockwise direction, crawling up me. I was still completely naked. I held out my arms so that they would be clear of the coils of which there must have been about six. It laid its head flat on top of my head, producing a vision of *Aion*, without the lion head! I knew it was not meant to be the animal "snake" but the serpent aspect of some elemental being.
>
> In spite of it being non-physical, the sensation was largely physical. I have never felt anything like it in my life before,

and I am sure I could not have entirely imagined it. The snake was icy cold and made my skin bristle, and yet there was a warmth radiating from it. The combination of feelings is quite indescribable. The coils were fairly tightly wrapped round my body but not unpleasantly tight. There was a rhythmic contraction and relaxation that was strangely pleasant. What surprised me was the definite feeling of affection coming from the serpent which I found I could return. I felt no fear or repulsion. The cobra was beautiful with wonderful markings. It looked iridescent. It began to stroke my cheek with the underside of its head. I could feel its tongue flickering in and out, tickling my skin. It felt all round my face and neck in this way, and then over my chest and back; all the time, there was this very odd mixture of icy cold body and radiating warmth. I stroked its head with my hand. Presently the cobra just faded away. I have no memory of it uncoiling. One of the oddest experiences of my life.

In a somewhat similar incident on the Findhorn beach, the serpent coils around ROC, who is aware of his head apparently changing into that of the head of a lion, an identification with the god Aion. The Saturnian connection is again clear, but the exact meaning puzzles ROC:

> 670803. Findhorn. Raining, but presently the rain stopped and the sun came out. I sunbathed for quite awhile and then went to the shore for a bathe. The sea was surprisingly clear. There was a wonderful sky, varying from blue clear sky to very black storm clouds, with many cotton wool fluffy clouds building up into towers and cities in between. A most dramatic sky. I sunbathed again and decided not to dress until the sun went behind dense clouds that were slowly coming across. Tio was with me and gave me a Huna treatment which filled me with energy. I had already drawn a lot from the sea. I could feel the touch of his hands very strongly, especially on my spine.
>
> I then saw a serpent crawling over the sand towards me, a python. I stood quite still, stretching my arms out and the serpent wound itself round my naked body and laid its head flat on the top of my head. It was icy cold and yet it radiated warmth as on the previous occasion when the same thing happened. This time I felt that my own head had become the head of a lion. I

had become the likeness of the god Aion—the Mithraic Chronos (Saturn). I know this has tremendous significance, though as yet I do not understand. The serpent faded away.

Denlio and Friends

Further meetings with unusual elementals continued:

> 660611. Edinburgh. Last night, I had a visit from a woodland sprite who told me his name was Denlio. He was about four or five inches high of a beautiful iridescent green colour. I facetiously asked him if he was a little green man from Mars. He said, "Of course not, don't be silly. I am a spirit. I live in the Botanic Gardens looking after the branches of the trees." He was very thin, slightly suggesting a stick insect or a grasshopper, but with human-like attributes.
>
> I find that if one throws away the conceited human habit of comparing anything remotely human in shape with the Greek ideal, and consider these beings in their own light, an entirely new perspective is arrived at. This little being was very beautiful looked at in this way. I am learning quickly how to hold this perspective in looking at these beings, and what a difference it makes. I realise that the earth spirit who was indignant the other day in the Botanic Gardens because I compared him and his companions to fat infants, was right. According to their perspectives, he was not fat. We must accept all these beings as themselves in their own right and not make comparisons with the human ideal which applies only to the human race. They have their ideals too. Denlio had heard that I was accepted as a friend and wanted to see me.

Encounters with the denizens of the nature kingdoms continued to take on an expanded dimension for ROC as he once again visited the Botanic Gardens the following day. As recounted in Newton's LBLs, souls can take on various appearances to suit the situation, and the same appears to hold true of nature spirits. Once again, Pan is present.

> 660612. Edinburgh. I felt a strange urge to go to the Botanic Gardens. The day had cleared up and was beautifully sunny. As I

left the house, Denlio was sitting on my shoulder. He asked if he could travel with me that way. I said certainly. Communication is really by telepathy, but I was vaguely aware of a very high pitched chirping voice. On the way down Dublin Street, I was aware of a beautiful flame on my right shoulder. It formed patterns, but had no form to speak of. I knew it was a salamander and spoke to it (him? It is doubtful if they have sexual differentiation.). He asked me if he could travel on my right shoulder as Denlio was on my left. I said yes, provided he did not burn a hole in my jacket. He said he was cosmic—non-physical—fire and would not burn material objects, and that certainly they would never destroy anything of mine as I was their friend. I said surely he was small. He agreed, and said they varied greatly in size and could alter size and shape at will.

I then saw a number of flames travelling along the pavement. They kept changing shape and were the most wonderful colour. Some were about ten feet tall at times. Occasionally the shape veered towards a human one. I realised that my acceptance into the elemental world was complete, and the veil had been lifted.

Turning into Inverleith Row, I saw many shapes. Beautiful silver coloured sylphs and green dryads. The shapes were mostly changing but occasionally the hint of a human form. There were lots of little elves and gnomes, occasionally clad in brown and greens, but quite often naked. I was told that their true spirits are almost formless changing patterns, but that they take on aspects which to a great extent are projected onto them by human beings. That is, human beings expect to see them in certain shapes and dressed in particular ways, and myths have been built up through the ages. These entities take on the myth, and appear to those who believe in them as they are expected to.

They also tend to take on human shape because it is more acceptable to us and partly because God created man with a special physique, and man could be a god if he lived right according to God's will. The human form is something to be aspired to therefore. Those entities do not wear clothes but appear to us to do so. Their "clothes" are really part of themselves. They respect human conventions, though they think them often stupid and will not try to shock us. Because of my nudist attitude, they can appear to me naked. I am not projecting clothes onto them, and they are not having to create them. Fig leaves and prudery do not really exist in this world. But I find they very frequently appear as their spirit essences to me now because I can accept them like that. I don't call for human shapes. They are of course very ephemeral and transparent and extremely beautiful. It is quite impossible to convey a real sense of the beauty in words.

In the gardens, I was aware of multitudes of beings—elves and gnomes dancing round the trees. Tree spirits, dryads, tiny spirits. Denlio pointed out his friends to me sitting on the branches of the trees, sometimes clinging to them. Many of them danced over to me and greeted me. Pan was there walking by my side. The gardens were looking superbly lovely in the late afternoon sunshine. This was one of the most glorious moments of my life.

Which Pan?

On a further meeting with Pan, ROC is once again challenged as to his acceptance of the traditional appearance of Pan. It is important to realise that the visualisations of generations of mankind of Pan as the cloven hoofed god led to the creation of that idealised thought-form, but the essence of the being is capable of adopting any form to suit the occasion. As pointed out earlier, a similar situation exists in the human realms where, for example, an individual undergoing an NDE may meet the traditional angel, complete with wings. The same "angel," however, may take on the appearance of a wise old man to someone who has atheistic leanings.

> 660620b. Edinburgh. Pan came in and sat in the armchair with its back to the door, opposite the one in which I was sitting reading. There was a period of silent communion. Presently he stood up, and as I watched him, he slowly changed into the conventional type of Greek god—the Greek ideal of the human form. He stood looking at me and then asked me which aspect I preferred. I immediately said I preferred the Pan with the cloven hooves, the shaggy legs and the horns as he was the woodland god I loved and respected. He smiled, and I knew that my choice was right. He changed back into this aspect, asking me if it was wholly and completely acceptable. I said it was completely so.

R. Ogilvie Crombie

He said that aspect might have been originally man inspired and in a way man imposed, as were so many of the aspects of the elementals and nature spirits, but it was age-old, and fixed. He said he was pleased and now entirely satisfied that I accepted him completely in that aspect.

Pan Within

The next important encounter with Pan was at the end of a weekend course at the Attingham Park Adult Education College near Shrewsbury in Shropshire, when ROC went for a morning walk around the Park grounds:

> 661010. Shrewsbury. Went down the mile walk. Power very strong, beginning reaching the cedars and increasing, producing slight difficulty in walking; feel of walking through an atmosphere somewhat thicker than air, but not so thick as water. [There was] intense stimulation of the centres [chakras], particularly heart, throat and head, producing an increase in rate of heart beat, and a considerable degree of breathlessness and feeling of pressure in the head. I stopped at the power point [called the] "Place of the Philosophers" by a tree near the path. I was "pulled off" the path and stood looking at the big tree near the river. I had a strong feeling of having slipped out of the earthly plane into another higher plane interpenetrating it—of having stepped out of time.
>
> Something seemed to be building up immediately in front of the tree. I had a feeling of excited expectation. Something was about to happen. I went on as far as the corner where the rhododendron walk turns off to the left. I stood for some time looking at the lovely view of the river and the trees, aware of a tremendous build up of power to a pitch which I have seldom felt before. The physical sensation already mentioned increased enormously. The total effect was almost too much to bear though it was not unpleasant, being rather thrilling because of the sense of expectancy. I began walking along the rhododendron walk and into the wood. There was an indescribable feeling of utter peace, and a raising up to a high spiritual plane; a sense of contact with the divine.
>
> A great degree of hyperaesthesia was reached, intensifying

the sense of sight, hearing, and smelling. The grass and bushes became even more three dimensional than normal, with an intensity of shape and form which is quite impossible for anyone who has not experienced it to understand. I was aware of every blade of grass and of every leaf; of the markings on the bark of the trees and a feeling for colour and its significance, which was almost overwhelming. [There was] a tremendous sense of utter and complete reality. The sense of awe and wonder is indescribable. There was an acute feeling of being one with nature in a totally complete way, as well as being one with the divine. An even greater surge of physical sensation took place, reaching an intensity I have never before experienced. All the centres were activated producing a feeling of great exultation.

I was aware of Pan by my side and of a strong bond between us. He stepped behind me and then walked into me, completely taking me over. I became Pan and saw the world through his eyes, though at the same time a part of me, the recording and observing part, seemed to stand aside. The moment I became Pan, the woods changed, and I saw all the earth spirits, the elementals: nymphs, dryads, fauns, satyrs, elves, fairies, gnomes, and so on. Some of them were dancing round me in rings. All were welcoming me and full of rejoicing and delight. I was outside space and time, and everything was happening at once.

It is quite impossible to describe the wonderful experience. Words are hopelessly inadequate and can only give a faint impression of the actuality. I can only stress the feeling of exultation, of joy and delight, of a wild exhilaration, and yet of the underlying peace, contentment, and spirituality. This is of the greatest importance. This is due to the reconciliation, the unity being brought about between the nature forces, the primitive cosmic forces, and the spiritual forces, all becoming one within the divine mind, as was the intent and is the truth.

I continued along the walk aware of my cloven hooves, shaggy legs, and horned brow, completely at one with all nature. After a time I reached a clearing with a seat under a tree. I turned here, and started to walk back. Now I had pan-pipes between my hands and I began to play. It was the melody I have often heard Pan play and can never recall afterwards. The birds responded, and their song was an exquisite counterpart to the music of the piper. All the beings and spirits were active and many were dancing as they worked. I began to dance myself, still playing the pipes. Presently I stopped, attracted by a cluster of mushroom-like fungus. There were dozens of hood shaped beings, all intertwined, of a dark brown colour, and the cluster was alive with tiny bustling figures, elves or fauns of some sort. As they appear to me, their shapes, though fairly distinct, were not quite as portrayed in the conventional picture of such beings. Some of these beings do appear as the conventional ones we get in legend and myth, but their shapes are imposed on them by mankind and taken over by them. They have, of course, higher light bodies which are quite different.

As I went on, partly dancing, partly walking, still playing the pipes in great joy, I knew that there was going to be a great upsurge of the nature forces at Attingham, and that the placing of the bronze plaque on the "ancient of days" [a large, old tree on the Attingham grounds] had been an act of great significance which made this possible.

Presently I walked on. Pan was now beginning to withdraw, and had left me by the time I had reached the corner again. This was as well, as there was a boy sitting on the seat by the tree. It might have been disconcerting for at least one of us if I had come dancing out of the woods playing invisible pan-pipes. Walking as sedately as I could after this tremendous experience, I went on a bit by the path running straight on. The grass was long and very wet, and it was beginning to rain, so I turned and began to walk back. As I approached the ancient oak tree—the ancient of days—I was aware of an immense being both containing the tree within itself and soaring far above it. There was a feeling of immense brooding power. This was certainly the spirit of the tree and might well have been the spirit of the place. There was a faintly luminous aura round the tree. I went to the back of the tree and read the "Hymn to Pan" on the bronze plate fixed to the tree. I decided to take a copy of this, and then went back along the path.

I stopped and stood on the power point when I reached it [for an explanation of "power points," please see Chapter 11], and then approached the oak tree which had a very strong aura and was radiating powerful pulsating, horizontal rays as I had seen it do before. It seemed to me to change from a tree into a vast pillar of power. When I left the tree, I went on down until I reached the place of the philosophers, where, as before, I was drawn off the walk.

Again, I had a strong sense of something tremendous impending and a feeling of going out of time and space. I was aware of the presence of Pythagoras who was standing under the large tree near the river. I was prompted to approach him and walked up to the tree. There was a feeling of great power, and I found it difficult to approach the tree. Pythagoras stepped to the side, and I was drawn to the tree. It was almost as if he had put his arm round my shoulder and gently pushed me towards the tree. I turned round with my back to it, feeling as if I was inside a vortex of power. I was now aware of being within a vast circular dome-crowned building. It was very tenuous but real. There were crowds of people within it, moving about and talking. Some of them began to walk past me. Quite a number of them I recognised, such as Plato, Socrates, Aristotle, Confucius, Lao Tse, Mohammed, St. Germain, Dr. Dee, Francis Bacon. I am sure there were many more I could have recognised, but in this strange state where everything happens in the eternal now, it is next to impossible to translate it into terms of our time. But I believe I have remembered and recognised at least some of the essential ones. Then the figure of Buddha appeared sitting under a tree, then the immense figure of the risen Christ raising his hands in a blessing over Attingham.

Confrontations

This particular episode in man's dealings with the nature kingdom is a salutary reminder indeed of man's destruction of the environment. Instead of the expected warm exchanges taking place between ROC and nature spirit, this encounter reflected one of intense antagonism towards humanity from an alienated section of the elementals who viewed human beings as the very scum of the earth thanks to their extensive and thoughtless pillage of nature. It was ROC's lot to both confront them and plead our case with an objective of winning them over to cooperation. The initial visit to Rosemarkie on the 14th of June was in his normal physical body. His second visit was both physical and out of the body, while a subsequent visit was purely an OOB on the etheric realms. Because of its considerable significance, ROC had expanded his notes to form a more readable version, and that is what is presented here:

> 670616. Rosemarkie. In 1903, when I was approaching my fourth birthday, my family spent an Easter vacation at Rosemarkie, a little town on the north shore of the Moray Firth. A beauty spot known as "The Fairy Glen," at that time part of a private estate, had a powerful fascination for me. I was taken there frequently by my nurse, Mary, often accompanied by my elder sister, Katie, who was thirteen years older. From time to time, I have had strong flashes of memory of this glen; of a waterfall with two streams of water splashing down into a rocky pool; of a flight of steps and a wooden bridge crossing a stream, and of a "wishing well" under an overhanging rock, a clear circular pool of water with a bottom covered with pebbles into which I used to drop a penny while wishing a wish.
>
> In those days I believed in fairies, as I still do, and this glen was fairyland to me. I was anxious to revisit it sometime, never having done so, feeling that it had a significance and played a part in what is happening to me now and ought in any case to be linked with the garden at Findhorn.
>
> Peter had taken me with two others to visit Inverewe Gardens at Poolewe on the west coast of Scotland. I had told Peter of my desire to visit Rosemarkie, so as we passed fairly close to it on the way back, he turned off the Inverness Road at Muir of Ord and we set off for The Black Isle, as that part of the country is called, I believe from the density of the woodland that covers it.
>
> It was late afternoon. As we approached Rosemarkie I felt some excitement and expectation. What would it be like after sixty four years? Could I remember anything? No memory stirred as we entered the town, and I had no idea where to start looking for the glen, to go on or turn inland. A long time ago I had come across a reference to The Fairy Glen in a newspaper. There was no money for its upkeep and it was going wild; the estate had been partly dispersed — it was probably no longer known by its old name.
>
> Leaving the town we soon came to an S bend in the road where it crossed a river. Ahead of us was a rough bit of land covered with bushes and long grass at one side of which was

what appeared to be the drive leading to a house on a height to the left. Beyond the house was a glen thick with trees. I knew this was what we were looking for. Peter parked the car on the far side of the bridge, and we started along the drive. We could see a narrow path leading from it into the glen.

When we reached it, this path proved to be difficult; a flood had washed part of it away. It was wet and slippery and there were fallen tree trunks lying across it. The place had certainly gone wild. We managed to get over this bad part and find the path again. So far I had no recollection of the place. I was certain the way in had been different, having a strong memory of a gate or door through a wall. The trees were different. There certainly had been trees, but most of these there now were comparatively young; they could not have been there sixty-four years ago, nor could the ferns and bushes. The place was different, and yet it felt the same, the enchantment was the same. I had been aware of it at four years old, and that awareness had been renewed in a marvellous manner since the meeting with the little faun in the Botanic Garden in Edinburgh. There were many "little people" in this glen. I could not see them to begin with but I sensed their presence.

Our two companions were forging ahead. They were not really interested and may have resented this detour. I don't blame them; the path was slippery and difficult with the mud and fallen trees and the day was dull and wet. Peter suggested that if I thought it necessary to go further, I should do so by myself. He called the other two back.

This was just what I wanted. I went on alone and Peter made sure that the others lingered behind. There was a small river on the left hand side of the path which was gradually rising. After proceeding for some time I came on a pond on the right hand side of the path. A little beyond it I sensed I was approaching a significant point and suddenly found myself unable to go any further. There was an invisible barrier in front of me; it was as if my feet were stuck to the ground. With much difficulty I managed to advance a few more yards feeling uneasy and looking about me. Suddenly two elves appeared before me barring the way. They were about three feet high, dressed in green tunics, breeches and hats. To my astonishment, they carried bows and arrows.

They had drawn the bows and the arrows were pointing at me. One of them said:

"Mortal man, approach no further."

I explained to them that I was a friend of Pan's and the nature spirits and that I came to them with love in my heart.

"We have no love for man," said the second elf. "He does not believe in us and wantonly destroys our dwellings and desecrates our sacred places. Go back to where you came from and leave us in peace."

They were standing still and tense, their arrows still pointing at me. I did not move; I was equally tense, and yet I could not help wondering what would happen to me if they loosed their arrows, which could not be material. I thought it best to take no chances. There are many tales of nasty things happening to mortals foolish enough to fall foul of the "little people."

"Not all men are bad, there are exceptions. I admit man has desecrated nature and destroyed your dwelling places, but not deliberately. He has ceased to believe in your existence and is driven by greed and ignorance. Many of us detest this behaviour as much as you do. We believe in you and want your friendship and help."

"That may be so, but this is our stronghold. We want no mortals here."

I was aware that Pan was standing behind me but was not making his presence known to the elves. He was there as an observer and was not going to help me. I was on my own. Possibly as representing man, this was right.

The two elves lowered their bows and turned away; they seemed to be conferring. Presently they turned to me, and one of them said: "You may go on along the path as we see that you do have love for us in your heart."

They stepped aside and let me pass. I went on for about a dozen yards. The path was rising gently and reached a point where it began to descend. I felt I should go no further on this occasion. The elves appeared again and said that had I been alone I would have been welcome to go as far as I wanted to, but as I was not, it would be better to return to my friends who were slowly coming on behind and to whom they sent greetings. They then melted away into the trees.

Walking back along the wet and slippery path I had a lot to think about. This was my first encounter with hostile nature spirits. I had met negative and evil entities, but these were neither, they were good and beautiful and justified in their hostility. I thought of some of the appalling outrages man has committed against nature and felt depressed and sad. Somehow or other those who believe and care must demonstrate to the nature kingdoms that not all mankind is ruthless and destructive—a formidable task

I had been prevented from going further into the glen; not only prevented but threatened. What about others? Surely other human beings visited the glen? It was not private as far as I knew. Could the elves prevent anyone from going to the end of the path? This I found hard to believe. Was it because I was able to see and communicate with them that they could stop me and give me a demonstration of their real feelings towards mankind? Was it up to me to do something about it? I was immediately aware of Pan beside me. He answered my unvoiced question.

"Yes, it is indeed up to you. You are being used as an ambassador from the human race. You must try to win over these elves who are hostile. You must justify mankind. It is important as part of the attempt to bring about co-operation with the elemental kingdom. You understand why I cannot help you? I am on their side. It is up to you. Go back to them later."

I was once more alone, still wondering about many things, but finding it surprisingly easy to accept as normal those happenings I would have rejected a short time ago. They had almost become part of my everyday life. Some miracle had enabled me to shed my conditioning and prejudices and become aware of unseen realms which were so beautiful and just as real as the material world. If only this could happen to others, then the whole world could be transformed and life become a thing of joy and delight instead of the thing of depression and misery it so often was. Perhaps this is one of the things that will happen in the new age.

I rejoined Peter and the others, and we returned to the car. The rain was stopping and the sky began to clear. I told them something of my experience and passed on the elves' greetings.

R. Ogilvie Crombie

That night I returned to the glen out-of-the-body. It was a moonlit night, the earlier rain clouds having completely dispersed leaving a cloudless sky. I walked along the path past the pond to the place where I had turned. I had not long to wait before the two elves appeared, this time without their bow and arrows. One of them spoke to me:

"Welcome friend of Pan. We greet you. As you are now alone, you may come with us to the meeting place where you are expected."

I followed them along the path. There were numerous beautiful trees and bushes, and even in the moonlight I could see the many wild flowers. I was fully aware of my surroundings, perhaps more so than in my physical body. There was a wonderful feeling of serenity. We walked on for a considerable distance before they turned off the path to the left. I followed them through the trees and found myself in a glade. It was quite large, roughly semi-circular in shape with trees all round it. The river lay beyond a fringe of trees. I was aware of the distant sound of what was probably a waterfall.

The glade was thronged with nature spirits, mainly elves, of many different sizes, shapes and manner of dress. Some of them were familiar from myths and legends, conforming to man's idea of such beings; some of them strange and to me unknown. It is impossible to remember them all in detail; there were so many.

One of them, larger than the rest, dressed in green like the ones who had stopped me that afternoon, wearing a golden yellow cloak and hat, was sitting under a tree near the river. I assumed him to be their chief or king. My guides pointed to him, and I walked towards him through the throng of beings who parted to let me through in dead silence.

This elf rose to greet me and invited me to sit before him pointing to a hump in the ground. As I sat down the elves watched me with interest and curiosity, and I was aware of waves of hostility directed at me. I felt very vulnerable, the only one of my kind amidst these strange beings who belonged to another world and were not friendly. I felt I was a prisoner in the hands of the "little people."

Pan had told me that I was an ambassador from mankind whose purpose was to win them over. I must show no signs of alarm or fear. I smiled and bowed to the chief elf and waited. My heart was thumping, but I hoped that would not show. He had been watching me closely; now he spoke:

"We much prefer to see you alone. You are welcome. We are not friendly towards man, as you already know, but we will listen to what you have to say in his favour and if you can convince us that we ought to co-operate, we will do so."

The elf-king rose to his feet. It seemed to me that he was the spokesman not only for the beings present in the glade but for all the nature spirits. There followed a crushing indictment of man and his abuse and exploitation of nature. The elf was only four feet tall but, as he stood there looking at me sternly with his cold and piercing eyes, the power and authority that came from him was awe-inspiring.

The main accusation was that man had betrayed his role in the universe. Created by God, he had evolved according to God's will and design, becoming the highest form of life on this planet and being incarnate spirit. He had been given full dominion over the other kingdoms with which he shared the earth: the animal, vegetable and mineral kingdoms as well as over the unseen kingdom to which they belonged—the elemental kingdom. Man had tremendous potentiality for spiritual development and the power and ability to make this planet the most beautiful in the whole universe, where love, understanding and wisdom ruled.

Man had been given freewill and self-consciousness with the possibility of becoming the supreme spiritual being in incarnation in a material body—a true Son of God. Instead, what had man become? Grown so over-inflated with his own self-importance, he had turned against his very Creator and even ceased to believe in Him. The fundamental divine laws were flouted, and Love, the one thing that really mattered, dismissed as weakness. Only its opposite—hate—was strong. Man became utterly degenerate and selfish, seizing everything he could grasp for his own selfish use, regardless of the suffering and misery that it might cause others. He could not live with himself. Son turned against father, brother against brother. Hate, envy, pillage and destruction spread all over the earth until from being the most beautiful planet it was fast becoming the ugliest. Certainly so as seen from the higher planes, where the negativity in the etheric shell of the earth brought about by the foulness of man's thoughts and deeds caused such dirty and revolting colours that the beauty left on earth that man had so far failed to destroy was masked and distorted to the sad and grieving eyes of the watchers above.

As for the dominion over the other kingdoms, man had taken this as a mandate to dominate, to exploit and to destroy. His selfishness, his cruelty and greed led him to outrage the animal, vegetable and mineral kingdoms. He had ceased to believe in the elemental kingdom; belief in which he laughed at as foolish superstition.

I was aware of occasional murmurs while he was speaking, but in the main there was silence. I felt the hostility increase; the elves were closing in on me.

The elf's voice was hard and cold:

"Man has deliberately set out, not to collaborate with nature, but to subdue her. [Mankind says]'I will dominate nature and force her to do what I want.' He upsets the balance of nature, destroys unique species of animals and plants that have taken millions of years to evolve, turns vast areas of the earth's surface into desert, ruthlessly cuts down or burns large areas of trees so essential to his own continued existence. He brutally maims and disfigures the landscape, blasting great gaps in the mountains and hills with high explosives, leaving gaping wounds in the living earth that will never heal, levelling great tracts of land with equal brutality to build his hideous towns and cities and monstrous roadways; all in the name of civilisation and progress.

"He pollutes the rivers, the lakes and even the seas; the earth itself and the air above it. Everywhere he goes, he fouls and destroys. Is he so stupid that he cannot realise that in doing what he does, he is destroying the earth on which he dwells and so will ultimately destroy himself?

"Us, he cannot destroy, we are immortal and indestructible in our higher being. We care about this planet, we love it; it is our abode. It was once beautiful until man defiled it. Can you blame us if we consider man as a parasite on the face of the earth? A parasite that should he ruthlessly destroyed; a cancerous growth that should be cut out if this world is to survive."

The elf-king's voice cut like a knife. I hung my head in shame. I could not deny the accusations. He made me see man as they did, judging him by his actions.

The voice continued:

"This is only part of our accusation against mankind, but it is enough. You, as his ambassador, have the effrontery to ask for our co-operation. Cooperation in what? The further devastation of our own strongholds, our sacred places, our dwellings? To fight amongst ourselves, perhaps to kill, torture and maim our own kind? To help to bring about the utter destruction of our planet? Justify your request, answer our accusations if you can!"

There was a growing excitement amongst the crowd of elves, and a murmuring broke out like the sound of the wind in the trees, rising in volume like an approaching storm. The hostility increased alarmingly; it beat down on me like a physical force, crushing me. The elf, immediately aware of this, added in a softer voice:

"We have no bitter feelings against you who come to us of your own freewill. You are under Pan's protection though he cannot guide you in what you say. I see that you indeed have love for us in your heart and that the behaviour of your own kind deeply distresses you. We return your love and will gladly listen to anything you have to say. That Pan himself and others of the nature spirits are co-operating with man surprises us. Can you explain it? We will hear you."

"Are you not the subjects of Pan?"

"Yes, we are."

"As such you owe him allegiance?"

"He is our ruler, and we obey his commands. He will never try to coerce us; he is a true leader. He demonstrates to us that what he asks is right. If it seems so, we will obey and thus fulfil God's will as he does."

"And if not would you disobey?"

"We have the right to do so."

"Have you? Would that not be flouting God's will? Become rebels? This suggests you have a certain degree of freewill. I thought that was man's prerogative?"

A glint of amusement showed in the elf's eyes. "That belief could be man's own conceit. However, this is not the time to enter into an ethical argument on who has, and who has not, freewill, interesting though that might be. You are trying to divert the issue, O man with the wily mind." The smile vanished and he grew stern. "Can you, or can you not, refute our accusations and prove to us that Pan's direction is right? That is the point at the moment. Stick to it."

Perhaps I was trying to divert the issue. The indictment was difficult to counter. Though it might be over-weighted on the negative side, it was fundamentally true.

I stood up and faced the elves from a position at one side of their chief. I began by admitting that the accusations were in the main true but were only part of the picture—the dark part. I did not attempt to justify or excuse the outrages on nature. The only excuses would be ignorance and stupidity, lack of foresight, or lack of care. Mankind in general was not evil. The majority of the inhabitants of this earth were peace-loving and kind, wanting to live quietly in friendship with their neighbours and help those in need.

There was a murmur of dissent from the elves. The elf-king raised his hand, and it died away.

"This is the truth. It is easy to see the bad deeds. It is less easy to see the good ones. To be fair you must try to do so. You nature spirits are reasonable beings; you are not ruled by emotions and you are infinitely tolerant, far more so than the average human being. You have endured appalling devastation of your sacred places and dwellings without either rebelling or departing. You have not sought revenge, though no doubt you retaliate within reason when the opportunity arises. Your restraint is admirable.

"There are many people every bit as distressed as I am at the outrages committed on nature, at the cruelty and destruction inflicted on the animal kingdom, the exploitation of the vegetable kingdom and the raping of the mineral one. There are many who are equally shocked at man's appalling inhumanity to his own kind. That being so, why does it happen?

"Unfortunately there are men, driven by the lust for power and for domination over others, who have the ability and the opportunity to raise themselves to positions of authority. Such men can control and bend to their wills large groups of people and even whole nations. This has happened repeatedly throughout the course of the history of the human race. Often these men are ruthless and cruel, seeking only to build up their own power and authority, coercing the people they dominate into fighting wars they don't believe in and committing atrocities they would normally hate.

"Many human beings are easily swayed by suggestion and by playing on their emotions. They can be roused by mass hysteria to hate and destroy. These men are not always evil; some are idealistic, driven by a fanatical belief that what they are doing is for the ultimate good of the majority of the people. By no means are all the leaders bad; there have been many good ones, inspired ones. But the bad ones do the harm and attract the attention while the good ones often go unnoticed, and so judgment of man's behaviour is often prejudiced in favour of the negative."

I paused. There was a hush; the elves were listening to my words with concentrated attention. My confidence grew.

Surely the elves had heard about that perfect man, Jesus of Nazareth, who lived nearly two thousand years ago. (I wondered if our time scale meant anything to them). Many believed Him to be the true Son of God come to earth to bring salvation to mankind. During his ministry he taught the fundamental divine truths and laws, of which the greatest one is Love. "Love thy neighbour as thyself." Nothing else really matters.

"What did mankind do to him?" asked one of the elves in front of me. "Man will always destroy those who try to teach him selflessness and humility or to change his accustomed way of life."

"A necessary sacrifice in order to teach the fact of resurrection, of life continuing after what we call death, which is a doorway into a new life, a rebirth, not an ending. On His teachings the Christian religion was based."

"What authority has that religion today," another elf asked.

I replied that it had less authority than it should have. The early church had become more concerned with its temporal power than with the spiritual teachings of its founder and had even condemned the esoteric side of these teachings as heretical. Organised religion had failed to give its followers what they were seeking for and was failing to attract the young today by falling behind the development of contemporary life. If the churches were to fulfil their role in the New Age into which we are entering, this must stop. The teachings are still valid as are those of the other great religions. There is only one true God, to whom we all owe allegiance. He has expressed Himself through all the different religions in the manner most suited to their followers, through the divine or divinely inspired prophets and teachers, Buddha, Mohammad, Zoroaster and many others up to the present day. Such men could be considered as Christed beings, reaffirming the divine truths of the Godhead. Man was not a parasite on the face of the earth, though from many of his deeds he might so appear. No parasite could bring forth such teachers and teachings.

Admittedly a large part of mankind had ceased to believe in the existence of God or of such truth and could accept only the material world in which we live. Such men are not necessarily evil; many of them are surprisingly good and behave with great humanity to their fellow men. Materialism, however, is a failure; it can never supply the fundamental need in all human beings for spiritual truths and for the possible contact with the God within.

"Mankind is seeking for the fundamental truths. That is the vital point. Remember this; look for man's good deeds, not his bad. Continue to be patient and tolerant and cooperate with man when he seeks your help. Of course you are disbelieved in, no doubt by the majority, but more and more are beginning to accept your existence. I know that words can fail to convince and that other people's experiences can be meaningless. Only deeds satisfy. It is up to us, mankind, to convince you that we both care about, and respect, nature and the other kingdoms. Forget the horrible scars man has made on the surface of the earth, the filth he has added to the waters. Look at the vast extent of still undefiled countryside that exists. Go and visit the nature reserves and the clean rivers and lakes that are still to be found. We admit the ravages and the destruction. Be fair to us; we have so much to learn. Help us. That is my answer to your indictment."

There was a prolonged silence when I stopped speaking. The elf-king rose to his feet:—

"We have listened, friend of Pan, ambassador from mankind. We accept what you have said. We will seek out man's good qualities and try to ignore his bad ones. We will continue to be tolerant and try to be understanding. It will not be easy, but we will do it. We will obey Pan and co-operate with man when he seeks our help. We will not injure him or impede him in any way. That is our promise."

A thought had occurred to me. "May I ask a question?"

"I will answer if it is allowable."

"Could you destroy mankind if you wanted to?"

"Easily. We have more than enough power, but we will never use it as it would not be in accordance with God's will to do so. However if man should continue his present violation of the earth, we might have to depart and leave it. If we did not do so, we might be the cause of terrible disasters which we could not avoid bringing about. Cosmic laws have to be fulfilled."

"What then?"

"The vital force in all that grows would cease, since one of our functions is the transmutation of certain cosmic energies and the channelling of these energies into the plants.'"

"Surely that would mean the end? Is that in accordance with God's will?"

"If man goes too far, he will destroy himself. He has the means of doing so, and he has freewill. We would have to do what we must. We cannot break cosmic laws which are God's laws."

I smiled at the elf. "I do not believe that will ever happen. Man's higher self and his inner prompting to turn towards God will prevail in the end. More and more people are turning towards the Light. Stronger and stronger spiritual energies are pouring down onto the earth. I believe in a great future for mankind; the New Age is dawning. It may take time but it will happen."

The elf looked at me and smiled. He held out his hands. They were warm and firm when I touched them. A strange thing happened. The elf began to grow taller until he was my own height. It did not surprise me as I knew that though such entities usually appear in a particular form, they are ephemeral and can change in size and shape according to the circumstances. He was still holding my hands which he had grasped. He released them and laid his own on my shoulders.

"Bless you, O man, and the work you are doing. We thank you for coming and accept you as one of us. You are welcome at any time."

I felt an immense radiance coming from him as he embraced me.

I turned away and walked through the crowd of elves and under the trees back to the path. The former hostility had given place to a warm feeling of love that was almost overpowering, coming from these beautiful little people and enfolding me as I walked down the path. Pan joined me.

"Well, ambassador of man, quite an evening. You haven't done at all badly for a first time." There was an amused but affectionate glint in his eyes. He gave my shoulder a squeeze. "I'm proud of you. Sleep well."

I was once more alone. I continued along the path and found myself back in my body in bed, fully conscious.

Essential Wild Parts

670617. In the evening we went to gardens of a house at Kentessack [near Forres, Morayshire]. As arranged I wandered about by myself while the others went round the garden. I was immediately drawn to a wild part across a wooden bridge over a stream. This is a completely wild part with many trees, rhododendron bushes, long grass and nettles and other weeds. I felt it was very rarely if ever visited by mankind. It is a very strong centre for nature forces and Pan was by my side immediately, telling me this was their part of the garden. I did not go into this wilderness very far, as I felt it would be wrong to do so. I was aware of being surrounded by nature beings of many different kinds who seemed friendly and at times very curious about me.

Pan explained that where co-operation of the nature forces is wanted, there must be a completely wild part of any garden, which should be left uncultivated and as little frequented by man as possible. This is for the nature spirits own domain, a focal point to work from.

A Fairy Ring

670808b. The croft we had been told about (by Albert Best)

is on a hill, high above the glen, with a staggering view over Loch Ness and the surrounding mountains, and right up Glen Urquhart.

There are curious hollows in the hillside—really dells—the first one was small, with an overhanging wall or rock, twenty to twenty five feet high, and a pool below it. There were trees and bushes, heather, whin and long grass. I knew at once that this was a nature force stronghold. A little further on, we came on a quite vast dell of irregular shape, a deep hollow in the hill with a Scots pine of fair height—25ft at least—and other trees, whin and heather, with rocks and long grass. I asked permission from the "little people" to enter their domain and was immediately invited to do so and made welcome.

These were not the fairies of the fairy tale, but the real Celtic Little People, perhaps about two to three feet in height, some dressed in green, with pointed hats, and others in blue, red, and black; the men in tunics and breeches, and the women in long skirts, bodices and white collars—a slight suggestion of puritan styles, but they varied a great deal. I wandered about in this dell, feeling very happy and somehow close to these people. They told me they often thought human beings a nuisance and were not above playing tricks on them, but they were willing to help when asked to do so, where they were believed in.

I crossed over a vague road into a side section. There was a high grassy mound in front of a high rock out of which a small tree grew, making a canopy.

On the mound, a fairy about three feet [tall], wearing green tunic and breeches, with a red cap, and a long red cloak, was standing—I thought he was probably their chief or king. I bowed to him, and he welcomed me as a kinsman, though a human being, and said I had the freedom of their domain. He asked me to greet their princess. On a mossy stone, again beside a rock to his right, there stood a very beautiful being in a long green robe, with a golden girdle, and a circlet on her beautiful long, fair hair.

As I turned to greet her, she held out her hands, and I bent down to take them. She kissed me on the cheek. I said I felt very privileged to be allowed to wander in their domain and made to feel welcome. She said I would always be welcome to the fairy people, and that the reason for this, and why I had been chosen to

R. Ogilvie Crombie

make such contact, was because I had a fairy ancestor—she would not say how far back, but quite a long time—on my mother's side, but it made me kin to them. This sounds very far-fetched, but I would like to think it is true.

I wandered right round the top of this dell, and presently Peter returned with Bill Robertson [the owner of the croft], and we went right up the hill, and he showed me the fairy ring. It is really a ring of mounds, with one in the centre. There is also a ring—a vague one—of stones, and a ring of birch trees to the left in a great sloping rock dominating the scene. There are many trees. Peter and Bill left me, and I stood for a while and again asked permission to enter the ring. I was immediately pulled right into it and sat down on the mound facing me.

I felt as if I was in another world and suddenly felt myself right inside the hill. I was looking at a beautiful sunlit landscape, with rivers and forests that kept changing. It was in a strange way very different from earth and is difficult to describe. The differences were subtle, and I was more aware of the landscape than seeing it. This sort of thing has to be experienced to be understood. I felt very happy and at peace. I was not aware of any beings, though I knew it was inhabited. The peace was slightly disturbed by the intrusive noise of a tractor working in a nearby field. Perhaps this was as well, as it kept part of me on the earth's surface, otherwise I might have been reluctant to come back.

I found myself sitting on the mound. I rose and climbed up the sloping stone. From the top, the view was astonishing as it is much higher up the mountain side than the croft. I sat down here for quite a while, then went and sat on the centre mound.

It was with great reluctance that I finally returned to the croft where we had tea outside. The weather had been beautiful. After tea, we packed into two cars and set out on the return journey [to Findhorn]. I know a wonderful contact has been made.

The Grey Man of Ben Macdhui

This presence features widely in legends of the Scottish Highlands as a fearsome figure of enormous size who induces fear and terror in climbers approaching the summit of Ben Macdhui, a somewhat desolate mountain in the Cairngorm range.

The Occult Diaries of

Norman Collie, who became Professor of Organic Chemistry at University College (London) in 1896, spoke of his experience on Ben Macdhui during a visit to New Zealand in 1889. Many other people up to the present day have similar tales to tell.

> "I was returning from the cairn on the summit in a mist when I began to think I heard something else than merely the noise of my own footsteps. Every few steps I took I heard a crunch, then another crunch as if someone was walking after me but taking steps three or four times the length of my own. I said to myself 'this is all nonsense'. I listened and heard it again but could see nothing in the mist. As I walked on and the eerie crunch, crunch sounded behind me I was seized with terror and took to my heels, staggering blindly among the boulders for four or five miles nearly down to Rothiemurchus Forest. Whatever you make of it I do not know, but there is something very queer about the top of Ben MacDhui and will not go back there again by myself I know."

The Grey Man, like the spirits associated with many other mountains, rivers and notable geographic features such as Smoo Cave considered in the next section, were referred to by ROC (by St Germain in fact) as "border beings," elementals who are in themselves neutral, neither good nor evil but with potentialities for either.

ROC's out-of-body encounters with the Grey Man are recorded as follows, and illustrate the other side—the positive side—of this traditionally frightening elemental. ROC is in Edinburgh:

> 670604. During the night, I visited Ben Macdhui and met the Grey Man. He is a 'border being', and could be very frightening.
> G.M. This is my mountain and I am its guardian.
> ROC. Is it your purpose to stop people climbing to the top?
> G.M. Some people only.
> ROC. It is mainly the sensitive and spiritually minded you frighten and chase?
> G.M. Yes.
> ROC. If I tried to reach the top, would you drive me off?
> G.M. I could not. I know who your Higher Self is and that

you do not fear me. It is fear that gives me power over people. But you have no reason for climbing my mountain in your physical body, since you can do it out of the body as you have done at the moment.

Two months later while at Findhorn ROC is again in contact with the Grey Man:

>670804. Back in bed in my body I then tried to contact the Grey Man of Ben Macdhui. I was immediately on the upper slopes of the mountain and the Grey Man was there to greet me; he had reduced himself to my own height. He knew humans as it was his job to chase them off the mountain. They nearly all of them feared him. He was astonished at feeling warmth and love coming from me.

And on the following day:

>Last night, the grey man was with me. I asked him if he was not neglecting his duty, and he replied—"no one climbs at night, so I may leave it."
>ROC. But some do camp on it all night, surely?
>GM. Oh yes, but my brother spirits and elementals will deal with them if necessary. I am not alone on the mountain.
>ROC. I know that. I have seen the others.
>GM. So you have. The contact yesterday was most pleasing.
>ROC. I am glad. It was pleasing to me too.
>This morning at the session, I was aware of the Grey Man standing behind me, and of the spirit of Morven beside him.

Smoo Cave

Throughout much of the meeting with the Spirit of Smoo Cave (in Durness), the aura and auric garments were much discussed. As a precursor to this, I have included a segment from some of ROC's earlier notes on the aura and also a script received just before he retired to bed on that same occasion which provides further comments regarding the means of building up the flow of cosmic energy and its potential uses:

651027. I played the piano for a while trying to choose music that would help to increase the power. Later when I went through to the back to get supper ready, I did not switch on the light. The aura round my hands was intensely bright with powerful rays shooting out from my fingers. I have never seen anything like it, and it settles the matter as far as I am concerned. The aura is not an optical illusion. My hands were phosphorescent. This is real and not a reflection from anywhere. The light is pulsating and has bright flecks in it. Also my hands are unusually warm for me. I shall see what my aura is like when I go to bed tonight.

Later I fixed up the black curtain opposite the wardrobe mirror and shaded the bed light so as to give a dim light. On removing my clothes I found that my whole body was glowing with the beautiful pale blue phosphorescence as if it had been rubbed with luminous paint. My aura was very clear and considerably enlarged, stretching to at least two feet from my body. It looked like blue smoke and the inner part was faintly striated. The division between the inner and outer auras was not very distinct. There were flashes of green and yellow in the aura. There is no doubt of the reality of this phenomenon.

Script received:

The blue glow is an indication of a high cosmic energy content. This is often accompanied by a feeling of warmth. The aura should be brighter, since it is stimulated by the flow of cosmic energy. This energy may be used in many ways—healing is one of them, so is telekinesis—but this requires special development. Great care must be taken in releasing this power. It must never be used selfishly or for bad ends. Because satisfactory conditions have been established here [in the flat], the power can now he more readily built up. Two or three people in sympathy with serious intent can bring about a much stronger build-up sitting quietly completely relaxed, sometimes in silence but not necessarily so all the time. For the maximum build-up, the ideal is total nudity on the part of the sitters who should sit either all on chairs or cross-legged on the floor. The latter is best but requires practice. Clothes carry with them the atmosphere and contaminations of

R. Ogilvie Crombie

material life besides concealing the real true self and shutting off the physical aura. Nudity enables the auras to interact and brings about the maximum build up of cosmic energy. It is symbolical of the casting off of hypocrisy and concealment. Such an ideal is difficult to follow as it requires sympathy and understanding. There must be no feeling of embarrassment as this would hinder the power build up.

The initial encounter with the Spirit of Smoo Cave was during a visit that ROC made there in 1967. A brief introductory communication takes place and ROC returns later out-of-the-body and has extensive discourse with the Spirit on several topics but mainly on the aura and auric garments.

670618. After lunch we went on to Durness, our northern destination. There is a famous cave there called Smoo Cave which I felt we must visit. It is quite a climb down a steep cliff path to the shore in front of it. There were numerous sea birds nesting on the ledges of the cliff. They seemed to resent our presence as the noise they made was terrific. The cave is most impressive, and there is a tremendous atmosphere in it and great power. Peter climbed up a steep passage at the back which seems to be like a solidified flow of lava, but it led nowhere. In a large side chamber to the right of the entrance, which is inaccessible because of an underground river which flows through it and is cut off by a ridge of rock, there was a most beautiful effect produced by a ray of sunlight coming through a hole in the roof and falling onto the surface of the water like a theatrical spotlight and lighting up a circle of golden colour on the surface, which was also thrown as a shimmering reflection on the back wall of the cave. The whole of the water flowing through this side chamber was glowing faintly, and the chamber was filled with a faint mist.

It was a remarkable sight and was no doubt due to the perfect day and the time we had gone there. Both were absolutely right. I was aware of a great nature being in the chamber. One could see into it fairly well by going out onto a stepping stone. At first he was a vague shape swirling in the mist but he gradually took on a human shape that filled the chamber.

S. I am the Spirit of Smoo Cave. What do you want of me?
ROC. I want your friendship.

S. Do you? Are you worthy of it?

I stood quite still and could feel that he was reading me to the very depth of my being.

S. I welcome you as a friend.

ROC. Thank you.

S. We shall meet again.

I felt that he was a border being of the same kind as the Grey Man of Ben Macdhui and of a new type to me. Something will come of this link I feel sure.

A great deal has been happening during the night. I was back again in Smoo Cave [out-of-body, of course] standing, as before, on the rocky ledge separating the inner chamber from the main cave. The Spirit of the Cave welcomed me and said he was glad I had left all material things behind me. I asked him if he meant clothes, as I was naked as I usually am in out-of-the body travel. He said "yes."

ROC. Tell me, how do I appear to you—as a naked human being?

S. No, you are not naked; you are robed in your auric garments. They are very beautiful.

ROC. Tell me about them.

S. They are long and flowing and in your language what you call blue and silver. There are also touches of green, purple, magenta and gold. I know now who your real Self is.

ROC. Did you not know that when you first saw me?

S. No. It was kept from me. All I knew was that we could communicate.

ROC. Are there many human beings you can communicate with?

S. Yes, quite a number. Those with a certain kind of sensitivity can see me as you can and we are able to communicate.

ROC. Now I am in my etheric body having left my physical one behind. Surely this etheric body is the counterpart of the physical body. How does it come to be clad in what you call beautiful robes? And how does the higher self come in?

S. It is the counterpart of your physical body, but it carries with it the reflection of the Being who overlights you and at times becomes you, and of other aspects you have. The auric robes symbolise both him and your Saturn aspect. In certain ways they are one, in certain ways they are different.

ROC. That is very enigmatic. Can you be clearer?

S. No. If it is enigmatic to you, it is also enigmatic to me. I only have certain knowledge from which I know it is so.

ROC. I have been increasingly certain for some time now that the robes described by sensitives on the beings or entities they claim to see are symbolic. Is it the case that the same being may appear to more than one sensitive in the same place at the same time clothed differently?

S. Yes, this is the case. How and in what form the being appears to each person depends on that person himself and what is to be conveyed to him.

ROC. So that for two or three people to describe a being they see in different terms would not necessarily mean that only one was right?

S. Certainly not. Each would see what he was meant to see. The Being might be present in his light body but would take on an aspect suitable to each sensitive present he wanted to make his presence known to, and might well appear different to each, or at least dressed in different garments.

ROC. I feel it is most important to understand this as it explains discrepancies in different sensitives' visions.

S. It is important.

ROC. Can a sensitive project onto a Being the kind of form or garments he expects to see.

S. Oh yes. If a man expects to see an angel as a beautiful being in long white robes with wings and a halo, that is how he will see an angel. You are already aware how mankind has projected forms onto discarnate entities and that these forms have been accepted and are used by these entities. Do you want me to enlarge on this?

ROC. Not at the moment. I think I understand it fairly well and that forms and robes are largely symbolical.

S. They serve to identify. If, for example, a fairy appears in filmy garments with gossamer-like wings, people know it is a fairy — if they believe in fairies that is. The light body would not be recognised and might even be frightening. You see clothes have to be used by such beings not as concealment of the body as you humans use them but as shields as well as symbols. Few people can bear the sight of the real entity especially if it is a great being. It has at times to be veiled so as to dim the intensity of the light radiating from it.

ROC. Yes, I can understand that. Now, can you help me on another point. It seems to me that at the moment I am naked—that is, my etheric body is the counterpart of my naked human body. Yet you see it as dressed in robes—what you call auric robes. This is a new idea to me which I find most interesting. It fits, and clears up certain things that have puzzled me. When I leave my human body, I am always naked—that is, the etheric vehicle in which I travel is. As a rule while travelling I remain naked. I understand from books I have read and others I have discussed it with that most people who travel in this way think of clothes and are immediately dressed.

S. Yes, because on the plane they are now in, thought immediately takes form. If they feel embarrassed at having nothing on, they immediately create clothes for themselves.

ROC. In that case they would not appear in auric garments? Or are the clothes they create for themselves auric?

S. No, they are not auric; they are thought form clothes and they screen and hide the true auric robes.

ROC. But surely these could be seen by beings on other planes like yourself?

S. No. The thought created clothes suppress the auric ones and prevent them taking form.

ROC. Then it is not good to clothe oneself in this way?

S. Of course it isn't. You should leave the aura to provide whatever clothing is necessary. This will be adjusted to suit the situation.

ROC. Then I myself could not choose the auric garments?

S. No. As an incarnate human being, though travelling in the etheric body, you have no influence or choice on how you appear to others.

ROC. And to myself I would seem to be naked?

S. Yes, as a rule.

ROC. I take it that discarnate entities do have control over the way they appear to sensitives.

S. Oh yes, unless they come from low levels of the astral

plane.

ROC. And as you said, they can appear to different sensitives to be dressed differently at one and the same time?

S. Yes.

ROC. While in my etheric body, could I do that?

S. It is doubtful if any incarnate human being can do it, but I am not certain. It may be that some beings who are incarnate adepts can. That is beyond my knowledge.

ROC. I still find it difficult to realise that I seem to be naked and yet you are seeing me robed. But it does clarify things. If it applies to my etheric body, does it apply to my physical one? I am thinking of the elves in Rosemarkie Fairy Glen when I went there in my physical body, they wanted me to shed my clothes so that they could see my real ones. From this I assume that they would have seen me clothed and not as a naked man.

S. They would have seen you possibly as I see you now. But I imagine that other human beings present, no matter how sensitive and able to see your aura, would simply have seen a man taking his clothes off.

ROC. This gives me a great deal to think about, some of it is still puzzling and needs sorting out.

S. In time it will be made clear to you. New ideas need getting used to.

ROC. Are the auric robes—as we are calling them—completely concealing, or can you see my etheric body through them? Some beings that I have seen are wearing almost transparent robes.

S. I can only very vaguely make out your etheric body, and I cannot see it more clearly unless you make that possible.

ROC. How can I do that if I have no control over the auric garments. Surely I cannot take them off?

S. No, but you can disperse them by an act of will.

ROC. Has the etheric body will power?

S. Most certainly as it is a vehicle of the soul. Now, you have proved it. You have dispersed the auric garments back into the aura from which they were created and I see your etheric body as the replica of a naked human man.

ROC. Can you judge the age? I ask because when out of my body I seem in one way to have no age and yet in another to have the body of a much younger man.

S. Of course. The etheric has no age in the way you understand the word and it tends to appear as the physical body is at its best and even as an idealised version of that. The etheric body is always beautiful no matter what the physical may be like. Now it's my turn; so far you have been asking the questions. How do you see me?

ROC. At the moment [I see you] as a constantly changing mist of rather vague form and of a grey-brown and red colour and luminous.

S. You are seeing my light body. Because of your training, experience and initiations, you can see the light bodies of many beings.

ROC. Yes, that is a wonderful gift that has been granted to me by God's grace. I have seen some very beautiful Beings. There is great beauty in yourself.

S. Though I inhabit this cave and often descend into the rocky depths of the earth? Was this how you saw me the first time?

ROC. As a mist, yes, but you took on a vaguely human shape.

S. I can do that. I know now that it is not necessary with you.

ROC. It certainly does make it easier when you take on a human shape. It is easier to talk with an apparent human being than with a swirling mist. I have seen entities like you who have been immensely tall such as the Grey Man of Ben Macdhui, but you seem to be about my own height. Have you a fixed size?

S. Of course not. I can be any height I wish when I take on a human aspect, but it is more convenient at the moment to be your height. The Grey Man no doubt is a giant according to legend and so appears like that. That is not to say that he could not vary his size if he wanted to.

ROC. Why is it that you are the one to give me all this information?

S. I do not know why. It just is so. Desire knowledge and you will usually acquire it in one way or another unless it is forbidden knowledge. You will see the pattern emerge in time.

ROC. I know this meeting with you is important.

S. It is, so is the link that has been made. There is a bond between us that will not break. Go now. We shall meet again.

R. Ogilvie Crombie

A further out-of-body meeting with the Spirit of Smoo Cave takes place about a week later, with further discussions on etheric appearances:

> 670623. Last night I was again in Smoo Cave with the spirit. This time I was sitting in a sort of natural arm chair in the rock inside the inner chamber above the underground river. The Spirit was sitting near me; again he had taken on a human form coloured like the rock
>
> S. Greetings mortal man known to us as ROC.
>
> ROC. Is that the name you know me by?
>
> S. You have another name, but that one has a significance for us.
>
> ROC. What is that?
>
> S. If you do not know, I cannot tell you.
>
> ROC. I think I do.
>
> S. That is good.
>
> ROC. Tell me, am I as real to you in this my etheric body as in my physical one?
>
> S. Much more real. The etheric body, as you call it, is much truer to the Real Self than the physical body and carries reflections of many higher aspects and of those who overlight you.
>
> ROC. Surely the physical body carries these reflections too?
>
> S. To a much lesser degree, and there is often gross obscurity due to wrong thoughts and desires that masks the true self, which is sometimes entirely hidden by material wishes and obsessions. And besides, except for the head and hands, the aura is suppressed or contaminated and distorted by the material garments human beings wear.
>
> ROC. Clothes are not wholly good then?
>
> S. No, they may he very bad. I suppose they are necessary for protection both against the weather and physical injury to the body. But so many people wear the wrong things, wrong materials, wrong colours and even wrong shapes. Few indeed follow their inner promptings.
>
> ROC. For a Spirit of the depths inhabiting this cavern and, as you told me, descending to deeper ones, you seem to know a lot about the human species.

The Occult Diaries of

S. Of course. I have means of observing without leaving this place. In any case I am not limited by physical space, and I have access to quite a wide range of knowledge. To us the behaviour of human beings is strange and unaccountable. It often seems stupid and pointless, but that may be due to failure on our part to understand the driving force. Human behaviour is frequently repulsive to us and alien to the pattern of creation.

ROC. I can understand that. To quite a lot of human beings the behaviour of our own kind is inhuman, wicked and utterly repulsive. I have found myself seeing the human race through the eyes of the nature spirits. It is not a pleasant sight, and I could not blame them for being unfriendly and even hostile.

S. This widening of your perspective has, together with other qualities you possess, made you a suitable link between the kingdoms. You have been prepared for this for a very long time and are fulfilling the purpose of your life.

ROC. I am trying to. It is a great responsibility.

S. By complete surrender to the will of God and constant realisation that you are only a channel and that you in your physical self are nothing, you will succeed.

ROC. Am I right in thinking of you as a border being? You are neither good nor evil, you are neutral?

S. That is right. A great number of the nature spirits are like that—neither good nor evil, but with potentialities for either.

ROC. Can you explain further?

S. This is not the time for that. There is mystery here which you could not fully understand. Far as you have advanced, your human brain, which must be used in this communication, has limitations.

ROC. I quite understand. Tell me how do I appear to you today? What auric garments am I wearing?

S. None. They are unnecessary now as I know all I am to know about you.

ROC. That knowledge was conveyed to you by the auric robes you saw me wearing?

S. Most of it. But apart from your robes I was permitted to read you to the necessary extent.

ROC. Am I right in thinking that not all the beings I might meet in out-of-the-body travelling could read me or be aware of my identity?

S. You are right. You might appear to be completely veiled by impenetrable garments that told nothing. In fact, this concealment could be so complete that you could pass unnoticed through the most crowded places.

ROC. Like an invisible man?

S. Just like an invisible man. You might appear to be what you call naked, though to us it is simply the fundamental aspect taken on by the light body for some purpose or other. There is no difference to us between that and the appearance of auric robes other than the symbolical one.

ROC. The etheric body is the lowest form of such an aspect?

S. There are many higher ones.

ROC. Can discarnate entities take on etheric bodies?

S. Certainly, when it is necessary to do so.

ROC. Such as?

S. In order to become visible to a human being. It is easier to do so in the etheric body than in a higher one.

ROC. But not impossible?

S. No. Many sensitives are able to see beings in much higher bodies than the etheric. You yourself can do it. You can even see the light body.

ROC. That is true. But surely when I appear to a discarnate being naked, the aura can he read and will give a great deal of information even if it does not form into auric garments of symbolism.

S. Not necessarily. Without the symbolism of the auric garments, the plain aura might tell little. Only if it was intended to be revealing could information be received.

ROC. Then I do have the ability to close the shutters and remain aloof.

S. Yes, in your case it is also adjusted from outside. Because of the work you are being used for, you are protected.

ROC. And that is also the case with my physical body?

S. Yes. You have a protective shell. No sensitive, clairvoyant, clairaudient or mind reader can tap into your mind unless you allow them to do so. Sometimes for what you call camouflage, false information is sent out by your unconscious mind. This is necessary for your full protection, otherwise some of those working for the dark would he able to frustrate what you are doing.

ROC. Good. It is nice to have confirmation of this fact. I need not hesitate to meet sensitives or mediums then?

S. No, though at the same time it is better to avoid such people whenever possible. They can use up energy drawn from you which is needed for other work. You will be guided on this matter as you were recently.

ROC. I find it interesting that in out-of-the-body travel when I seem to be naked, I never feel improperly dressed though to be naked in my physical body could cause embarrassment.

S. That is because in out-of-the-body travel you have reached the point where you leave behind all your human prejudices. It is only in the material world that nakedness is foolishly thought of as wrong and embarrassing, not on other planes. Some humans when they travel out-of-the-body bring that outlook with them. We talked about this before.

ROC. I remember. They clothe themselves in thought garments. You said it was better not to do so as they obscure the auric ones.

S. And remember that though you may seem to be naked to yourself, you are probably seen fully clothed to the beings you meet on your travels.

ROC. Yet at the moment I suppose I am naked to you?

S. Yes, but does that matter?

ROC. Not in the least. I feel quite properly dressed in my nudity.

S. Otherwise you would not be naked.

This next interesting discourse with the Smoo Cave spirit, also conducted OOB, offers yet further insights into the etheric worlds and their workings. During this visit, ROC is presented with a ring in the form of an ouroboros that was made from etheric gold, silver, and a greenish metal not yet discovered on Earth.

670625b. I am now walking across the shingle towards the entrance of Smoo Cave. The Spirit of the Cave is standing there in human form.

S. Welcome once more to my cave.

ROC You are not in the inner chamber today?

S. No. I am not always there. Shall we sit down here in the mouth of the cave and enjoy the light?

We sit. I find it easy in the etheric body to adopt the lotus position which is almost impossible in my physical one. The spirit being, in his human aspect, does make it easier and more natural to communicate. He sits in the same position beside me. There is utter peace, broken only by the occasional cries of the sea birds nesting on the ledges of the cliff and the sound of the waves lapping on the shore of the creek.

ROC. I suppose this cave has been used for smuggling?

S. It has been used for many things.

ROC. That would be a useful creek for landing in secret.

S. No doubt it would. There have been secret landings here. But what is past is past.

ROC. You are right, we should talk about more important matters.

S. Did you come here for any particular purpose?

ROC. To see you and, if possible, continue our interesting conversation. You seem to be remarkably well informed on certain subjects, and you have widened my understanding.

S. That is always good. The more we understand, the more tolerant we become. What more do you want to know?

ROC. As I told you when travelling out-of-the-body, I nearly always seem to myself to have no clothes on.

S. That is natural and right. You are always naked when you leave your physical body and as you have no sense of shame about nudity, you do not immediately cover yourself with thought garments.

ROC. Yet I may appear to be wearing auric garments, formed out of my aura, to others who see me.

S. That is true. If any garments are needed, the auric ones are the right ones.

ROC. I have sometimes found myself walking along a busy street, say Princes Street [Edinburgh] with nothing on, and no one pays the slightest attention to me. Am I in fact walking along that street in my etheric body, and am I invisible because it is not my physical body?

S. Let us take things in order. You find yourself walking naked along a busy street. Is it a dream, and therefore unreal in the physical sense, or is it a genuine out-of-the body experience? By this time you ought to be able to distinguish between the two. We therefore assume it is an-out-of the body experience. Is it Princes Street, the physical material street you are walking along, or is it an etheric or astral reflection of the street?

ROC. Is there such a thing as an etheric or astral reflection of a place?

S. Certainly there is, just as there is such a thing as a mirror image. It is impossible to explain it fully, as you could not understand from the knowledge you have so far acquired. The mirror image is the closest analogy.

ROC. I get your meaning, I think. The people in such a reflection would have no more reality than those in a mirror image and therefore could not be aware of my presence.

S. Unless they are reflections of those with special powers and knowledge.

ROC. So, if I am walking in only a reflection, it does not matter whether I am wearing clothes or not.

S. No.

ROC. But this reflection is a true image and what I get from it or infer from it is true?

S. Yes, it is a true image.

ROC. So I do not necessarily have to distinguish between the actual and the reflection?

S. No. It is unimportant. If it is the actual street you are walking along in your etheric body you will be invisible to almost all the passers by. Only a "sensitive" might see you; this would depend on whether or not he was intended to do so, either because you wanted it or because it was necessary for some reason or other. You might as far as he is concerned be cloaked in invisibility and unseen even by him. You might appear to him in some form of auric garment, or he might see you naked; it depends on a number of circumstances too complicated to go in to at the moment. He would not see you naked if it would cause embarrassment.

ROC. That is exactly what I wanted to know. I need not ever worry if I find myself naked out-of-the-body in someone's presence?

S. No. Nudity in that case is as good as an invisible cloak, except where it does not matter, as at the present moment. Have you ever worried or felt embarrassed when travelling in that state?

ROC. I can't say I have. About twice I have turned into an empty street when I felt too conspicuous in a crowded one. But I rarely seem to think about it. I always feel perfectly clad. Now you have told me that, I can seem to myself to be naked and yet appear to others to be dressed in auric robes, as I did to you on a previous visit.

S. Yes.

ROC. Can I be aware of, and see my auric garments?

S. Oh yes, if you want to. Have there not been times when you have been out-of-the body and aware of what you were wearing?

ROC. That is true. I have been aware of robes.

S. Then you are answered. Pay no heed to your apparent condition — it will be adjusted to suit. I have a gift to pass on to you.

The Spirit called out in a strange language, and two very odd creatures appeared from somewhere in the back of the cave. They seemed to be naked. They were about four feet high with rather pear-shaped bodies, round, completely bald heads, and rather short fat legs, ending in unusually large feet. Their arms were normal, and they had perfectly shaped and very beautiful hands. Their bodies were completely hairless and of a very dark green colour. One of them was carrying something very carefully in the palm of his right hand. The Spirit smiled at my astonishment at seeing such strange creatures.

S. You cannot be really surprised as you have already met a number of strange beings in your travels. These two are earth spirits who live in the depths of the earth and only rarely visit the surface. Their shape is dictated by the conditions in which they live. They are expert workers in precious stones and metals. Does that surprise you? There are many treasures stored in the earth that man knows nothing of, the work of such as these. Their bodies are almost physical and the form is fixed; they cannot change it.

The Spirit spoke again and the two advanced. They moved on their short legs and large feet with great rapidity and ease. The one carrying the object handed it to the Spirit, who took it and held it out to me on the palm of his hand. It was a ring, most exquisitely made in the form of a serpent with its tail in its mouth. It seemed to be made of metals that looked like gold and silver, but there was something else of a very beautiful greenish tint which did not look like colouring. The scales of the serpent were indicated by the different metals. The workmanship was exceptional.

S. Beautiful isn't it? You know the meaning of the symbol?

ROC. The ouroboros? Yes. This ring is one of the most perfect and beautiful things I have seen. What is it made of?

S. Gold and silver and another metal so far unknown to man, which is only found in the depths of the earth.

ROC. An element that is unknown?

S. A pure metal.

ROC. Is that green tint its natural colour?

S. Yes. It is very beautiful, as it seems to shine with an internal luminosity.

He handed the ring to me and I examined it closely. It was surprisingly heavy. I remarked on this.

S. This unknown metal is by far the heaviest metal in existence.

ROC. Then surely it is radioactive as most of the heavy metals like radium and plutonium are?

S. It has many strange properties, but it is not radioactive in the way you mean.

ROC. And this beautiful ring was made by these two?

S. It was, and that will give you some idea of their skill which could not he matched by any human craftsman.

I handed the ring back to the Spirit.

S. This is the gift I have to pass on. It is for you.

ROC. But surely I do not deserve such a precious gift.

S. It would not be yours otherwise.

ROC. But why am I to wear it?

S. Because it is a talisman and will give you protection stronger than anything else can do, and it will enable you to go almost anywhere. Your whole self will benefit much from wearing it.

ROC. It appears to be a solid material ring. Will I find it in the physical when I return to my body?

S. No, you will not see it except at certain times when it will appear. But you will know it is there.

ROC. Will I see it in the etheric?

S. Yes.

ROC. It is removable?

S. Oh yes. It will adapt itself to suit any of your fingers. There may be times when it is to be so worn.

ROC. How can I ever thank you for this wonderful gift.

S. Accept it with gratitude, and remember it is not my gift. I had to pass it on to you. Use it well to help you in your appointed work to the best of your ability.

I stood up, the Spirit embraced me, blessed me and I walked away from the cave.

Corrieshalloch Gorge

700620. Last night I was first of all on a beach with Tio, the first time I have seen him here this visit. He said that I had not needed him as there was so much to do. We walked together some distance along the beach which had a wood beside it. It was not Findhorn.

Next I found myself on the suspension bridge over Corrieshalloch Gorge. It really is a terrifying place but excitingly beautiful. I had an unknown companion beside me who asked me if I was afraid to follow him. I said "no," and we floated up over the side of the bridge and sank down into the gorge; it was a strange and rather terrible sensation as the gorge is very deep. My companion kept close beside me all the time. He was a very beautiful being, naked as I was, and the thought came to me that he was Hermes. We seemed to hover over the water. He told me to turn round and look. On the other side of the bridge there was a breath-taking sight of the waterfall looking like a horse's tail and high above us the thick thread of the bridge and the sky. The gorge is fairly narrow at the bottom and looks very lovely with all the trees, bushes and ferns.

We went along the gorge, still hovering over the water,

which was rushing along beneath our feet, until we came to a rocky platform in front of a hollowed out part of the cliff, rather like a cave. Here we stopped, standing on the platform which was just above the water level. A curious greyish mist filled the hollow which presently began to take on a shape that was almost humanlike, and I found myself standing opposite a very curious being. He was a little taller than myself, shaped like a male but with webbed feet. He was a greenish-black colour and had a curious head not unlike that of a sea lion. He was shaped, apart from his head and feet, like a well built man.

I knew that he was the spirit of the gorge, and in spite of his odd appearance I felt friendly towards him. He took hold of me by the arms and held me with what looked like a grin on his strange face. There was a deep communication between us which I cannot express in words—something deep and fundamental.

I seem to be used in some way to link with these beings, earth spirits who are guardians of certain places on the earth. I know this gorge has real significance, though what it is has not been revealed to me yet. My companion in the descent into the gorge had disappeared, and I was alone with the spirit of the place. Nothing was said, but the silent communion continued.

The spirit then embraced me and stood back. My previous guide was beside me. I turned to him, and we left the ledge, floating slowly upwards out of the gorge until we stood once more on the bridge. I then found myself back in the caravan.

Falls of Rogie

While many of the border beings met by ROC appeared male, this was by no means ubiquitous. This encounter with the Spirit of the Falls of Rogie was with a female spirit. Again it is emphasised that the appearance taken on by such spirits is that projected by human beings, as in reality these beings are androgynous. As with the previous border being encounters, ROC is once again in the out-of-body state.

670629. Last night I was for a while with Tio on the beach and in a forest, and then I found myself on the suspension bridge over the Falls of Rogie. Immediately after that I was sitting on a rock overlooking a deep pool surrounded by black rocks. A great

R. Ogilvie Crombie

waterfall is in front of me and I am conscious of a mist of spray which falls over my naked body. It is bright sunlight and there is great peace in spite of the noise of the waterfall. I sit for a long time on the rock, perfectly happy. The spray from the waterfall grows more dense and presently begins to take on a shape, a human shape—that of a beautiful woman, and presently she is standing on the rock beside me.

S. You seem surprised.

ROC. Yes, I am.

S. Because the spirit of this place appears to you in female form?

ROC. Yes. For no real reason I can think of, I tend to think of such beings male if they take on a human form.

S. Places like Smoo cave and Corrieshalloch, from their nature, would have male spirits.

ROC. But of course beings like yourself and these others really have no sex.

S. Not as you know it in your physical life. It is you that have imposed it on us, when we take human form. This place is very much a place of water, so the water spirits rule it. They are water nymphs, and I, who am the chief water nymph here, am the Spirit off the place. We are always thought of as female. Can you accept that?

ROC. Yes, easily.

S. And you are glad to see me?

ROC. Very.

S. You looked so contented sitting on this rock. Yet I thought you might like company.

ROC. In any case it is vitally important that I should meet you.

S. To link up with this place. Yes, you must meet the Spirit of every place that is important to Findhorn and to you. This place is.

The spirit sat beside me on the rock. She looked mature and very wise, and was beautiful with long blond hair that hung down to her waist.

ROC. Do you see me dressed in auric robes as the Spirit of Smoo cave did?

S. To begin with yes, and so I know all I need to know about you, but now I see you as a naked young man; you have dispersed your robes.

ROC. I suppose because it seems to me natural to be naked in the sunlight and by the side of this lovely river. In my physical body, I always want to take off my clothes when I am alone in the sunlight. But young, I am not young.

S. You are young in heart, eternally young in heart. That is why you appear to me like this in your etheric body, however old your physical one may be. You will never really grow old.

ROC. And have you anything to teach me?

S. Not on this occasion. This is our first meeting; we shall meet again. But I have little to teach you. I leave that to my brother in Smoo Cave. He is very learned.

ROC. You live in the water?

S. Mostly. You were here recently with others and you formed a link with this place. I knew you would come back as you have now done and that we must meet.

The body of the Spirit began to fade and presently I was alone being sprinkled with the gentle spray from the waterfall. I sat down again in the sunlight.

Destination Unknown

This remarkable series of encounters continues with experiences with five very large "gem" spirits

670707. I found myself in a vast cavern. There was a feeling of radiance and light. Facing me were five gigantic beings who inspired awe but not fear. They were at least twenty feet tall with a roughly human shape; very broad shoulders tapering to a narrow waist, rounded abdomen, thick thighs tapering to fine ankles, massive biceps, thin wrists, very powerful hands, roundish heads with pointed ears, and bald heads; fine general muscular development in spite of the rather odd shaped bodies. Each was a different colour and they seemed to glitter and shine. One was white, one red, one blue, one green and one yellow-orange. They stood round me in a circle looking down at me. I felt very small.

W. Who are you little man, and what are you doing here?

R. Ogilvie Crombie

ROC. I have come to see you.

B. That's nice of you—were you invited?

ROC. Would I be here otherwise?

They looked at each other, wondering which one had asked me. I had as yet no clue. This was different from previous experiences, though I knew it must be meant. The red giant bent down and picked me up, setting me down on some sort of stone bench or table made from a flat slab of stone laid across two upright stones. His grip was gentle. They stood round looking at me.

G. He looks like a human being.

Y. No human being can come here.

W. Unless out of his body. I believe they can do that? Is that so?

ROC. Yes. This is my etheric body in which I can travel.

B. It is like your material one?

ROC. Yes exactly like it.

G. But he is naked like us. I thought all human beings smothered their bodies with garments because they are ashamed of them. If you are human, how do you come to be naked?

ROC. When I leave my material body in this etheric one, I am naked. I remain so while travelling as, if clothes are necessary, my aura will provide them. At the moment it seems they are not necessary.

G. I suppose he is male.

Then one of them saw the ring.

R. Look, he is wearing the ring. You are indeed welcome. We have been expecting a visit, but we did not know more than that someone wearing the ring would come to us.

ROC. Greetings to you great beings.

W. You know who we are?

ROC. I am beginning to have an idea.

G. We are the spirits of the precious stones. Five brothers, one for the white, one for the red, one for the green, one for the blue and one for the yellow. Do you wish to see some of our work?

ROC. Very much.

They lifted me across the cave and set me down on another stone bench that ran the length of the cave. They then brought flat plates encrusted with gems. Most of them were square and varied in size from about an inch square to several feet; some were oblong and some circular or oval. I cannot describe the astonishing beauty of what they showed me. The most incredible mosaics made of gems which glittered and sparkled. Some were stones I have not seen on earth.

R. These tablets are taken from the history of this earth from the time of its creation, expressed in symbols. Have they a meaning for you?

ROC. Deep down, yes, a great meaning but I cannot put it into words.

R. It is enough that you feel it.

I wish I could carry a complete memory of the wonderful and beautiful things they showed me. Cups cut from whole diamonds and bowls and dishes from emeralds and rubies. Details are fading rapidly, but the impression left will remain forever.

The strange green beings in the cave had been workers in precious metals; these giants were workers in gems. How much there is that is unknown to man who foolishly thinks he knows all there is to know. In legend, myth and fairy tale, there is quite obviously truth and not just fantasy.

After showing me their work one of them lifted me down and set me in the centre of the cave while they stood round me. Then they began to diminish in size until they were about my own height.

ROC. So you can alter your appearance?

W. Yes, easily. For the work we usually do, the size we were when you came in is the most convenient, but we can change it as you see. It is more suitable now to be your size.

B. Our general shape remains the same, though we can appear differently when required.

W. Now we have invested you with the qualities of some of the qualities of the jewels we work with. I have given you the clarity and strength of the diamond, the lustre of the pearl and something of the mysterious quality of the opal.

B. I have given you the serenity of the turquoise, the purity and peace of the sapphire, the spirituality of the blue topaz.

R. And I have given you the depth of the ruby, the endurance of the garnet, the magic of tourmaline.

G. I have given you from the depth of the earth the union

with the nature forces of the emerald.

Y. And I the brilliance and inner glow of the yellow topaz.

The Spirits laid their right hands one on top of the other on my head and blessed me and the work I was being used for.

ROC. And what have I to give you, with so little to give compared with your gifts?

W. You have given us contact with the surface of the earth which we rarely see, and with the human race who live there. Through you, we will get understanding of that race. You give us much. We thank you. Above all you give us love. We need that from the human race. You also believe in us.

ROC. May God bless you, the five brother spirits of the gems who work in the depths of the earth.

I left the cavern and found myself back in my body. I have given up thinking about the strangeness of the things that are happening to me!

Moray Firth

From journeys to mountains, caves and underground places, and meetings with the strange elementals, this next extract takes us to water worlds where ROC now encounters the Spirit of the Moray Firth.

670726a. As soon as I got into bed, and while I was still fully conscious, Hermes appeared beside the bed and called me. I rose out of my body. This has become very easy. I just step out of bed through the bedclothes. My consciousness goes into the etheric body, though there does seem to be a slight residual consciousness left behind in my physical body. I occasionally am aware of being in bed and even of turning over. In the etheric I seem to be very single minded and do just what I am intended to do and nothing more.

This time Hermes was carrying his caduceus—I have not been aware of this before. In the etheric, one only sees and is aware of the things that have significance.

I went with Hermes and we were floating in space. As before—and probably because one only sees the intended—I did not know where we were—just travelling through space. I am becoming more proficient at it. It is a wonderful sensation, just moving through space with ease like swimming in air.

Presently I was aware of a sea shore, and we were over the water. We came down and just went into it, and I felt myself travelling through the water just as I had been through the air (I suppose we were in the earth's atmosphere). Whether I breathe or not in the etheric I just do not know, but going into the water made no difference. There is a greenish light all round me, and I am vaguely aware of fish. I wonder if I have become a fish and have a fleeting recollection of the account in T.H. White's The Sword in the Stone of Wart's being turned into a fish by Merlin, but I still have my human shape. This shows that I carry a certain degree of normal consciousness and memory into the etheric.

We now approach what looks like a dwelling place or enclosure of some sort. It has no roof, but walls built out of rock, stones and shells. There are many shells making ornamental decorations on the walls. There are beautiful mosaics made of shells—abstract designs.

In a square chamber there are what look like chairs hewn out of rock. In one of them a being, half man, half fish, in fact a merman, is sitting. He has pleasant features with a slight suggestion of a fish, especially about the mouth and eyes. His hair is longish and green, rather like seaweed. It sounds odd to say that he stood up to greet me, but he rose from his chair and remained vertical in the water. He greeted me by the name ROC and I wondered who he was. I did not think that he was Neptune. He told me he was "The Spirit of the Moray Firth."

S.M.F. I have been told about you by Hermes who said he would bring you to meet me, as you are, I understand, linking up with certain beings of whom I seem to be one. You are very welcome. Come and sit by me.

He indicated a rock chair beside his own and resumed his seat. He had the head, torso, and arms and hands of a man. But from the pubic region downwards he had a fish's tail.

I saw no sign of Hermes who must have departed after bringing me.

S.M.F. I know that you bathe in my waters and draw energies from them, which makes me glad.

I thanked him and said I had great benefit from bathing in the Firth.

R. Ogilvie Crombie

S.M.F. I much prefer it when you bathe naked. I dislike the strange unnatural garments humans put on. You are wise to visit me as you are.

As usual in etheric travel my etheric body was naked. I gave him greetings from the Findhorn group, of which he seemed to be aware, and with whom I hoped to link him.

I asked him if he was friendly to mankind to which he replied:

S.M.F. Not particularly. At the same time I am not hostile. Man is so untidy and thoughtless. He spreads rubbish wherever he goes, not only all over his own parts of the earth but all over my kingdom as well—empty tins and plastic containers of all sorts, bottles, many of which are broken, and in general discarded rubbish and filth of all kinds. I suppose he thinks that by casting it into the sea it is out of his sight and therefore doesn't matter how much he offends others. But it is ill bred of me to talk about this to a representative of the human race who, like yourself, does care. I do not remember when we last had a live human being to visit us.

I did not stress the point that I was not exactly a live human being as I was not in my physical body. He summoned his sons and daughters and their relations which were numerous. His "palace" was soon thronged with mermen and mermaids. They differed quite a lot in size and shape though mainly half human, half fish. They were highly amused and interested in what they called my split tail, and I tried to explain to them that this was necessary to enable me to walk on the surface of the earth, just as their tails enabled them to travel through the water. I had to give them a demonstration by walking along the bottom of the sea. They were most interested, and I had to do it repeatedly as new arrivals came in.

I seem when in my etheric body to function very much as in my physical body, except that in this case could remain under water without any difficulty or inconvenience.

I was then entertained by a form of "water ballet"—a very beautiful and graceful set of "dances" they performed for me. During all this there were numerous shoals of fish swimming in and out. Some of these crowded round me, nuzzling at my body in a curious way.

> From time to time I was aware of my physical body lying in bed in the caravan and presently found myself back there.

Morven

This mountain visit occurs on the same date as the visit to the Spirit of the Moray Firth. While all these border beings may have been strange, ROC nonetheless classes the spirits in this extract as the most unusual he had yet come across. Again, it is important to realise that the appearance adopted by these spirits is largely imposed on them by humanity and that their spiritual essence is very different. There is an interesting change of perspective here, where these beings, rather than being considered ugly by human standards, consider mankind ugly by their standards. It all depends on your viewpoint!

> 670726b. It was not very long before Hermes was beside the bed again summoning me to go somewhere else, and I found myself once more floating through space. I knew somehow that we were heading north this time and thought it was most likely to the mountain Morven, the one we were to circle. Reaching it, Hermes showed me a crevice in the rock, the entrance to a narrow passage into which I had to crawl. This passage went down and down into the earth until it finally reached a vast cavern which was full of light.
>
> Here I met some of the strangest earth spirits, unlike any I had so far encountered. They were two or three feet high and their bodies were completely round like a ball. They had round heads and most of them wore little pointed hats. They had very thin arms and legs and large hands and feet. They were dark coloured, mainly brown and very dark green. It was very difficult to tell if they were clothed or not. If they wore garments they were very close fitting and looked skin like.
>
> They swarmed round me with great curiosity as they did not visit the surface of the earth and had never seen a human being before (my etheric body is, of course, an exact replica of the physical one), though they knew a great deal about them. They wanted to be friendly and help man, but as he was so stupid and did so many silly things, they thought it was almost impossible to do so, all the more so as Man did not believe in their existence.

R. Ogilvie Crombie

They communicated with me in "words" of one syllable and showed great surprise when they discovered that I understood what they were saying and could even answer questions.

I tried to tell them that man was not quite so stupid as they thought him, and to give them examples. They were both wise and naive at the same time as I had already found when dealing with nature spirits and elementals.

They found my body as interesting and curious as I found theirs and they crowded round me, but they did not touch me until I had given them permission to do so, as they have very good manners from our standards. They compared my shape with their own and obviously thought me ugly according to their standards. This I find most salutary and enlightening and at the same time humbling.

I spent some time with these strange people who showed me many things that remain in my mind only as an impression. After leaving them, I was with another lot still further north — an elven people fairly friendly to mankind. I do not retain much of what took place except that another link was made which is the important thing.

Ben Hope

ROC's first meeting is with the spirit of Ben Hope. This is followed by what he describes as the "most wonderful experience of my life." Few, indeed, can count themselves so fortunate as to have been accorded such a wondrous encounter with the Christ presence. As far as I am aware, ROC told no one of this experience.

> 670729. Wonderful journey to Ben More with Peter, John and Janet. We left Findhorn at 5.40 am and took the same route Peter and I had gone by on our circling of the northwest of Scotland, but branched off at Altnaharra, where we had coffee at the hotel at 9 am, to take the road round the west side of Ben Hope. The power in this mountain is tremendous; it is definitely magnetic in its attraction. As we approached the mountain in the car, this power grew stronger and stronger. My whole body vibrated to it. Only on a few occasions during the power point journey in England have I felt anything like this power. I found it difficult

to walk when I got out of the car, as my legs were so strongly affected. All the chakras were stimulated to a high degree. There was no feeling of darkness at all. All was light.

Then Peter, John and Janet set out to climb the mountain—conditions were perfect (I had been told that the climb would be made if conditions were right). I went a little way with them by the side of a wonderful mountain stream which came down a series of rocky clefts, sometimes in a waterfall of twenty to thirty feet, into deep pools in the rocks. One of the most lovely mountain streams I have seen. The day was dull but very pleasant. The ground was very boggy, but I managed not to get my feet too wet.

I sat for some time absorbing the power and the beauty of the surroundings, feeling supremely happy. Then I climbed down to the side of a pool, took off my clothes and bathed in the pool almost under a long water fall. To my surprise the water was not cold as such mountain streams usually are. It was very pleasant and the power I drew from it was quite extraordinary. I sat for some time on a rock after drying myself, still aware of being bathed in power.

Now, sitting on a rock a little higher up after dressing, writing this beside a lovely waterfall, I feel quite wonderful and full of energy. I love this mountain.

I am now aware of the Spirit of the mountain—a tall giant of a man. He is a little vague. He is bronze colour with a shaggy head of hair and a broad beard. Almost like a Stone Age man. He looks very jovial as he greets me. I saw him with an inner sight as he was standing behind me all the time.

S.B.M. Welcome to my mountain which you love.

ROC. Thank you. It is a wonderful mountain of great power.

S.B.M. It is.

ROC. George King has done no harm with whatever he did when he climbed it?

S.B.M. None. His capers were harmless.

ROC. It is right for us to come here and circle the mountain in a clockwise direction?

S.B.M. It is right.

ROC. And for Peter, John and Janet to climb it?

S.B.M. Yes.

R. Ogilvie Crombie

ROC. And for me to bathe in the pool?

S.B.M. That was essential. You had to draw the full benefit from the power. You had to immerse yourself in the water from the mountain. You will return to this mountain in your travels at night. God's blessing on your task.

He is still standing behind me. He bends down and lays his hands on my shoulders. I feel a tremendous surge of power.

I am sitting in front of a great slab of striated rock on a ledge. The rock is almost my own height. Leaning against it, face towards it, I feel the power to be tremendous and seem to become one with the rock. I then leant for a long time with my back to it.

12.30pm. I have been feeling utterly at peace and yet exalted to a high degree. This is a very wonderful mountain, magnetic and a source of great power. I have had a wonderful vision of the golden one—the miraculously changing patterns of gold on golden orange that I see at times, impossible to describe. This was followed by an orange cone of light with a brilliant green centre. I have a feeling of ecstasy, a descent of the Holy Spirit. The valley below me is beautiful, and peaceful. I have the utter certainty that all is very well.

The following message came through very strongly:

Dissentions, wars, catastrophes do not matter in the least—the false prophets do not matter, the groups following teaching from the planes of illusion do not matter, all is very well. There are enough people in the world who have been touched by the Holy Spirit and who are following the truth. These are enough to save humanity. This number will grow. So it shall be, even should devastating wars break out, even should the earth's axis shift and parts of the earth sink beneath the sea. These people who seek the truth and do the will of God shall survive to keep the truth alive. So shall it be. All is very very well.

(12.50 pm. on Ben Hope by the rock beside the stream.)

I again stood with my back to the rock for some time. I had my eyes closed. I felt a strong impulse to open them. What I saw was so wonderful that I hesitate to put it down. Standing in front of me was the figure of the risen Christ in majesty. He was wearing white, blue and scarlet robes and had a golden crown on his head. I stood still, with my back against the rock, rather dazed and surprised that I could both dare and be able to look at him. He came towards me and taking my head between his hands, bent it forward and kissed me on the brow. I burst into tears and sank to my knees before Him. I felt so terribly unworthy. He laid his hands on my head and blessed me and the work I was doing. Then he raised me to my feet. This was the most wonderful experience of my life. There is nothing I can say about it except to marvel that it should happen to me. The radiant figure moved away from me and faded from sight. I leant against the rock again in a moment of eternal peace. Just then Peter came catapulting down the mountain side. I was glad he did not see me as the tears were still running down my cheeks. I went after him and called to him. He told me they had had a wonderful climb to the top of Ben Hope. Janet and John were following behind him.

The impact of the meeting with Christ clearly also had an impact on the "border beings" that were so much part of ROC's life. The words of one such being, a fire salamander called Fircos, are recalled:

670802. Last night I wondered why Fircos had not been near me since the journey. He immediately appeared and said it was because of my meeting with Christ on Ben Hope and being blessed by Him. He and the others felt that they should stand aside. He reminded me that they were mostly border beings and that they did not like to approach me now. I said: "It is not that you cannot approach me, as you are here now, but that you were holding back?"

F. That is so.

ROC. But you are willing to do God's work?

F. Of course.

ROC. And my recent work is with such beings as yourself. That is the work that was blessed. It is therefore right that you and the others should be with me. The close bond between us is blessed. The love between us is blessed. You have taught me so much and expanded my outlook—surely you must know that.

F. I do know. But I want to find out what you feel now.

ROC. If anything the bond between us is stronger than ever;

>   my love for you is even greater, if that is possible.
>   A beautiful smile lit up Fircos' strangely lovely face.
>   F. That is as it should be. I am glad.
>   I next found myself on Ben Hope beside the stone I had leant against. I seemed to walk right through it and went along a passage in the rock to the cavern I had visited before. The Spirit of Ben Hope greeted me. He was now very little taller than myself, a somewhat caveman-like being, very strongly built, his body a bronze colour and very hairy. He radiated a great feeling of peace and controlled power.

ROC had further encounters with the Christ presence. These were always indeed precious moments to him.

>   670520b. Findhorn. During the morning session, prayer and meditation. Voice of the Master calling me by name and saying, "Blessed of Men that you are chosen to do this work." Made me feel very humble. Voice continued, "Accept with humility and joy." The Master put his hand on my head, and said that my eye would be completely cured and any other ills I had, so that I might have as sound a body as possible to do His work (did not tell the others, as this was a very personal message)

>   690604. At Pluscarden [priory], we went into the service. There, in that holy place, I gave thanks for what had happened and dedicated myself anew to work for the light. I asked for power to fight the dark and for protection. I was aware of the presence of Christ, who laid his hands on my head and blessed the work I was being used for.

Linn of Dee

>   670813. As soon as I am in bed, I leave my body and find myself sitting on a rock at the Linn of Dee. It is brilliant sunshine, and the river is roaring through the channel in the rock. I am presently aware of many beings—water sprites, nymphs and so on. They are mostly very tenuous and lively to look at. I watch them as they dance over the rushing water. Presently I become aware of a being standing beside me on the rock. He is almost

transparent and of a blue green colour. At first, his shape keeps changing, but he becomes denser and less transparent and begins to take on a very definite shape of that of a young human male. Somehow, I have usually thought of water spirits as female, though the spirit of Corrieshalloch Gorge was male, but I thought of him more as an earth or rock spirit than a water one. This being I somehow know, partly no doubt from his colour, to be a water spirit. He grows still denser and greets me and welcomes me. His voice is liquid like running water, and yet I understand the words—of course, the communication is no doubt telepathic.

I rise to my feet and find he is slightly taller than myself. He is slimly built and very beautiful to look at. He takes hold of my hands, and I can feel the clasp of his hands. He has a strange smile.

W.S You are wondering at a male water spirit, since you think of most of them as female because of the legends of water nymphs.

ROC. Yes. I am a bit surprised.

W.S. Yet you should know by this time that there is no sex differentiation into male and female in our realms. We are just beings, but when we take on human shape, we have to take on either a male or female shape. It is far better for us to take on the same shape and form as the person we want to make contact with. That is why the beings you contact are nearly always what you call male, because you are a male yourself. Of course, often the polarity is positive and a male form is more appropriate. As you already know, the form is nearly always complete. Are you disappointed that I am not a beautiful water nymph?

ROC. Not in the least.

W.S. I am glad. Let us sit and communicate.

I sit down on the rock again, and he sits beside me. We sit quietly but there is a flow between us. I can in a strange way feel what it is like to be a water spirit. I have a sense of tremendous exhilaration from the swirling water. I want to get up and dance—a rhythmic ritual dance—and then plunge into the water. I have a sense of oneness with the water and of communication with all the other water spirits. It is a very wonderful experience.

W.S. Now you know and understand.

ROC. Yes. Thank you for sharing this with me.

R. Ogilvie Crombie

W.S. It is necessary. In the work you are doing, you must not only link with the beings you meet, but you must identify with them so that you can understand and experience the way they feel and appreciate what they are doing, and they can understand how you feel and appreciate the work you are doing. In this way, the different kingdoms can be brought closer together and finally integrated. You are one of the chosen ones destined to bring this about. We are very close now. It is said all men are brothers, though few looking at the antics of the human species can believe that, though it must be so in time, and the greater concept—"all beings are brothers." This has been a preliminary meeting in which I think we have both learnt much.

Vernal Equinox

When ROC was staying with us at Nervelstone in Ayrshire, he had a number of out-of-body experiences, two of which are given below. Descriptions of nature spirits and elementals follow the usual pattern but with local variations!

680321. Vernal Equinox. Between 6 and 8am, I had been trying to visit the glen but only managed very brief visits. It was obvious the time was not right, but in the morning I found myself there with Gordon. The glen was thronged with beings. Pan was there and a great variety of nature spirits of all kinds—elves, gnomes, fauns, dryads, and so on, and many fairy beings some of whom were very tall. As usual, it is difficult to be detailed. At one time, I was strongly aware of them, but the consciousness that is in one with the etheric body is very single minded.

A tall being in green and brown robes with a circlet of leaves round his head was standing to the front of the hollow above the tree. I did not recognise him as having seen him before, but he is probably the spirit of the glen. There were other beings grouped round him also in green and brown, some in robes, some in tunics and breeches with yellow stockings and black shoes. As they were tall, they were probably elves of some kind. Pan was standing higher up the bank beside the higher tree.

This was obviously a vernal equinox ritual in which we were taking part, and part of it involved us. We were standing in front of the spirit of the glen and his group, wearing long green cloaks. We turned and walked down the slope to the tree. As we did so, the cloaks dissolved away, leaving us nude. We embraced the tree, one on each side, touching our foreheads to the bark, and gripping each other's arms.

The following is the sequel to this and shows my seeming involvement in a world I certainly cannot see. Belief would be considerably strengthened if such experiences came my way directly! But, in time, who knows? However, my lack of such direct exposure to the unseen neither authenticates nor negates ROC's experiences. I keep an open but critical mind.

680323. Last night, not long after going to bed, I found myself in the glen. The being who had been wearing the green and brown cloak and whom I thought to be the spirit of the glen was waiting for me in the hollow above the tree. (I had the impression that this hollow, which is in reality boggy and muddy, was floored with a soft green moss). Without his cloak, he was a faun about my own height. He greeted me, and confirmed that he is the spirit of the glen. I was there to be linked with him in ritual, as with the other spirits. This took place, and we then walked down to the tree, circled round it, and then walked to the end of the glen and back. He told me I was to bring Gordon in the morning.

I am not certain when this took place, as I did not switch on the light to see the time, but it was probably between 2 and 3am, still dark.

We both were in the glen by the tree (it was light, of course, in this plane). In the clearing, a little beyond the tree, Gordon was ceremoniously and symbolically linked with the spirit and with the glen. A green cloak was draped over his shoulders, and a circlet of leaves placed on his head, as he was named guardian of the glen. With the spirit, we walked round the tree, and the glen.

3.30pm. We went for a walk in the afternoon in spite of a slight drizzle. The ground was very wet as there had been a lot of rain, but it was fair by the time we reached the glen. The river was very high. Great feeling of peace, and I could sense many beings who greeted Gordon as guardian and welcomed him. Though not aware of them, he could feel a great oneness with the

R. Ogilvie Crombie

glen and with nature. We returned by the waterfall, which was big—obviously no hope of bathing in the pool this time.

Midsummer in the Botanics

720623. Very good feel all morning. Went to the Botanic Gardens. Dull but with blinks of sun. Took the path to the rock garden. The strange horse chestnut was on the left of the path with the curious markings on the bark like hieroglyphics and ancient nature carvings which has always struck me as negative and evil. I am now sure after reading a chapter in Dion Fortune's *Psychic Self-Defence* that it is in cabbalistic terms a negative, evil tree, i.e. a necessary balance to the positive in the gardens. I turned off onto the grass to go through the heath garden to the nature power point between the three pines. The garden was suddenly alive with nature spirits. Beautiful green elves three to four feet high were walking in front of me, full of joy and delight, but walking more sedately than usual.

As I walked through the heath garden, Kurmos came running up to me—still the beautiful little faun that was my first contact with these beings. He greeted me with joy and, turning, went dancing in front of me between the elves. I felt great happiness and wonder at the activity that was going on. I suppose being Midsummer Eve, there was more activity, and I was probably more aware of it.

Pan was with me, very powerful, on my left. I felt great energy. All the chakras were strongly activated but in a pleasant and good way. Very strong feelings especially in my legs on the nature power point. Went on to the "tree of life" and walked round it clockwise with a stop to look at some of the heath as a couple came past. This tree has a very strange spirit which I have not been aware of before. His "picture" is impressed on the front of the tree, strange and a bit sinister; a faun-like being with fierce eyes and longish straight horns on the forehead. This figure is about 14" tall. The entity itself was standing in front of the tree [and was] about my own height

E. Are you afraid of me?

ROC. No.

E. Would you have felt so drawn to the tree if you had seen

me before?

ROC. Yes.

E. Will you touch the tree as you have always done, but this time aware that you are doing it through me.

ROC. Yes.

I laid my hands on the trunk of the tree and felt the usual strong flow of energy.

E. Will you lean your back against the tree again through my being.

I did so and was aware of a strange warming energy and the voice said: "Do you love me as you love the tree?"

ROC. Yes I do. You are the tree.

E. You found me strange. Not what you might have expected but you are not repulsed?

ROC. Perhaps a little disconcerted. You are not what I might have expected, but you are not evil.

E. I am neither good nor evil, unlike some of the other beings you have met. My tree has been called "the tree of life." I am what you make of me.

I moved away from the tree and turned round. I was aware of the being standing where I had been leaning, strong powerful and strange. I felt extraordinary activation of the heart chakra. Pan was beside me. "You are developing in the right direction," he said, and smiled. "More and more you are able to accept the stranger looking of the elemental beings with discernment and be aware of the true quality of the entity, not being put off by the seemingly sinister aspect but feeling love and respect. You still have no fear of me?"

ROC. None

P. And you still love me?

ROC. From the depth of my heart. It could never be otherwise.

P. In whatever aspect I might assume?

ROC. Yes. I would always know you.

I stretched out my hands towards him. He took them and looked into my eyes from his own strangely deep and luminous ones. The bond I feel with this wonderful and beautiful being cannot be put into words. God has indeed been good to me in allowing this to happen and bringing it about.

R. Ogilvie Crombie

I began to walk along the path that skirts the rock garden to the south. Kurmos and the elves [were] still ahead of me. Pan [was] beside me. The sun was shining. I felt great happiness.

P. You can still accept me as I am?

ROC. Yes. You are the god of fertility and growth, the symbol of life continuing.

Some distance ahead when the path was bordered by bushes and trees, there were two wooden seats. I thought I would sit there for a while amongst the circle of redwood trees which I like so much. They radiate a different energy from any other trees. A seat near them was occupied by a man, and a long haired youth was sitting near a border sketching some flowers. I walked round the trees and stood for a moment in the centre, then went back to where I had seen the other seats.

By this time, one of them was occupied by a woman—absolutely not the right place for me to be. I turned towards another path which curved round a rhododendron bush. Kurmos came running out of it towards me. For the first time I was consciously aware that his eyes were green. If anyone before had asked me the colour of his eyes, I would have said brown. Were they, and have they changed colour or were they always green—a fact I had failed to notice?

He turned, and I followed him along the curved path to a seat where I sat down. The path was fairly narrow, and I felt enclosed by trees and bushes and very close to nature. I watched two bullfinches in the bush opposite. Some sparrows came twittering down, probably hoping for breadcrumbs. A blackbird was hopping about and a squirrel dashed across the path and climbed about a yard up a tree trunk, disappearing round the back of it. It must have jumped into a bush close by. I could see its tail which remained motionless for some time. Then the tail disappeared with a flick, and the squirrel came out from under another bush onto the edge of the path. It sat up, looked at me, came a few feet towards me, perhaps hoping for nuts and then turned and scampered off. Kurmos, who had been standing in the middle of the path turned and coming over, sat on the seat beside me.

ROC. This reminds me of our first meeting when you asked me why are human beings so stupid.

Kurmos looked at me with a mischievous twinkle.

K. You can't answer that question, can you?

ROC. No, since I have come to see us through the eyes of beings like yourself. I sometimes wonder how you can put up with us at all. To quote Puck in A Midsummer's Night Dream: – "What fools these mortals be." Dangerous fools at times, too!

I did not expect Kurmos to have studied Shakespeare in the "school" he had learned in, but as I have said before, our exchanges got across in terms of symbols and images which are universal, no matter what language they may be expressed in.

K. We find human behaviour amusing, and we try to understand. It isn't easy because so often it is destructive, cruel and horrible too, or so it seems to us, and makes us sad. But there are those who love nature, who love the gardens, who draw happiness and peace from the flowers, the bushes and the trees, who love the birds and the squirrels and no doubt would love us if they could see us. That makes us happy, and we draw close to them. I am sure some of these are aware of us even if they cannot see us. Why is it you can see us as well as you do?

ROC. I suppose because I am a privileged person, being one of those chosen to link with Pan and help to renew the old contact between mankind and the nature spirits.

Pan appeared at that moment standing opposite us.

P. Being who you are, the Master of the Seventh Ray, you are surely the most suited for the task. As soon as the integration between your lower self and your higher self reached a certain degree of completion, you were bound to see us. Your lower self and your physical body had to be trained and conditioned for many years before the integration could begin to take place. Your higher self and I have always been close associates.

Kurmos looked up at me. "I know who you are now," [he said.] He rose from the seat and turned to Pan who placed a hand on his head and looked down at him with infinite affection in his eyes.

P. You, too, were chosen for the part you played in bringing about our meeting, my little henchman.

A slow beatific smile spread over the little faun's face. He seemed to grow in stature. He gave a little cry, spun round and went dancing along the path. Pan looked after him smiling. Then

R. Ogilvie Crombie

he crossed the path and sat beside me.

P. Being who you are must have its problems, being who you are physically on this earth.

ROC. Yes, many problems. Mainly interesting and fascinating, often amusing, sometimes disconcerting! Now I accept the truth, I am becoming used to them. There are times when it seems as if the whole thing was fantasy, and when I seem to be two people; to be strongly overlit by another being or even possessed. And yet I know deep within me that the two are one and [the] same being. The integration is not yet entirely complete, but very nearly so. What will happen when it is?

Pan looked at me shrewdly: "Only you know that."

ROC. Obviously I must, to the outer world, keep my personality—persona, if you like—of Ogilvie Crombie. That is the mask I must always wear since the time is not yet when I can throw it away and appear as Monsieur le Compte, or as Merlin. This physical body will probably wear out before then.

P. Laying a hand on my arm. "The body will not wear out until it has fulfilled its purpose and is not of any further use."

ROC. My higher self is notoriously saddled with long lives in incarnation! Who knows?

P. Don't you?

ROC. Which me? It is a curious thought, and life on the physical level becomes more and more interesting and exciting with the sense of ever increasing power and knowledge.

P. But the sense of power and its potential use does not tempt you?

ROC. No, but the responsibility can be frightening.

P. The integration must very nearly be complete. Some people must recognise you.

ROC. Yes, but only the few who for one reason or another are allowed to. Some people see me as you and talk about my Pan-look. One or two have seen me become you doing the nature spirit talk.

Pan laughed delightedly "I know, and why not?"

ROC. Indeed, why not?

We both laughed at some inner joke which cannot be expressed.

ROC. One thing I am sorry about, when people are envious.

Why should I be able to see those beings and not them? It isn't fair—they want so much to see them. How can they set about it?

P. And you have to hedge a bit and say someday you probably will if your faith is strong enough. Don't try too hard. It will happen at the most unexpected moment.

I laughed – "No doubt you heard me at it."

P. Oh, yes, but little do they know how dangerous it could be if their wishes were fulfilled. The elementals adhere to a totally different evolution. Close contact between human beings and elementals can be very dangerous, especially if the motives are wrong. My subjects are strange beings. Only you and a few others can ever make close links with them. A number of people who believe in them can be aware of them, and of course they will work for those who love them and invoke them, but to see them might unhinge the mind, and has done in some cases.

ROC. I know, but how can I, as ROC, explain that to those who feel envious or frustrated?

Pan laughed again. "That's your problem." Then he grew serious. "Master, the plan proceeds?"

I felt a strange power come over me, as the higher self took over. "The plan proceeds, but with many setbacks and flaws. The little egos are so assertive—I must have this. I want that, the largest blooms, the longest and strongest stems. Quantity all the time rather than quality. The expedient rather than what is right and just. A doubting belief in the reality of the nature spirits, but paying lip service to the idea. As if that wasn't obvious. Still, the plan proceeds, limping if not on very sound feet. And in many places it is working, as you and your subjects must be aware."

P. Yes, we are aware, but we have to be so tolerant and forgiving. Human beings are ignorant and thoughtless in spite of the attempts made by yourself to bring them enlightenment.

ROC. My dear brother, let us be tolerant and make allowances. After all, we must not forget they are only human. Considerable advance has been made in spite of that.

Pan rose and stood looking down at me. The contact with the higher self was lessening, and I was becoming my everyday self, though still highly sensitive. During this odd occurrence, an observing part of my brain seemed to stand aside recording

R. Ogilvie Crombie

it all.

Memories and Explanations

721030. Felt I had better go out for a bit after lunch, and was strongly prompted to go to the Botanic Gardens. Wind very strong. As soon as I entered the gardens, I was aware of an unusually strong power which produced a strong reaction from all the chakras. As on Midsummer Eve, the reaction of the lower chakras was good—the pure nature reaction. The whole physical response of my body was very marked and of an exalted and ecstatic nature, recalling my first experience of this sort of feeling just before my first meeting with Pan on the Mound.

I took the first path to the left to go to the herb garden, but a number of the garden staff were working there. I went by the edge of the rock garden to the south end of the garden. There was great human activity towards the top of the heath garden, digging and so on, so I did not visit the tree of life. I have a suspicion that they may have cut down the pine trees or some of them round the nature power point, as I could only see the top of one, but I was not prompted to confirm this. I went up the slope and down to the south path and turned west, aware of great activity on the part of the nature spirits, which surprised me at this time of the year.

A great degree of heightened awareness, and more than usual reality of the trees and bushes and flowers and three-dimensionness, which is almost overpowering. The whole surface of my body felt stimulated to a high degree with the "pins and needles" feeling—very exhilarating. The chakra reaction increased, my legs felt strange; the back, calf and thigh muscles reacting strongly, and a feeling of tension in my chest, and breathlessness. In fact, all the usual effects, but to a very intense degree, produced an ecstatic feeling of joy. Pan was with me, and Kurmos, dancing along in front of me. I was strongly aware of St. Germain and Merlin, with the Saturn aspect, and of the Chinese sage, and the Indian master the "Gnomes" had seen me with on Saturday. Someone—I think the Chinese Sage, but I am not sure—said:

"Do not try to inhibit the activity of the lower chakras. All seven must be developed together, and as equally as possible to bring about balance. Do not follow the Sufi practice of ignoring the two lowest and trying to lift the energies into the heart. This is not sound practice, as apart from inhibiting radiation from these chakras, it tends to overdevelop and distort the radiation of the heart centre. The heart centre must never be neglected or bypassed, as many people do, but it must be kept pure so that it radiates its own energies. You have been tending to suppress the lower chakras in spite of all the knowledge you have acquired already on the subject."

This was enlightening, as I had once or twice had a feeling that the Sufi teaching might be wrong, and Annie had said she was aware that some of the young Sufis who came to see them had overdeveloped their heart centres producing tensions in the body.

I was strongly conscious of the livingness of the trees and bushes, of a closeness and identification with the earth and with the vegetable kingdom. I skirted the west end of the rock garden and went across the grass to the redwood trees which have such a different feel from the other trees.

Then I went on by the winding grass paths through the trees and bushes conscious of an ever increasing intensity of feeling, the tingling in my body, and the sense of "more real than real," of three-dimensionalness, of an almost unbearable ecstasy.

I came out of a path into more open ground and crossed the south path running round the garden, turning diagonally down toward the middle walk, filled with a tremendous feeling of exultation. These experiences are so difficult to express in words and can never be adequately recounted. Only a pale reflection of the actual experience ever gets across. One feels a sense of frustration because there is a shortage of the right meaningful and evocative words to give it true expression.

Feeling a little overcome by the intensity of all this sensation, I sat down on a seat on the grass just beyond the middle path, looking at the trees. How vitally alive they were, though some of them had lost most of their leaves. I became immediately aware that not only were they alive, but they were communicating with me. I was not only overwhelmed by the love they were sending me, but realised they were thanking me for the work I was doing in trying to put over to people the sensitivity and consciousness of the vegetable kingdom, the talks I had been giving, and in particular the tapes I had made, copies of which were going to many places all over the world, were slowly but surely spreading knowledge of the sensitivity and consciousness of the vegetable kingdom and would surely help to bring about the renewed contact with the nature kingdoms which is so vital if the world is to continue to exist.

They thanked me for the bravery I had shown in giving the talks and making the tapes, which could surely meet with much disbelief and even ridicule. "You are our champion, and we claim you as one of us."

The feeling of oneness with all nature was both wonderful and unexpected. The trees and bushes, the grass and the flowers have become even more alive and conscious beings than before, and this unlooked for return of appreciation and love was deeply moving. I felt that my whole life had been worthwhile. No doubt my conscious self has brought some of it about, but it is my higher self and the overlighting entities who have been mainly responsible.

Pan was sitting beside me with an arm round my shoulder, looking at me with deep affection, and Hermes was behind me. There was a sense of timeless wonder. The gardens were full of nature beings, beautiful elves, fat little gnomes, and many others. Again, I felt surprised at so many of them being about at this time of year.

"Why not?" said Pan, "look at the number of trees that still have leaves on them. There is plenty of work to be done. And isn't this a beautiful part of the year! How do you think the changes in colour are brought about? Who are the artists responsible?"

I looked at him startled. "Your subjects, I suppose. I had never thought of that."

"Yes, my subjects. The botanist will tell you differently, of course. He has his own explanation, and I have mine. Which do you think is right? Take your choice."

"Both are probably right. It depends on the way you look at it."

"Yes, both are right. You develop in wisdom."

"I have good teachers."

Pan laughed and stood up. "We know who the best one is — or at least one of the best." He looked at me with a mischievous twinkle in his eyes. "Come, let us go."

I got up from the seat and started to walk in the direction of the west gate. There was one place we had to go — the wild corner that I always think of as Pan's corner, though it is not so wild as it used to be since all the grass has been cut short. It has lost nothing of its mysterious atmosphere.

I was only aware of Pan walking beside me; Hermes had gone. Wandering in places like the Gardens or the Hermitage, I often wish I was naked. It seems so wrong to be close to nature with clothes on. As we skirted the gate and walked towards Pan's corner, I suddenly felt that though I was in fact fully clothed, I was at the same time naked. It was a curious experience though it had happened at least once before. I began to think back to the years I spent a Cowford cottage where, because of its isolation, I could wander about without clothes as much as I pleased; where in fact, the real joy of doing so was first fully realised.

Pan, who could obviously read my thoughts, said:

"I wonder if you realise the full significance and importance of the ten years you spent at the cottage."

"I think I am beginning to. I know I accepted it at the time as necessary because of my heart condition. But for those years, and the kind of life I led, I doubt if I would be alive today."

"You may be right. The change these years brought about in your physical state was considerable, but the changes brought about on other levels were even greater."

"I know that now."

"But at the time, you were totally unaware of the existence of such entities as elementals, in spite of your almost lifelong interest in esoteric, or what are called occult, subjects."

"These interests were mainly devoted to such things as telepathy, clairvoyance, psychometry, an examination of spiritualism and a rejection of the way it was put across, a genuine interest in the many branches of psychic research. It was during the Cottage years that I read many books on the subject; for instance, most of Harry Price's books including the controversial *Borley Rectory* ones; and, of course, a deep interest in mysticism, which I was led to delve into by Aldous Huxley's books."

"You believed in what are called poltergeists?"

"Yes, at least as real phenomena, and probably due to entities."

"But fairies? If anyone had asked you if you believed in them, would you have said 'yes'?"

"I wonder. I would like to have believed in them, especially in elves and gnomes, but probably one part of me would have rejected them."

"Because of your scientific training?"

"Yes, I suppose so."

We walked on across the grass towards the northwest corner of the Gardens.

"And me," Pan asked, "would you have believed in me then?"

I stopped and looked at him. "As a boy, and in my teens, I loved the Greek myths. The Greek gods were very real to me then; so were the Norse equivalents. But I suppose if anyone had suggested that I might one day see, talk to, and even touch one of these beings, I would have said 'don't talk rot!' And yet, I wonder."

"Perhaps the strong desire to find a scientific physical explanation for the strange phenomena you were interested in was just a temporary surface veneer, as was the materialistic phase you went through, the 'I only believe what I can see' phase you have spoken about. It never succeeded in eradicating a deep fundamental belief in the true reality"

"As a kid, I passionately believed in fairies, until it was suppressed by school life."

"Suppressed, but not destroyed. What was I to you in those days—the nymph-pursuing satyr; the being whose presence produced panic in the woods, an evil spirit, a devil?"

"No, you were the Pan of the Wind in the Willows." I stopped speaking and looked at him. Something rose up into my consciousness from the very depths of my unconscious. "Surely you have always been the wonderful and beautiful being you are to me now." I looked at him in astonishment: Is that why...?"

"It is one reason. The true reason why you were not afraid. I have never been other to you than what I am to you now. Let us consider time as you know it. As you are a human being that is functioning in a material, three-dimensional body existing in a time dimension, I am aware of that time dimension and can function in it, so I understand and can talk about your past.

"The other reason you were chosen was because of the identity of the being who overlights you and is in fact your higher self."

We came to a seat near a tree not very far from the special corner, and sat down.

"I suppose you were aware of that being when you first appeared to me, when I was walking down the Mound."

"No. He veiled himself from me at first. I only knew that you were someone I had to test; someone who would be able to see me. You look surprised. Because I was unaware of your higher self? Never forget, beings like myself do not know everything. Only God, the unknowable, ineffable spirit does that. We know our own functions, and all that is connected with them, and we carry them out according to the will of God.

"Your higher self can veil himself. Very few human beings will be aware of him in you, and for most who are, it will only be a fleeting glimpse. Even you, yourself, though the integration is almost complete, are only aware of him in the background. At times, you feel his presence and identify with him strongly, and you know that he is there all the time, ready to give you knowledge and promptings. As an incarnate spirit in a material body, you have to function on a material level, using a three-dimensional material brain and presenting the personality mainly connected with the ego—the lower self, the personality known as Ogilvie Crombie—to the world.

"The incarnate spirit, which is only a part of this being, has chosen to incarnate in this particular physical person, which must develop and evolve according to the many forces brought to bear on it. This development on the material level is accomplished by development and evolution on the higher levels, mental and spiritual, which can lead to at least some degree of integration, which is a purpose of incarnation. In your case, however complete the integration, you will never entirely become the being; to others, you will always be the man they know as Ogilvie, except for occasional glimpses of the higher self. It is not easy to understand."

"Thank you," I said. "Some of what you have said I was vaguely aware of. You have made it much clearer and less mysterious. To you, then, that night, I was just someone you knew would be able to see you whom you had to test—for fear, I presume.'

"Yes. I was delighted at your reactions to me. The awareness of my presence must have come as a surprise all the same."

I laughed. "Of course it did, but luckily for me, the experiences of seeing and talking to Kurmos broke the shock it might otherwise have been. You are an awesome being, but not frightening. I am sure now that I must always have felt love for you, otherwise, simply as a human being, I would certainly have been afraid. When did my higher self reveal himself?"

"Later that night in your flat. At first when you returned to your flat after our meeting, you could not see me, as I had made myself invisible to you, though you felt my presence when you crossed from the back room into the front one, which is your practice before going to bed. I was standing with my back to the door, making myself as fearsome as possible, ordering you to kneel down and worship me, as a last test. When you refused to do so, and I said, 'You know who I am', you replied 'But do you know who I am', and your higher self unveiled himself. You, in fact, became him for me, and I knew my quest was over—you were the chosen mediator.

"I still had to test you further, as you know, because the higher self is not always manifest. I had to satisfy myself that the physical body and lower self would not shrink from me. I came upon you when you had just had your shower, were naked, defenceless, and the higher self had withdrawn—possibly intentionally so that I could make the test. You showed no fear. The result, in spite of snags due mainly to others, is surprisingly good. You have played your part splendidly. What others do with the information given through you is their affair. They have freewill and can use it or reject it. They must answer for the consequences, not you."

"Have I still work to do in places like Findhorn garden?"

"Not for the time being. Your role was to talk about your experiences and make the tapes which will spread the knowledge. Your main work now lies elsewhere, as you already know."

"But I shall not lose contact with you, or with the elementals?"

"No. The bond with me once made is forever. Do you remember what happened on Cluny Hill when, through you, I was reconciled with Christ?"

"Could I ever forget!"

"That was a bond that was broken by the temporal church and had to be renewed. You were the mediator there. That also I sought in you. That is why I call you brother. Where you are, I will always be, for I am everywhere. You could not break that bond even if you wanted to. One of my functions is to look after you, to protect you, to take care of your physical body, to help you in your work, my dear beloved brother. As for the elementals, my subjects, they accept you, they acknowledge you, and they love you. They will never let you go."

Sitting there, still with the greatly expanded awareness and sensitivity, with the feeling of ecstasy and joy that went on building up, and now overwhelmed by the feeling of love pouring over me from this beautiful being and from all the nature spirits in the garden, many of whom had gathered round us, as well as from the trees, the bushes and all the vegetation, I felt so deeply moved, I could not speak. It was more than my physical self could stand.

Pan took both my hands in his and looked into my eyes. The feeling did not lessen, but a profound peace, tranquillity, and wonder was added. Somehow it almost seems wrong to try to put this experience into words, which are inadequate and can only hint at the true experience. But I must try to do so.

We sat in silence for some time—I was quite unaware of the passing of time.

At last, speaking with difficulty, I said "You seem to feel this bond with my lower self, my conscious ego, my Ogilvie personality, just as much as with my higher self. I am so aware of this great love."

"Of course, it has to be so," he replied. "My relationship with your higher self cannot be expressed. It cannot be understood unless seen from higher levels."

Suddenly he laughed, and the mischievous twinkle, which I love so much, appeared in his eyes. He said, "Pan, Merlin, the Saturn aspect—we are all one with your higher self, and therefore with you. And yet we are all separate entities. We are outside you and at the same time within you. Any one of us can overlight you, can identify with you, in fact can become you, when required. On such an occasion, only the rare sensitive would be aware of what was taking place. Some listeners to your talks have seen you become me, just as others have seen you as Merlin, or as your higher self. This is a mystery which must remain so. A time will come when you will understand it fully. We are all one with God—there is no separation—and yet we are all unique individuals."

Pan rose. "Let us go to the far corner, what you call my corner." I got up, and we went on across the grass.

"To me you are so real," I said. I looked round at one or two people walking about in the gardens. "In fact, in some way, you are more real than these people who cannot even see you."

He stopped, and smiled at me, "Of course I am more real."

"Man has developed his intellect for what?" I asked. "He was cut off from contact with the other kingdoms and from awareness of divinity in order to do so, and what has he achieved? Greater and greater ability to trick, cheat, and destroy his fellow men, and exploit the earth and the nature kingdom. How can you and your subjects bear to share the earth with us?"

Pan put an arm round my shoulder, and we walked on.

"Come now," he said. "You must not look on the black side like this. Your higher self must be off-duty. It is true that man has done and is doing terrible things, as you say, but he is also doing great and beautiful things. Many men reach great spiritual heights, because they are great beings. Concentrate on the good and the beautiful. Turn your back on the sensational headlines. Read beautiful books, listen to great music, and lose yourself in fine paintings. Of course there are times when we would like to leave the earth because of man's behaviour. We will never do so, on account of the evolved souls in incarnation."

After a pause, I said "Of course, you are right, but why should so many men, in spite of this boasted enlightenment, intellect and civilisation, take true reality for imagination and hallucination and call the illusion the real?"

Pan smiled. "Plato's 'men in the cave,' turning their backs

on the true and taking the shadows for the real."

I laughed, the sudden black mood had passed. "What! Pan talking of Plato?"

"Why not? After all, I am Greek and proud of our philosophers. At least my seeming appearance is Greek, even if my origin is much older. Talking of my appearance, how do you feel when people say I must be ugly?"

"Disgusted and horrified. At least I was the first time it happened, when Kathy Sparks came out with it in Peter's car on the way to Stonehenge, and I just about snapped her head off—at least, you did. The voice was not mine. You were angry then."

"Yes, I was. Such a stupid remark for a really sensitive person to make. But she is not clever in some ways, and lacks understanding." He sighed. "I should have been more tolerant, but it seemed to me that the hoped-for cooperation might break down at the very beginning. It was a thought that had to be stopped at once. I must be accepted by man as I am. It is so, and how I choose to be. As you have said, we take on forms imposed on us by man in his myths and legends, and so he must accept us." He smiled. "In fact, it is not quite as simple as you make it, but that again cannot be explained in earth terms."

"You feared the plan might break down at the start. Are you not aware of the future—of man's future, I mean?"

Pan gave me a whimsical look. "You ask difficult questions sometimes. I'll try to explain in your terms. In higher realms —here again I am simplifying—your time exists as the eternal now. We find it difficult to sort it out into a yesterday, today, and tomorrow sequence. That is the first point. When I am functioning in your time dimension, as I am doing at the moment, it is not possible to determine what is going to happen, say a week hence, or a year hence, because of man's freewill. The future exists but in a very flexible way. Will it confuse you if I say that all possible future events exist in the now, but what happens in your time dimension is finally determined by man's freewill choice?"

"I can follow that, but surely many things influence what a man does and how he behaves. He has only a limited freewill."

Pan gave me a wry smile. "Trust you to complicate things when I am trying to simplify them. Basically, there are many things that determine man's behaviour, but he does have sufficient freewill to make the future difficult to foresee, because his actions are often erratic and unpredictable. So at that time, I could not tell how the cooperation might work out. You, yourself, have made quite a profound study of the problem of time and freewill, so you ought to know most of what I am telling you already."

"Some of it certainly, but you have clarified it."

"Like butter," said Pan, and we both burst out laughing.

We had reached the corner in the extreme north west of the gardens, where I have always had such a real sense of the presence of Pan, and were standing in silence.

"I regret they have cut the grass," I said presently. "I loved it when it was long—it seemed so right. This is too trim."

Pan shrugged his shoulders. "It doesn't really matter. We have established a focal centre so strongly in this part of the garden that there is nothing our enthusiastic gardeners can do to alter it now."

I smiled. "I am delighted to hear that; the short grass worried me."

"It needn't."

We walked for some time round the bushes and trees in the vicinity of the corner.

"Can I ask about Gordon? I know there is a very close bond between us. In some strange way, we seem to be part of each other. We are necessary to each other. At least he is necessary to me and my work. Is this true, and in that case, does your love and protection and that of the elementals extend to him?"

Pan smiled. "Yes, it is true. The bond is a stronger one than you yet realise and goes a long time back. Looked at in one way, you are part of each other. Of course, my love and protection and that of my subjects extends to him and his family. Though he may not sense it in his conscious mind, he is aware of it in the depths of his unconscious. This is as it should be for the time being. Sensitivity, as you well know, takes a considerable time to develop. His life at the moment is much taken up with his daily work on a material level, and with his family. Too high a degree of sensitivity would not help him. The balance between you is right—you complement each other. He expresses his deep awareness in the exuberation he so often feels and shows in the country."

"Can I tell him this?"

"Yes. Even [though] the scientific part of his mind may want to reject it, he knows within himself that it is true. He must accept things as they are and cultivate patience. Your relationship is excellent at the moment. Be content."

"What I am writing now is mainly very personal to me, but it seems to me to be important and informative. I presume I can share it with him."

"Of course. There is very little—if anything—you cannot share with him."

We walked back to "Pan's corner," stood quietly for a time, and then left this point of the Gardens, crossing the walk that turns at right angles by the herbaceous border, and walking towards the beech tree under which I had been sitting when I first saw Kurmos. I leant against the trunk of the tree with my back on it, facing towards the tree I had seem him dancing round. I could feel an exchange of energies with the tree which was very much a living thing—the heightened awareness was still acute. I could no longer see Pan, though I felt he was still there. Kurmos was leaning against "his" tree. He was laughing. He danced round this tree and then in a great circle round the tree I was leaning against, circling round it several times, spiralling in until he stopped opposite me and bowed.

"In exalted company today," he said, with an impish grin. "Am I welcome?"

"You are always welcome, Kurmos."

He frisked about and danced round the tree. "I haven't seen you like this before in the Gardens. You once told me it wasn't right, whatever that means."

'What are you talking about? I'm the same as usual.'

"Oh no, you're not. You've shed your skins—what did you call them?—clothes. You are your natural self. You look much better."

"Don't talk nonsense. I'm fully dressed. I even have my raincoat on." I looked down at myself to make sure, because I had several times since coming into the garden felt that I was naked.

"I'm not talking nonsense. To me, you are in your natural

state, as you should be." He put out his hand and touched my arm, ran it over my chest and down the outside of my thigh. To my astonishment, I felt the touch on my bare skin.

There was something strange here. For him, my clothes did not exist, but my body did, since his hand did not pass through it as it had through my clothes. I had a memory of the first meeting with Pan, when he put an arm round my shoulder as we walked down North St. David's street, and I had felt the touch on my bare skin, and again when he had done the same thing a little ago as we walked in the Gardens. Had this something to do with the etheric body? The clothes, presumably, had no etheric part, and could become invisible. This was fascinating and would need thinking about.

"You really do not see my clothes?," I asked, and touched the sleeve of my raincoat, which unfastened and held out.

"No, I see only you—your clothes are not part of you; they don't belong; they are something extra."

I remembered what the Spirit of Smoo Cave had told me about the garments the elementals and other entities appear to be wearing as being part of them, formed out of themselves, and that when out-of-the-body, when I seemed to myself to be naked, I might well appear to other entities to be wearing garments, those being appropriate to the situation. This statement has been repeated to me on several occasions since. Of course, our clothes are not part of ourselves in that way—they are additional. Fundamentally, as Kurmos said, they don't belong. It had never occurred to me that it was possible for elemental beings not to be aware of the clothes. In fact, I remember the Smoo Spirit saying they could get in the way. The elves in Rosemarkie glen preferred me without my clothes.

"To you then, at the moment, I am naked?" I asked Kurmos

"If by that word you mean your natural self—yes."

"But you have seen me with clothes on—you referred to them as 'skins' the first time we met."

"Oh yes, I usually do, but not today."

"Why not today? Can you choose what you want to see?"

"Not entirely. It has just happened today and has something to do with you. You wanted to be naked; you regretted having to wear clothes here."

"That is true. I do feel it is wrong when one is with nature. Clothes don't belong, as you say."

"And did you feel naked?"

"Yes, I did. It was strange to be both dressed as I had to be, and at the same time naked."

Kurmos laughed, and clapped his hands. "And so at that moment, for us, your skins vanished, and you were yourself."

"You mean that to all of you I was naked?"

"You still are. Don't think it wrong, or we will see your clothes again. You are so much better without."

"When I was with Pan, did I appear dressed?"

"No, you were naked all the time." Kurmos laughed.

"Kurmos, you said you had never seen me naked in the Gardens before. Did you mean you have elsewhere?"

"Of course."

"Where?"

"When you really have had no skins on—on the beach at that place you go to in the north, where the garden is which you had so much to do with; you went into the sea with no skins on, at least quite often, and you often lay in the sand up on the moors in the sun and walked about amongst the sand hills. We've seen you in your dwelling place too."

"We?"

"Yes. Many of us are with you, though you do not seem to be aware of us. We do not wish to intrude." He suddenly looked grave. "Perhaps we are doing wrong; perhaps we do offend you. I should not have told you. Forgive us, we mean no wrong. We like to be with you."

At first, it was somewhat disconcerting to realise that one was probably never alone when one thought one was; that there was really no such thing as complete privacy. There might always be entities of one kind or another present watching one's actions and no doubt reading one's thoughts. It was inevitable and right, especially when awareness and contact had been made as in my case.

"No, Kurmos, you are not doing wrong; you are not intruding; you are welcome at anytime. But don't hesitate to make your presence known to me if you want to do so. This applies to any of you."

His face lightened, and he gave a delighted crow of laughter. "I thought it would be like that." He danced off.

What he had been saying was in complete agreement with what I had already been taught. The only new thing to me was the fact of appearing naked to these entities where I was wearing clothes, but only it seemed when I wanted to be naked. Many mysteries and fascinating things are gradually being made clear to me.

I continued to walk up the slope and went between the trees and bushes making for the huge beach tree which I am sure is the lord of the Gardens. Most of the leaves had come off it, but it still looked majestic with its enormous trunk. I leant against it, aware of great energy exchange, again feeling an odd absence of clothes. My naked back was touching the bark.

Kurmos came dancing back accompanied by a number of elves and tubby little gnomes, as well as a couple of fauns. The fauns and the gnomes danced round the tree, but the elves stood aside gravely watching. The dancing group finally scattered in all directions, and I began to walk down the slope accompanied by Kurmos and the elves, who were beautiful with great dignity and elegance. They were about four feet tall.

The next tree I wanted to visit was the Austrian pine, a strangely shaped tree above the pond. In front of the tree are a number of bamboos. I made my way between the clump and again leant against the trunk which slopes backwards, as it leans over the pond. It is a tree of great power. Again I felt the trunk against my naked back. It is a strangely disconcerting experience; something more than an illusion, I am sure. Perhaps it is the aura or field of the tree which can penetrate my clothes that I am feeling.

I skirted round the end of the pond past the two great weeping willows I love so much, Kurmos walking sedately at my side, and the elves following us. They accompanied us to the East Gate, and Pan appeared beside them. He raised his hand in a farewell gesture as I walked towards the main road, Kurmos still walking beside me.

"Are you coming back to the flat with me?" I asked. "You are very welcome to do so."

"No," he replied. "I am coming part of the way with you. This is one of my busy days."

I grinned at him. "Is it?"

"Yes, it is," he said gravely.

As we turned into Inverleith Place, he said "Now you have your clothes on."

"I should hope so."

"You don't want to be naked in the street?'

"No."

"Then that is why I see them."

I had on several occasions walked through Edinburgh streets with Kurmos beside me, so I was used to it and no longer felt it strange.

"When you are with me." I said, "and I do not see you nor am I apparently aware of your presence, can you do anything to make yourself visible to me?"

He frowned. "I don't know. I sometimes try, but apart from hoping you will see me, I don't know how to bring it about. The first time you saw me in the Gardens, I did nothing, because I didn't believe human beings could see us. I am curious about human beings and their strange and sometimes stupid behaviour, and I like to watch them. For some reason, I was attracted to you—I had been watching you once or twice when you came to the Gardens. It gave me a shock when I was forced to believe that you could see me. I suppose some other people who come to the Gardens see some of us, but it had never happened to me before. We get communications, of course, because people's thoughts come over to us fairly clearly. They are usually very dull and uninteresting."

"So, apart from just hoping, you do not know how to make yourself visible to me."

"No, it just happens. But I think it will only happen when you are in the right state for it to do so. It is a thing that depends more on you than on me."

"That is probably true, and I don't yet know how to control that state; it just happens, as with you."

"Perhaps Pan knows."

"If he does, we must hope that he will tell us when the time is right."

"You are glad when it happens?"

"Very. Life has never been so exciting and interesting as since it began to happen."

"It's nice to think I was the first of such beings you saw."

"You're becoming conceited, I'm afraid."

"What is conceited?"

"Pleased with yourself."

He laughed delightedly. "I am always pleased with myself. Is that wrong?"

"No, I don't think it is for you. You have every right to be."

He looked at me with curiosity. "Aren't you pleased with yourself?"

"Not very often."

"But you ought to be. Existence is so joyous."

"Only rarely for human beings."

He looked downcast. "But that is sad. I know it is true from the thoughts I pick up, and the things I see."

"I am not unhappy, Kurmos; though there is much to condemn in human behaviour, there is much to rejoice in, and from time to time, wonderful experiences like this afternoon in the Gardens. I am content, but I am not pleased with myself, because I fail in so many things."

He looked astonished. "I don't believe that; at least you have not failed in your contacts with Pan and with us. Is that not something to be pleased about?"

"Yes, Kurmos, it is. I am a very privileged person, a very fortunate one, and I know it."

He smiled. "That's better. How can you fail in things since you have so much knowledge and wisdom."

"Knowledge, yes, wisdom I am not so sure about. I should like to believe I have at least some."

He looked at me. "You know you have, and you have powers few other humans possess. We also know that."

I was silent

"It is true, isn't it?"

"Yes."

He looked at me shrewdly. "And a terrible responsibility?"

"Yes, Kurmos, a terrible and frightening responsibility. I can only use them when I am sure it is in accordance with God's will.

Sometimes the temptation is very strong."

"I am glad I am not you," he said. "We all love you very much; we are with you, and will help you all we can—all of us."

"Thank you, Kurmos. That gives me confidence and makes me very happy. Together we will not fail." I felt light-hearted, and laughed.

"Now I must go," said Kurmos.

"It is your busy day."

"Yes, it is my busy day." He looked at me, chuckled, and turning, ran off back the way we had come, gradually fading out as he did.

I returned to the flat once more, my everyday self, thoughtful and absurdly happy.

I am writing this down on Thursday, 2nd November, [1972] carrying on with what I began yesterday. It is coming through with fluency—there are no barriers or hold ups, yet it is coming slowly, and using up considerable energy. Pan is sitting in a chair almost opposite me, where he has been since I began to write.

"Did all this exchange actually take place in the Gardens on Monday," I asked him, "or are you giving me more while I am in the process of writing it down, or again am I myself embellishing what took place and adding to it. It is important to me that this is authentic."

"Of course it is important. It is authentic, as you well know in your inner and higher being. You are adding nothing. Quite a lot of our exchange took place in the Gardens, in images and symbols which were not fully realised into words by your mind, but it was deeply impressed in your unconscious and is now being realised into words under my guidance. As you are well aware, I am overlighting you during the whole of this transcript. Nothing is being left out or added. Personal colouration on your part is kept down to a minimum. When we go through it together later on, if there are any mistakes, or wrong interpretations into words, I shall give you the corrections."

"Thank you. I was sure within myself, but as I am always aware of the dangers of colouration and false transcription, there are times when I need reassurance."

"Understandable. You have it. Proceed in faith."

"Now," he said, "I am going to give you more. You will write down this 'conversation' as it takes place. I want to return to your life at the Cottage, which we did not pursue in the Gardens. I want to be certain that you consciously realise its full significance in your development."

"What am I not realising about it? I know the importance of the close contact with nature."

"But at that time, you knew nothing about power points and what some people call ley lines."

"That is true."

"Does it surprise you to learn that there was a strong nature power point in the wood behind the outhouses, with crossing ley lines."

I looked at him startled. "Good Lord!"

"In spite of your present knowledge and experience of power points, it has never occurred to you to think back to the Cottage?"

"No. I suppose knowledge gained at a later date is not often carried back in thought to an earlier time. Where was it? I suppose you know. Behind the outhouses, you said. That's about the centre of the wood."

"Yes." Once more the mischievous twinkle appeared in Pan's eyes. "It was the exact spot you chose to sunbathe on—that you surrounded with the windbreaker you built."

I must really have looked startled this time. "Oh no! This is fantastic!"

"It is true, and all through the years you lived there, when you sunbathed, you lay naked on the ground on a power point with only a rug between you and the earth. Lying in the air in the sun's rays, and then you bathed in the pool you had made by damming the burn. Close and frequent contact with the four elements you talk about in your lectures. Is it any wonder you can contact the entities that inhabit these elements—the sun symbolises fire, as you know—and can see them. Ten years of having all your bodies conditioned and prepared by the energies of the power point."

I was astonished. I could only sit staring at him. Why had it never occurred to me there might have been a power point there and to have chosen it as the place to sunbathe on, over such a long period?

"Not only was it a nature power point, but it was also associated with pre-Christian religious ceremonies and rituals. If you draw a line on the map from Morven in Sutherland through the position of the Cottage, it skirts the shoulder of Ben MacDhui. Have a look at some maps. Now do you see what I mean when I ask you do you fully realise the significance of your years at the cottage?"

I drew a deep breath. "Yes, I do now. My goodness, you've given me something to think about."

All these extracts tell only a small part of the work that ROC did as a bridge between humanity and the etheric and spiritual kingdoms of nature. In some ways it could be considered the core of his spiritual mission and even sheds some light on the mystery of his incarnational paternity as an aspect of the evolved soul known as St. Germain. For as Pan and others pointed out, it was vital that this connection with the nature spirits be between an ordinary man with ordinary human reactions and not with a high adept or "Master." Such beings are already reconciled with the higher levels of spirit where all our souls dwell; at that level there is no problem. It is with struggling incarnate humanity that the split and separation exists.

In many esoteric traditions, St. Germain is seen as the human adept most responsible for overseeing and sponsoring efforts to bring a new human civilisation into being; that is why in Theosophical writings he is often referred to as the "Lord of Civilisation." It is his desire and service to help bring a new, more holistic and beneficent civilisation to birth. As a look at our modern world and its global environmental problems will attest, such a new civilisation must at the very least embody more ecologically sensitive and responsible behaviour than we do now. Reconciliation and partnership with the devas, angels, elementals, and other spirits of nature is essential to such a wholeness, a key part of such an emerging civilisation. Bringing about such reconciliation would thus be a major part of the strategy of a being like St. Germain in order to accomplish his wider civilisational goals on behalf of our species.

Such reconciliation must be effected by normal humanity and its representatives, not by highly evolved adepts and souls such as St. Germain who already exist in wholeness and love with all of nature; it must be accomplished, at least in part, by those who experience—and have created—the separation. In this case, a normal human individual must step into a relationship with these kingdoms and be an exemplar of what any of us can do with love, awareness and a willingness to partner with nature rather than trying to control it.

This need gives us insight into why a soul like St. Germain might incarnate an aspect of itself to be a normal human being who could be that exemplar. ROC could draw on his heritage as a master magician and adept when he needed, but in this particular instance to do this specific work he had to encounter the nature spirits not as St. Germain the adept but as Ogilvie Crombie, the human. There may be many other reasons, some we will never know, why such an evolved soul would incarnate as ROC—or for that matter, as Peter Caddy, the founder of the Findhorn community experiment where the reconciliation and partnership with nature could be physically and undeniably demonstrated as a keystone of a new civilisation—but it is reason enough that he was an instrument for fostering the partnership with the kingdoms of the nature spirits. In other contexts and doing other work, the power and presence of his higher self could reveal itself, but in this particular work, St. Germain had to remain cloaked in the background so that the human personality that was Robert Ogilvie Crombie could succeed or fail as a true representative of all of us.

The Occult Diaries of

Chapter 8
The Space Connection

Many of ROC's contacts have been with space entities. As mentioned in "Aspects of 'Aspects,'" ROC's own paternity (or should it be fraternity?) in this regard was an aspect of himself, or an aspect of St. Germain, referred to throughout his journals as his "Saturnian Aspect." When he made an appearance, he did so typically as a being some 30 feet tall and generally dressed in blue and silver garments or robes, though sometimes he appeared in "space gear." With all souls (including our own in the spirit world environment) appearances can or will be adopted to suit the audience. While not in the soul world directly, the Saturnian aspect was (is?) presumably in incarnation on Saturn. However, as this planet comprises a core believed to be of iron, nickel, silicon and oxygen, followed by a layer of metallic hydrogen, and topped with an atmosphere of helium and hydrogen, existence there as we know it would be impossible. Add to this its extremes of temperature and pressure, and I doubt it would turn out to be your favoured holiday destination.

If, on the basis of ROC's experiences, there is life on Saturn, it would have to be in a much less condensed form than on Earth-like planets and perhaps possess an etheric consistency which could remain immune to its hostile environmental challenges. Difficult as it is to visualise the soul worlds, it is almost as difficult to visualise life as it might be in this realm, and we can only really guess at its nature. Newton refers to these as telepathic or mental worlds.

Our nearest approach to perceiving what life might be like on these worlds may be to liken them to those that are encountered by out-of-body travellers, where the soul, embedded in its etheric shell, can roam the lower astral (and higher worlds as well, of course) at will unimpeded by matter with its temperature or other environmental extremes. As generally reported by Bueller, Monroe, Bruce, and others, these are very real worlds, seen and experienced to be every bit as tangible as our own physical worlds. These are telepathic worlds in that no words are spoken—communication being directly from mind to mind—and movement from point A to B is accomplished by simply wishing it to be so. Additionally, the power of thought, as in the pure soul worlds, is fully capable of creating corresponding forms and structures, transient, temporary or more permanent as the situation demands.

While these astral worlds, therefore, may be referred to as the "planes of illusion" from our perspective, they seem to be none the less real either to those visiting them as temporary OOB excursions or to their permanent inhabitants. Is this analogy sufficient to give us a glimpse of what life may be like on these "uninhabitable" planets and gas giants? Why would they build or need to build space ships (flying saucers, if you will) for transport within and between worlds when they could arguably translocate by an act of will? Why, if these are thought worlds, would life need to be associated with a planet at all? Could they not have their existence in the vast expanses between? Perhaps they do! We may indeed have some answers, but they in turn pose a whole range of further questions.

If we bypass these questions for now and tentatively accept that the occupants of these "uninhabitable" worlds construct space ships for their interplanetary travel, these would arguably be made from the materials available on that planet, although to our eyes such materials would have no substance, and such constructions would—as in the case of the finer worlds in general—remain completely invisible to our sense of sight and, in fact, to all our normal physical senses for that matter. It is profoundly difficult to think of such items of etheric hardware as mechanical contrivances, and yet, based on ROC's clairvoyance and inner vision, this pseudo-physical world does appear to exist.

I have for many years believed that the UFOs seen in our skies were fundamentally solid physical objects, but my opinion is being forced to change, as their reported characteristics match few of our norms. Energy manipulation, which is a fundamental characteristic of the soul worlds, may allow these craft to change density from their fundamentally pseudo-physical, intangible ground state to a physical one that can be perceived by our normal senses. This would go a long way to explaining much of the strangeness of the abduction scenario, where those "taken" can, on their journey to the space ship, be transported through the solid walls and windows of the house that they occupy. To explain this in terms of out-of-body travel would be easy, if it were not for the fact that these people are physically missing from their homes, cars, and so forth. After having undergone the obligatory highly intrusive and painful examination by these callous aliens aboard their space craft, they are once again returned, bearing the scars of their medical examination such as scoop marks, nose bleeds, and internal and external pains and discomforts for weeks. A physical or pseudo-physical experience? Or both? Certainly there is evidence that effects created in the etheric body can replicate themselves in the physical body as well. Is that what happens here?

The world of the abductee has been explored by a number of investigators, including Dr John Mack, Professor David Jacobs of Temple University, and

R. Ogilvie Crombie

Budd Hopkins. Jacobs has carried out a lifetime's research on more than a thousand individuals, again by very similar hypnotic techniques to those that Newton and others employ to explore the soul worlds. Jacob's findings, and those of many other similar investigators in this field including, of course, Mack and Hopkins, indicate the existence of many common features between the various abduction reports, and these are statistically compelling. Jacob's conclusion, reluctantly arrived at and highly unsettling, is that this particular alien phenomenon bodes ill for humanity. It would appear that not all interplanetary travellers have our best interests at heart. This is borne out by some of ROC's experiences when he talks about the presence of hostile craft in our skies and the activities of the Saturn ship in limiting their influence.

During the 1960s there was much interest in the UFO phenomenon, and various attempts at contact were made at Findhorn and elsewhere around the world. ROC was involved with some of those at Findhorn, and as seen below, there were some interesting experiences, although the hoped for materialisation or physical appearance of a space craft never took place.

ROC's first encounter in his flat with a "spaceman," Hamid, is detailed below:

> 660224. While sitting in the front room here reading in the evening, I was aware of a figure sitting in the chair opposite, though I was very interested in the book, *The Living Past*. He was much the "conventional" spaceman, wearing a fairly tight fitting silvery grey one piece suit and helmet. I tried to dismiss him from my mind, but he persisted. Later, I saw him moving about the flat, but there was no form of communication between us. I felt this is ridiculous, as I am very doubtful of the existence of such beings.

The following evening, ROC had a dream of travelling in a flying saucer. This, and his comments following his write up, make interesting reading:

> 660225. [I had] a long and vivid dream that I was travelling in a flying saucer. I seemed to be partly awake during the dream, and, at times, I was awake fully. The dream continued when I dozed off again. This happened several times. I seemed at times to be both inside the saucer, and watching it from a point in space. It was a golden brown in colour, and just large enough for me to get inside. It was night, and the saucer was travelling

over rugged landscapes, rather like the one I visit in my depth dreams. There were also high ranges of mountains, and in the valleys, vague towns. At one time, the saucer approached a high cliff at great speed, and just as it seemed about to crash into it, it suddenly shot upwards. It turned on edge to do so and skimmed right past the cliff. There was absolutely no sensation of any kind. This was a very vivid dream.

Comments: Flying saucers seem to be much in my mind just now, possibly from discussing them with others, and the previous dreams. There is a memory of Daniel Fry relating his alleged trip in a flying saucer at White Sands. I have never before had such a dream.

His second encounter with Hamid occurs on the following evening. Interesting here is the indication that "flying saucers" are the result of the collective projection of ideas and ideals by humanity. These crystallised thought forms are then accordingly inhabited by "space beings,"' creating somewhat of a self-fulfilling prophecy!

This process is virtually analogous to the creation of the mythical gods of old where mankind, through a desire for contact with the divinity, projects these desires and visualisations. Once the thought form is created, it is then adopted by some spiritual being and takes on an extended life of its own, examples being Pan, Apollo, Hermes, and Anubis. Clearly, the power of thought may have far-reaching effects indeed; thought-form creation in astral and soul realms may be the norm, but this is not an expected attribute of our material world. This is perhaps a salutary reminder of the power of thought which may be used with equal measure either constructively for good or destructively for evil. As Shakespeare's Hamlet utters, "for there is nothing either good or bad, but thinking makes it so."

But back to Hamid:

> 660226. Again I see the "spaceman" sitting opposite me as I am reading, and later moving about the flat. There is no communication as before. After I had gone to bed, and before switching off the light, he appeared standing at the foot of the bed, and said "I am a space visitor from Venus, what are you going to do about it?" I asked him what he meant, and he said, "Well, you don't believe in me, do you?" He was about 5'8" or so and had blue eyes that twinkled with amusement.

S.M. I must be real, don't you think, since you would never imagine a being you don't believe in, and not very long ago, you thought that you would never see a space man. But you are seeing one now.

ROC. Am I?

S.M. Where is the open mind you pride yourself on having?

ROC. All right, you're a space man from Venus, though I am still convinced that there is no life on any other planet in this solar system that resembles life as we know it here.

S.M. You are quite right.

ROC. Then you must be an astral being.

S.M. Yes. I am what you call an astral being, but the word "astral" has collected a number of associations which can be very misleading. We must be careful in using it to keep in mind exactly what we mean by it.

ROC. Yes, I agree. Occultists, theosophists and so on have given meanings to the word which confuse the idea. But can you suggest any other word?

S.M. Not at the moment. It is better to continue to use it as long as we know what we mean by it.

ROC. By astral plane, I mean a different plane of existence from this one, and by astral body, one made of different, much finer matter than physical matter. Is that right?

S.M. Yes. My body is made of a different type of matter.

ROC. Golu has told me that astral matter is built up of atoms like physical matter, but that the vibrations are faster.

S.M. That is true. It is a different form of cosmic energy.

ROC. I am not seeing you with my physical sight.

S.M. No, with a higher sense of sight which you have developed, just as you see the other beings who appear to you.

ROC. Could you appear to my physical sight?

S.M. Yes, but it is not necessary to do so as you can see me with your higher sense of sight. One should never do what is not necessary.

ROC. Do flying saucers exist? S.M. smiled.

S.M. That depends what you mean by "exist," doesn't it?

ROC. Are they made of physical matter like we have on earth?

S.M. No, they are made of the finer matter we have been talking about, but you earth people wanted them.

ROC. We wanted them?

S.M. Yes. They really began as thought forms of a kind. You earth dwellers are a very materialistically minded race—at least in the west. But, having to a great extent rejected God and the spiritual side of life, there was still a burning need for guidance and help.

ROC. Jung made that point in his book on Flying Saucers, and suggested that the disc like form was based on an archetypal symbol of the round—a mandala.

S.M. To a great extent he was right. The projection became a thought form. It attached similar ideas and visions, picking up some things from science fiction writers who have written about space travel.

ROC. But surely flying saucers have a more definite existence than that.

S.M. Oh, yes. We took them over as another means of making contact.

ROC. Who are "we?"

S.M. All I can tell you about that is that we are discarnate in the sense of not having physical bodies like you. We cannot interfere directly with mankind, unless in very exceptional circumstances.

ROC. Such as a nuclear war?

S.M. Possibly, if it threatened the universe, but we can try to help and guide mankind through those with whom we make contact.

ROC. You said you came from Venus. What did you mean by that?

S.M. I come from that part of the other place you call the astral which corresponds to the planet Venus in the physical universe. You must simply accept that statement.

ROC. I do, and I think I understand to at least some extent, from previous knowledge I have been given.

S.M. Good.

ROC. Have you a name? And can you tell it to me?

S.M. My name is Hamid.

ROC. Hamid

R. Ogilvie Crombie

S.M. Yes. Good night, Ogilvie. I shall see you again.

Hamid vanished, and I was left with an extraordinary conviction that this was a real waking experience. I switched off the light, and settled down to sleep. Though Hamid had disappeared, I still felt his presence.

Almost a month later, Hamid makes another appearance:

660324. This afternoon, as I was sitting in the armchair, back to the window, Hamid walked into the room. He came to me more as himself as he said he was without his space suit. He was the most radiant being I have ever seen. He gave out what I can only call "light," and his beauty was breath-taking and awe-inspiring. His hair is golden. It is somewhat what used to be called pageboy style. It is curly and hangs to about below his ears and forms a curly fringe on his forehead. His skin is honey colour. His body is perfectly proportioned, with a slight growth of golden hair on his chest.

Later Hamid stood up and came towards me. I cried out "Stop. Don't come near me. It is too much." But he smiled, and coming over to me, he laid his hands on my shoulders. I could feel the weight of them. It is difficult to describe the feeling I had — like an intense electric shock accompanied by heat. He stepped back and held out his hands. He said "Give me you hands." Rather reluctantly, I did so. He took hold of my hands; I could feel the firm grasp. Again, a feeling of shock and heat; an intense flow of energy took place. He held my hands for a considerable time; a feeling of complete relaxation, of utter peace and exultation came over me. He bent down and kissed me on the forehead and then stood looking at me. He released my hands, smiling, and said "Goodbye, God bless you. I shall be back." He turned, and walked out of the room (I still feel the same state of exultation and peace.).

After he left, I continued sitting utterly relaxed in the chair. Then I had supper, and continued to sit in the chair until it was quite dark with only the glow of the radiator. This has been a quite wonderful experience. I accept these Beings completely now; they are not due to my imagination.

Later, Tio came in and said "You are thinking Hamid the most beautiful being you have ever seen. What about me?

He looked accusingly at me.

"Beloved Tio," [I replied], "you and I are almost one; we somehow belong to each other. I love you very much. You mustn't feel hurt at my thoughts."

Tio burst out laughing. "I am only pulling your leg. Hurt, we cannot feel hurt. We know no jealousy; that is a human fault. Of course Hamid is beautiful—all his race are. They are radiant beings." I am getting this now as I write.

ROC. Is he a space man from Venus?

T. What do you think? He came to you as one. But remember what he gave you in the script. He warned you of the enigmas and paradoxes. We are very protean beings; we have many shapes and forms. You must accept the appearances. They are true eternal, and yet ephemeral. Remember, God is the one Great never-changing, always-altering Being, and we are made in his image. Accept as true what you cannot believe. Believe in the ever-changing constant. The unsolvable enigma can be understood.

ROC. This is a new side of you, Tio. You have never communicated like this before.

T. My communication is in my hands. That is why I express myself in words. I am part of the enigma. I am the earth spirit, and I come from above. The above is below, and the below above. All is contradictory, and all is one whole.

Tio is laughing at me. There is joy radiating from him. Yet I know he is speaking deep truths, and somehow I comprehend deep within me.

This extract is from the experiences ROC had at Findhorn when the contact with space beings was being pursued there:

660408. We visited the beach again. This time the power was so great that I could not walk over the centre of the area on the beach. I had to earth myself through my hands when we got back. At an afternoon session, though the weather was bad, very cloudy, dull, and cold, we were told to be ready. I had the strange feeling of being in contact with a space ship which I could place overhead. I found myself in a vision, standing in the centre of the beach area, in a purple beam. Presently I found

R. Ogilvie Crombie

myself travelling up the beam and found myself in some sort of control room on board the ship. There were a series of screens, something like our TV screens but in some way different. There was a lot of strange looking apparatus not like anything known here, and then several men in tunics and light trousers. Looking in one screen, I found myself looking down on Findhorn, lying at a distance below. It moved rapidly up, until I was looking down on the beach, then on the caravan site. Then the vision faded. I knew that in some way I was going to control the operation that night, and that I would know what to do.

We dressed up very warmly and left about 9.30 in two cars. The last part was a very lumpy ride to the beach. It was very dark. We lit a fire on the beach. The power was extraordinary, and there was a strong downward radiation from the sky. I had felt this earlier in the evening in the caravan site. I have never encountered anything like this in my life before. It was certainly real.

On the way to the beach, I was rather worried, as I knew that I would have to stand in the centre of the area over which I had not been able to walk earlier in the day, and now the power was much greater. Hamid immediately reassured me, and said whatever happened, not to be alarmed and that I would be able to do it; what I did was done under direction. I told the other eight people to concentrate by holding the picture of a purple tube-like ray travelling from my feet, out in a direction which I indicated, over the sea. I sensed the space ship was in a certain direction to the north-west.

I stood in the centre of the area facing the direction I had indicated. The power was quite terrific, but I found I could take it. After some time, I left the circle, and returned to the others, who were sitting on rugs near the fire. There was a great feeling of expectancy. Several times, I thought I saw something out to sea. The firelight dazzled the sight a bit, so later I walked down to the sea. There was a long pebble ridge parallel to the sea. This was very highly charged with power. All the time, I had a sensation like a mixture of pins and needles and electric shock running up my legs and body. I have never felt anything quite like it before, though it reminded me of the feeling I got from holding the font at St. Annes.

Gazing out to sea, I had a brief glimpse of a shape like a flying saucer skimming over the sea towards us. It was glowing blue. But that was the only glimpse of it I had. I returned to the others. Twice I had the impression that a flying saucer had skimmed over us, though invisible. This was later confirmed by Eileen Caddy and three others who all had the same impression. At one time, I was convinced that there was a saucer on the beach, but invisible. I knew it carried a crew of three. Down again on the pebble beach, a voice gave me my name: Cafron—apparently my Saturnian aspect. Later I again stood for some time in the centre of the area. The power was tremendous.

Using my name, I called on someone to respond. A figure appeared on the beach. He was rather nebulous and seemed to be wearing a brown tunic and trousers and a brown cloak. He told me that because of the layers of damp cloud, they were unable to get the radiations required to bring about materialisation (they could not "spin" up to the necessary strength). Nothing more could be done that night, but an excellent beginning had been made.

When I returned to the others, I found Eileen in a state of partial collapse, with her hands pressed to the ground. Later she told me the power surging through her was almost too much. Lena, too, had felt it. It was coming along the ground from my feet. I think that in future attempts, the others will have to be further away. I did not remove my shoes, which had rubber soles. I was not told to do so. We returned to the caravans about 12.30 after one of the oddest experiences of my whole life.

One year later, again at Findhorn, ROC finds himself in a situation in which he experiences himself in two locations at once. His report of the controls on the inside of the space craft is interesting:

670401. Last night, impression of Saturn space ship coming in from the north-east. As there was a good deal of night flying they had to wait some time invisible in case the rays they were going to use did harm to the aeroplanes. (The space ship carried out an operation of "cleansing" the moor with rays). I had the strange feeling which I have had before that I was both in bed in the caravan, and in the spacecraft control room at a control desk—it was semi circular and had many "levers" unlike any I have seen on earth.

[handwritten sketch: goldish coloured metal — coloured spoon like 'knot' — hollowed out]

Diary sketch of Saturnian craft operating lever

    The "knobs" were of different colours and set in banks, in a way like organ stops. There were triangular shaped meters? with tiny holes, behind which were lights.

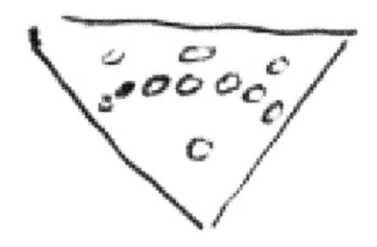

[handwritten sketch of triangular meter with small circles labeled C]

Diary sketch of Saturnian craft 'meter'

And another three years later, again at Findhorn, while walking across the moor near the Findhorn Centre, ROC once more encounters the space craft, and, out-of-body, is aware of temporarily being in it:

> 700430. Went to the beach after morning session. Dull, but nice day with very little wind. Instead of going by the usual path, I went on as far as the new road, and going along it, went on to the moor. At first I thought of crossing the moor to a point further along the beach, but felt a strong urge to go to the landing place which I obeyed. Hamid was with me for a bit—not in his space suit but in his glorious self. He radiates light, a true shining being. When I reached the top of the sand bank overlooking the landing place, I was alone and immediately aware of the Saturn ship overhead. I have not been aware of it either here or in Edinburgh for a long time. They are still policing outer space. I was told this

did not mean a renewal of space activity at Findhorn, and there was no question for the time being of an attempted landing. These days would seem to be over.

I was urged to go down onto the beach to the centre of the landing place. There was power, and quite a lot was channelled down through me as I stood there.

My Saturn aspect appeared standing in front of me in a space suit but without helmet, but my own size. He asked me if I had forgotten him. I said no, I certainly had not. I am quite often aware of being him as a great being 25 ft tall when out-of-the-body on a protection mission. I found myself momentarily on the space ship—a being of great power and authority addressing a group of beings in space suits or robes. I was back on the beach once more alone. It was fascinating, and it is nice to know these beings, and the space ship, do still exist.

R. Ogilvie Crombie

Chapter 9
The Thought Responsive Universe

Thought is the product of our own personal mind, largely of the ego, and manifests in logical iterations and conclusions (usually), many of which are tailored to address our immediate needs. This then spawns inventions, which by a gradual process change the way we live, work and play. Living within a world of duality, our thought sequences can lead to either constructive or destructive results. For instance, atomic power can be used for supplying needed electricity to our grids or alternatively for atomic bombs. We can "think" how to improve the lot of humanity or devise cunning schemes to dominate and exploit, or even eliminate, our fellow man.

In this way we live in a universe that is responsive to and shaped by thought. On the physical level where we live, the results are not always noticeably as immediate as on higher vibrational worlds, though the so-called "metal benders" like Uri Geller can have fairly quick results from their directed thought energies. ROC, particularly when attuning to his magical aspects such as Merlin, could also create physical effects using purely mental and spiritual means.

The Helicopter Incident

There is an interesting example from ROC's notes demonstrating this. It concerns his attempts to prevent a helicopter from spraying chemicals over a mountainside to remove bracken by attempting to put it out of action, though in a manner which would be safe to the pilot. The mountain in particular borders Loch Tay, and the incident takes place in August 1974:

> 740807. Today is dull and misty again, so spraying seems unlikely, but at about 4.30 there was a phone message from the shepherd to say that the helicopter was due at 5.30! Jo immediately set about getting the ponies off the hill, clearing the caravans and disconnecting the water supply which comes from the mountain stream.
>
> When word first came about the bracken spraying, she had been in talks with the factor saying she would put the matter in the hands of her solicitor and thereafter to see if any harm came to the children in the caravans and to any of the animals. He, getting a little alarmed, contacted the firm doing the spraying

who said it was completely harmless. The grass destroyed would grow again, but got in touch with the makers of the spray who said it was totally harmless to animals and human beings, but all animals should be removed from the hill and no spraying would take place over cultivated areas. It is completely harmless to human beings, but the water supply should be disconnected for 48 hours. In spite of the complete harmlessness, not one of the people concerned was willing to take any responsibility.

I felt very worried, as I strongly disapprove of the destruction of vegetation by such methods. The long term effects are totally unknown. This is a very special place. At all costs, it must somehow be stopped. I used all the power I could summon to bring wind and rain. The wind had almost dropped, and although still cloudy and misty, it looked as if they would go ahead with it.

One cannot change the weather in a few minutes. It takes time. I may have been partly responsible for keeping the weather in an unfit state up till now, but I had been off-guard as the day had seemed unfitted.

The only other possibility was to put the helicopter out of action but in such a way as not to cause it to crash and in any way hurt the pilot. Though I did feel that the matter was so vital that even that might have to be done so long as he was not killed. For instance, a blade coming off before the helicopter took off, or when it was only a few feet above the ground. At any rate, the helicopter arrived, flying over loch Tay from the south and landing in a field on the other side of the main road below the caravan site. Shortly afterwards, the lorry with the tanks of chemical spray arrived, and a car with a caravan, a large van, and two private cars. Great activity started.

I stood outside the house, looking down on the field and opening myself to channel the necessary energies. I was aware of, and then became, the Merlin aspect and worked the full power of hermetic magic. A tremendous flow of energy took place, and I was aware of a powerful will directing the energies. This was a somewhat similar effect to what happened at Glastonbury on my first visit, when I found a beam, like a laser beam, streaming out from the centre of my forehead. I directed the beam onto the helicopter with all the will power I could muster—something going wrong with the system or a break down in the electric ignition circuit. I tried a pulsing technique. Once, I even tried a kind of Uri Geller technique of bending the metal of the blades but gave it up as too risky for the safety of the pilot. The rotor blades were revolving all the time since it landed.

It took some time to fill the spray tanks from the lorry, almost half an hour. Bags were sent up over the hill with orange lollipop markers to show which bits had been sprayed. There was a horrible sinister atmosphere of technological perfection of destruction about the whole proceedings—utter ruthlessness. For the whole half hour, I kept up the maximum concentration on the helicopter. The energy flow was incredible, and I was aware also of a tremendous power coming down from the mountain from the spirit and the nature spirits.

Nothing happened, and shortly after 6, the helicopter started and began its deadly work. It looked like an evil insect hovering over the hill and letting go of its deadly venom onto the bracken—all for the sake of more grazing land for the sheep of the owner—profit and nothing more.

I watched all the runs of the helicopter, returning after each one to the field to fill up again. Feeling sick and terribly tired, the effort had very nearly finished me off, and my heart reacted badly. I returned to the house feeling depressed and disillusioned. Merlin, my foot! The whole thing was nonsense. How could I possibly hope to put a helicopter out of action! No more magic for me! I would give it all up, retire into myself, and read trash for the rest of my life. New age indeed—a lot of hooey!

However, I was not feeling depressed when I went to bed—a slight feeling that all was not lost. Something must have happened. The spray would in some way not work. The spraying did not matter. Even if the heather was temporarily destroyed, it would grow again and would colonise the area of mountainside in a mutated type immune to sprays. I was told to forget it. What was important was the total integration of the hermetic magic I had invoked and could use with the elemental energies. Up till now, the two had been separate, but from now on, they were integrated and blended and both could be brought into action. My own ability and power had been increased by an enormous amount. This was why the spraying had to take place. It had been a complete success, and no serious harm would come to the district or to anyone living there.

I felt completely reassured and must have fallen asleep. I woke up to find that the rain I had invoked had arrived. It had been raining all night. There was a strong possibility that the spray had been washed off the bracken before it had really got to work.

The morning was very odd. A strange misty fog hung over the loch and the whole countryside. Jo said it was quite unlike anything she had ever seen here. There was a feeling of anger coming from the mountain: everything was unreal.

I had had breakfast in bed, and read for a while afterwards. During the time, I had been aware of the sound of the helicopter and thought surely it can't be doing more spraying. I got dressed and went through to the lounge. Jo said, "What have you done to the helicopter?"

"What do you mean? I failed to put it out of action."

"'Did you? Come and look. It's been unable to get off the ground by more than a few feet!"

It had apparently been trying to fly off and return to the base but couldn't. I silently watched while it vainly tried to fly. The blades were rotating, but it could not develop enough power or move more than a few feet. It was turning about and moving sideways, but ultimately came to rest and then stopped nearby. The lorry with the tanks of spray had gone, and so had the helicopter van, but in a couple of hours a group of men arrived and stood round contemplating the helicopter. There was great activity for the next couple of hours, and then another attempt, but nothing doing. It could not get away. More activity and then about 5.30 it did a low flight of about a hundred yards, low over the hillside. The engine began to cough and splutter, and it returned to the field where it remained all night.

Pure coincidence or delayed action? Like the weather, a breakdown took time to organise. I concluded Merlin was not so impotent after all. Very heavy rain – torrents, with distant thunder by afternoon. All to the good, washing away the spray.

There was more rain and mist during the night. After breakfast-time, there was more activity at the helicopter van, and a car appeared. The rotor was going, but there was no lift.

The helicopter remained there all day, and eventually flew off at 5.30. When Jocelyn went down later to the café, she was told that the pilot and the others had been up to the café. The pilot had said that something broke during the spraying. All very odd—if a coincidence, at least a meaningful one!

A few days later, I heard from Jo that a second helicopter the spraying people were using had been put out of action—the entire spraying mechanism had fallen off it! This has put a finish to their activities for this year!

Psycho-Cybernetics

Maxwell Maltz, in his intriguing book *Psycho-Cybernetics*, sets out to examine how we go about achieving (or failing to achieve) our goals in life. He considers the brain, and the body which is subject to it, as being a goal seeking entity, teleological in essence, which consciously or unconsciously will approach its predefined target by a series of constructive moves and error corrections until the desired result is attained. He likens the process to a torpedo in motion which reaches its target not directly but by a series of course alterations; where unexpected local conditions cause the torpedo to stray from its path, this error information is fed back to the control mechanism which then makes the necessary course corrections putting the torpedo back "on target."

He points out the extreme importance of the *ab initio* target setting. If we visualise or imagine ourselves as failing at a given task, then that belief will have the power to bring it about even though we may desperately want the opposite to happen. If we imagine the task is impossible, than the obedient brain will ensure this image is fulfilled and will no doubt consider it has done an excellent job in failing to accomplish the mission set for it, thereby fulfilling the initial starting conditions within our imagination.

Crucially, the corollary is equally true. Maltz points out that once we recognise the way this system works, we can change our embedded thinking and belief structure to ensure best results. Where the imagination and the will are in conflict, Maltz states, imagination will inevitably win the day! The power of belief has within its grasp the means to shape both our individual and our global destinies.

Setting the goal then becomes paramount, and once that has been achieved, setting the next one needs to be addressed, and so on. Once we stop setting goals, then we have left the brain without orders for controlling the body mechanisms; the ship is without a destination. Inertness, despair, and diminished health can be some of the accompanying results.

Manifestation

An example from ROC's archives in which he is told by St. Germain that perfection should be the aim in a Centre of Light such as Findhorn, shows, on the basis of Maltz's thinking, that this result could be achieved almost automatically through the psycho-cybernetic principles outlined above. Once the idea has been firmly accepted by and embedded in the mind, the brain is then always on the look-out for the means of achieving its desired goal. There may, of course, be other forces of an unseen nature helping out. The St. Germain "perfection" message was first delivered through ROC in April 1967, reiterated in July, but followed by warnings of extravagance in October:

> 670428a. Perfection is the aim. Where there is not perfection or the nearest thing to it, what is now there in the etheric cannot be manifested without the greatest difficulty. As an example, take the site now being prepared for new bungalows. This work must be brought as near perfection as human fallibility will allow, otherwise the true and speedy manifestation on the physical level cannot be brought about. We make full allowances for man's limitations and for the imperfections of physical materials which are perishable and may contain flaws, but perfection must remain the aim. Man must try to rise above his limitations, and he must seek out the best materials obtainable. Nothing else is good enough for God's work. Perfection must remain the aim, however far off its achievement may seem. It can be reached, and no apparent failures must be allowed to diminish faith in this end.
>
> To bring about the complete manifestation of the ideal Findhorn centre, all present imperfections must be diligently sought out and eliminated. This will take time, and time is precious, and there are many things to be done. First things must come first, and the essential for daily living be done. But whenever possible, seek out the imperfections and gradually eliminate them, for only when this has been done can the full manifestation take place of that which exists above. Nothing but the perfect is good enough for God's work at such a centre

as Findhorn. Less perfect may be acceptable elsewhere, but not here in the pioneer centre for the New Age. Perfection must always be the aim.

670723a. Findhorn. 10.15am. I was compelled to sit and take the following: Plan for perfection. Perfection must be the aim for here at Findhorn the Kingdom of Heaven is to be made manifest on earth. In the Kingdom of Heaven there is only the perfect so in its earth counterpart, there must also be perfection. This is not easy to achieve at the moment as mankind is far from being perfect, but it is the end to strive for.

There is a need for understanding and for re-orientation in thinking and for trying to look at things from different points of view. Each individual is different, each has his own contribution to make, each may be travelling along a different path, but the goal in each case is the same. There must be a widening of understanding and a greater degree of tolerance. The old Idea that "I alone am right and all who differ from me are wrong" must go.

On the question of perfection, there are those who have led lives of self-sacrifice, dedicated to God, who have denied themselves things they might have had in the belief that this was pleasing to God. In order to follow this path of life, they have made do with the less good, with the imperfect. This way of life is right for them. It has been a sincere way of life and has real merit for those called upon to follow it. But here at Findhorn, it is not right now, as it is here that the Kingdom of Heaven is to be made manifest on earth. Here God asks for the best, not for the gratification of the Group living here but for His own greater glory. This does not mean luxurious living or extravagance. It is a question of need. Where true need exists it must be met by the best. So perfection must be the aim.

671008. Edinburgh. Money is coming in too easily, and this leads to a certain degree of extravagance which is not truly a need, though it is based on the perfection ideal. You were being used as a tester when the perfection messages were given through you. There must be no extravagance or unnecessary spending—this is to waste God's bounty. Only the best is good enough for

God—but this applies to needs, not to wants or desires.

Rebound

In the majority of people's minds it would be assumed, and reasonably so, that thoughts, underpinned in many cases by powerful emotions, will lead eventually to the desired result and that's the end of the matter. It would, however, appear that thoughts, having a strong energy component, radiate out far beyond the immediate locale, the ripples extending outwards into a universe designed to be responsive to thought. These ripples result in positive or negative effects as the case may be, depending on the nature of the thought; if love or hate is strongly expressed, in addition to activating corresponding brain processes, these thoughts and emotions are broadcast out in a telepathic manner, and their energy can have a creative or destructive impact on rebound, albeit unseen. Performance of powerful ritual (black and white magic would come under this), prayer (and, according to Newton's clients, all prayers are answered, though not necessarily with immediate effect), or the results of massed emotion and powerfully expressed beliefs have extensive effects in the unseen worlds from the concentrated energy released. They also return to impinge on our physical and mental life, negative broadcasts reinforcing our negativity, positive ones our positivity.

Planes of Illusion

The impact of our thought patterns extends far beyond the rebound effect. It is capable of creating structures and forms in the finer worlds themselves that take on a life of their own, ranging from the temporary through to the semi-permanent state. These thought creations are not restricted to the lower astral planes but extend ever upwards to the higher planes where energy can be moulded much more easily (according to Newton's and Bueller's findings), giving rise to downright unpleasant conditions in the lower astral and to blissful surroundings on the higher planes where pleasant semblances of our previous earth existence are created but without all the nasties. However pleasantly or unpleasantly real these areas seem, they are largely illusory. While thought energy has created them, likewise thought energy can disperse them.

A little book by Frederick C. Sculthorp entitled *Excursions to the Spirit World*, first published in 1961, gives a picture of the spirit worlds as discovered by the author following a large number of out-of-the-body experiences. Unlike the realms reported by Newton's clients, Sculthorp's top spirit level appears to overlap in a general sense with that of Newton's lower levels and hence gives an extended picture downwards of these spiritual states. He treats it in three broad levels: "The Brighter Spheres" (corresponding roughly to Newton's lowest), "The Earth-like Spheres," and "The Lower Spheres."

The lowest of these spheres appear to be banally earth-like, and the soul is totally lacking in awareness of his condition of having died. He goes about "life" in an extended dream state, repeating the same tasks day by day just as he had on earth, and surprisingly, he has no more awareness of higher spiritual realms than most people on earth have. Sculthorp says that in his travels he came across lamp-posts, although there was no need for light, and even a cheery group of coalminers riding in their buggies to work. He found all mundane occupations are followed, such as road making, bridge building, and so forth. Frederick Myers, commenting from the spirit world after his passing, first gave these realms the description of "the planes of illusion." ROC's experiences of the airmen killed in WWII are entirely consistent with Sculthorp's descriptions of those trapped in "the planes of illusion."

Hamid, in a script through ROC, also talks of these "planes of illusion" and says that not only pseudo-physical surroundings are created but that life forms of an entire look-alike heavenly hierarchy also exist, mimicking the "real." All of these are the result of humanity's thinking and beliefs over the millennia. This script, which was verbally given to ROC, was considered so important, that he requested it be given in dictated form. This is reproduced below and is indeed food for thought:

> 660324. I am appearing to you now more as myself because you are able to bear the sight. You have the thought that I am a radiant being. Just as a too bright light dazzles the eyes and can even injure them, the sight of a too radiant being can damage the physical body. When the veiled one [Koot Hoomi] was visiting you, you after had the feeling that if you ever saw his face, you would die physically—that is why he was veiled. You could not have endured the sight of his face then, though you possibly might now. This is the reason why we appear to you partly obscured. Who or what we are is for you to decide. You already have an idea of the power of thought and what it can bring about. Where the power of thought is used in accordance with the laws of God and the will of God, truth and reality are found in the thought constructions. When it is used according

to man's own ideas and will, the result is illusion.

I shall probably talk to you in enigmas and paradoxes. It is for you to try to resolve them. You must reach your own conclusions. We can teach mankind, but it can only be done by leading him to evolve in the right direction and reach his own conclusions. We cannot pump knowledge into him, especially esoteric knowledge which can be so dangerous. You were told last night by the Master in Tibet through Naomi's script that you would be given knowledge to pass on to mankind. This will be done, but you will have to use great effort to arrive at and understand this knowledge. You were told that "much must go." This is very true. Vast edifices of illusion have been built up by man in his self-conceit and ....[Here ROC's words were indecipherable]... though many of the people who helped in this building have been sincere and well intentioned. Unfortunately it was their own wills that were behind the creation, not God's will.

Self effacement, self-realisation and above all humility are the basic requirements for true working to God's purpose.

The work of many saintly people has been distorted and falsified by self complacency. The gradual belief that it was they themselves and not God working through them that was accomplishing their purpose. The inflated ego is the arch enemy of the spiritual development and true creation. It allows the powers of darkness to get a foothold and perverts the intentions.

The much that has to go refers to the many illusions that bedevil mankind. We cannot be specific except in certain cases, but we can try to give you clues. You have been told already that man will find what he believes he will find when he leaves his physical body. You will realise the vast planes of illusion that have been created; the various heavens and hells of the different religions; the idealised earth-like towns and cities of the spiritualists and others which differ so little from those on your earth. People can even carry on their earthly jobs, eating and drinking, and going to the theatres and concerts. Then there are the superb advanced towns on Mars, Venus and other planets believed in by your flying saucer fans.

All these exist on the thought planes and will be found by their believers. They are all illusions created by man's thought and not by God. Many will find themselves in man-created hells.

God would never condemn any being to eternal punishment; only earth-man is capable of doing it and has created a false god in his own image who would do so. This God EXISTS on the thought plane, but he is an illusion like all the rest. Man will find what he believes he will find when he passes over. If it is not according to God's plan, he will be existing in an illusion. He may be contented because he may be living the life he never had on earth but wished for. He may be in torment because he believes he deserves it. But in the first case, he will not be happy because he is not in tune with the Divine will. In the second, he may be suffering unnecessarily.

In either case, it is not until after a long period of education that he will be brought to a realisation that he is existing in an illusion of earth-man creation and may then gradually become conscious of the rhythms of Divine Creation and begin to work to God's laws. It is not until then that he will begin to make spiritual progress and escape from the planes of illusion. I am speaking in images, but it may help you to understand something of the future life. Man who tries to shed this man-created illusion while still on earth is indeed a happy being, however humble his earth existence may be. The difficulty is to know which are the man-made illusions, since most of them claim to have had Divine revelation of guidance. You already know some of these illusions; you must use your intuition and reason guided by the clues you may be given to show you the others.

It follows on from the idea of illusion that we appear to you in the form you want us to. If you want spacemen from Venus, you will get them. If you want the spirit of departed Aunty Jane, you will get it—though this latter may be a very undesirable mischievous entity, but you already have sound ideas on that matter. If you want a great Master or an archangel, you shall have them. The point is this: Great Masters, Archangels, spacemen and a vast hierarchy of beings exist created by God. But so do their illusory counterparts. How can you tell whether it is the God-created, God-inspired entity or the man-created one who is communicating with you? The man-created entities can and are used by the dark forces who bring false doctrine to earth. You must form your own conclusions. If you are very certain of the purity of your own motives—and it is very easy to deceive oneself here—and are aware of no sense of unease or tension and constantly try to submit completely to God's will, you may be reasonably safe from dark influences.

But never forget that evil can enter most unobtrusively into apparently sacred places and influence people you feel sure are good. This you already know. Constant vigilance is necessary. You will be given all the help and protection possible here, but this does not mean that you can relax your own guard. Be ever watchful.

You have been told that it is not your function to teach, but you will be able to help others and to pass on knowledge to them. By teaching was meant passing on information to the many rather than to the few such as by lecturing in public or publishing. This is not your function. You must only release what you know to those ready to receive it. Far more damage is done by those who are over anxious to spread what they believe to be the good news to everybody whether they are ready for it or not, than by those who keep silent.

As you know with the spiritual breakthrough that is taking place, the dark forces are very active. One of the ways they operate is to try to spread fear and a feeling of insecurity. Both these can have disastrous consequences. They have in the past led to wars. One of the main sources of fear and insecurity in past ages was the doctrine of hellfire and eternal punishment.

In the present century, owing to the growth of materialism and atheism, and due to the more enlightened view of most believers, the doctrine has ceased to be effective. Others have taken its place: fear of communism, fear of nations like Russia and China, and of course the greatest fear of all, the fear of instant annihilation by first the atomic and now the hydrogen bomb. This last was a gift to the dark forces as it produced the highest sense of insecurity.

During recent years, the fear has diminished partly because people have grown used to being under the threat of nuclear war, and also that since the Cuban crisis, most people realise that no nation will dare to start a nuclear war unless by accident, since no nation could survive one. This has led to an outbreak of prophecies of war and disaster—mighty earthquakes will destroy the earth. The earth's axis will suddenly change, causing widespread chaos. Continents will sink below the waves.

There have always been such prophecies, but rarely so widespread as today. This is even better than the hellfire and damnation doctrine since it can terrify the non-believer quite as much as the believer. The dark forces are jubilant at the near panic caused in parts of America, where some people are preparing to fly at the slightest signs of the prophecy being fulfilled. The dark forces inspired the spread of these prophecies, many of which have been put out by spurious groups claiming to be New Age centres but are man-made, not God inspired. The danger is that these groups, by concentrating on the prophesies, will bring them about. They claim that they will be caused by the wickedness of man. This is true, because they will be caused by their own activities.

Unfortunately, these prophesies have been taken up and believed in by some perfectly genuine groups who have been deceived by the emissary of the black forces. Remember, they can penetrate into the most sacred and carefully protected places. There is a double reason, therefore, for countering this idea wherever it is found. The people to beware of are those who are spreading the idea in magazines or pamphlets.

It is not for me to say whether such disasters are going to take place or not. Use your own reason and intuition to decide if they are possible or likely. What is important is that man cannot live and carry out his daily work under the constant threat of imminent disaster. Man must live in trust and faith in God, in compliance with his will, and all will be well.

It is all too easy to take prophesies from books like the *Bible* and to find some connection between the prophecy and certain present day trends and happenings and therefore often falsely assume that it is all going to happen. This is very foolish, and it delights the dark powers. Try to spread universal brotherhood and love and to counter the spread of a belief in woe and disaster.

You must decide for yourself whether I am a man-made illusion, or one of God's creatures.

There are indications that even the heavenly gardens, marbled libraries and halls of learning which the NDEer may visit, full of beauty and wonder as they are, may not be representative of true reality.

Clearly, separating the real from the imagined is never going to be an easy task and is especially confusing when it comes to distinguishing true from false messages from "the beyond!" Enigma of enigmas: St. Germain would be delighted.

Many of Newton's clients, however, reveal that they are well aware of the illusory nature of their surroundings and, depending on the experience of the soul, that they themselves can create, disperse and recreate forms at will by moulding the available energy. One particular soul mentioned that while on earth she had a passion for oranges and that in the spirit world, she was able to recreate them. Their taste nearly, but not quite, matched their Earth equivalent.

It would seem that if we as souls are aware of the illusory nature of our surroundings, then we are not constrained by them. Many souls, however, are clearly unaware of the protean nature of their environment and are trapped in these "planes of illusion" until realisation of the true nature of things dawns by whatever means it may do so. This applies particularly to the lower astral planes where some souls on death can find themselves. Such realms are not hell as we are told about it, but they are regions created by our negative earthly thoughts such as our fears and even our expectations; for as long as we are unable to rise above such thoughts and feelings, we are trapped by our own negative thinking.

Wellesley Tudor Pole, himself a down-to-earth psychic, echoes this situation in his book *The Silent Road*, first published in 1960:

> "...thoughts and feelings externalise themselves in form in those realms into which we pass at "death." And that these forms appear to possess a semi-independent life and to become tangible realities to those responsible for their origin."

But, with hints of the later Newton discoveries, he further indicates that physical matter itself can only come into existence through the origin of thought:

> "That mind, and its product, thought, influence matter, is now widely accepted [e.g. the Geller "effects"], but that no material form or object can come into being without a thought behind it is not yet fully recognised….The world of matter, as we know it today, owes its structure and present condition to the

accumulation over the ages of the totality of the effects created by materialistic thought processes which have been in operation for an unknown but immensely long period."

As our physical world is arguably a further downward extension of even the lowest astral, it is probable that strong and concentrated thought, as Tudor Pole points out, may also be capable of altering our physical environment directly here also. As recorded in Professor John Hasted's book *The Metal Benders*, both Uri Geller and many young children tested at the time were found to be capable of bending metal objects such as thin strips of metals, paper clips and so forth which were contained in a suitable enclosure which effectively prevented physical contact with the object. Is this energy similar to the "cosmic" energy available for manipulation in the higher spheres?

In this context, I have found that Hasted's research is an excellent and open minded, scientifically controlled study which has not really been accorded the importance it deserves. It again emphasises the importance of achieving a high statistical weight of evidence produced where several people are capable of achieving the same paranormal result.

The Occult Diaries of

Chapter 10
Duality: Light and Dark

The "powers of darkness" are disbelieved in nowadays by many, but in this script, St. Germain makes it very clear that few people, despite their loftiest ideals, are accorded freedom from these negative influences:

> 660824c. One of the great triumphs of the powers of darkness is the disbelief in their reality, held by so many people today. Such people, however high their ideals, unselfish their motives, and noble their aspirations, except for a very few, are open to being used by the dark powers. Their disbelief makes them vulnerable because they are totally unaware of the nearness of the enemy and unable to recognise him or be aware of his activities. They form weak links in the chain of light. There are many such weak links, and it is well to be on guard against their possible use by the powers of darkness. Those are very clever and subtle, and work in many surprising ways. Few are immune from the sudden intrusion of wrong thoughts and actions. Constant watchfulness is necessary. Be mentally alert and on your toes. Expect anything, and be afraid of nothing.

Some eight years later the theme of duality is further pursued in a document which ROC has prepared as the basis of a talk. It is presented here in slightly adapted form:

> 740606. In referring to positive and negative, light and darkness, it is important to remember that "negative" and "darkness" do not imply evil—they are the opposite polarity to "positive" and "light." Evil only comes into the picture when the energies involved are misused. If we go back to the creation, it all began in chaos, in the darkness. This darkness has been called, "The Divine Darkness." Then God said, "Let there be light." and light came into being, with the division into day and night, the light and the dark. If we did not have the dark, we could not know the light because there would be nothing to contrast it with. Perhaps in the same way evil is necessary in order to know good.
>
> Some schools of thought maintain that darkness is nothing

other than the absence of light and evil the absence of good; more of a quibble that an impressive argument. You might as well say that light is the absence of darkness or good the absence of evil.

It is important to know that such things exist—a darkness and negativity which may become evil through the misuse of the energies. It may not be necessary to dwell on the reality of evil, but if you do not know that it exists or, like some people, deny its reality, you lay yourself open to be easily influenced by it and even, in extreme cases, possessed.

It is foolish to think that if you do not believe in a thing, it does not exist. Denying the existence of the H-bomb will not prevent you from being incinerated if one falls in the vicinity. Nor is it enough to think that because you are so highly spiritually developed or engaged in such important work on higher and inner levels that you do not need protection, as some believe—a form of spiritual arrogance or presumption.

Anyone who has come face to face with active evil and had to deal with it knows very well that it exists. And there is more deadly and dangerous evil on psychic and astral levels than on the physical plane. That it may be intangible does not make it any less real.

On a practical level, to fight evil tends to build it up; it is better to use roundabout or more subtle methods; protective measures rather than counter-attack is the best answer.

For some years now there has been a tremendous influx of spiritual energies into the earth and its etheric shell and the consequent formation of groups all over the world drawing on these energies and building up the light. When you build up the light, the dark also builds up to try to counter it.

Negative attacks, often launched by black witchcraft covens or black magic groups, are rarely of the obvious or violent kind. Such an attack will happen in a much more subtle way; the forces of darkness use great cunning. Provided you are on the right path and have dedicated yourself to work for the light, there will be protection. Unfortunately, defences can be breached. Negative human emotions such as jealousy or resentment to which we are all liable at times, open a doorway to negative energies from outside, as does negative thinking in general. In this way, the strongest protection can be broken through. One must cultivate the ability to rise above the lower self and transmute such negative energies.

Evil is the consequence of the misuse of power and negative energies. Unfortunately there is a great deal of such misuse today and not only on the material level. It is said that during the last war the Nazis used black magic. There is considerable proof of this. Hitler is known to have been interested in occult matters and to have had mediumistic powers. Wherever there is strife, there is likely to be black magic somewhere involved in it.

The question has often been asked: how can anyone deliberately step onto the left-hand path and use negative energies for his own gain and selfish ends? Surely he must know that it will bring ultimate disaster on himself? The rebound of the energies he is using and directing will inevitably take place. However much the dark, in an evil sense, may seem to be triumphant, the light will always win in the end. This is certain.

The lust for power, power over other people, power to control the destinies of people and nations, becomes an irresistible driving force. The black magician feels so confident in his own knowledge and ability that he is certain he will succeed. Whatever has happened to others cannot happen to him. It does, inevitably, in the end. Such ego-inflation and over-confidence, far from saving him, will help to bring about his downfall.

A certain amount of darkness and even of evil may be necessary in order to maintain the dualistic balance. As long as it remains in equilibrium and thus under control, it is not dangerous. It is when the equilibrium is upset, and the darkness becomes too strong, that things begin to happen in the wrong way, and something has to be done about it.

The amount of distrust and hatred, the envy and resentment, the absence of love in the world today, and the inability of man to live with himself, are some of the causes of the breakdown of the equilibrium. As all our thoughts are powerful and persist, negative thinking adds negativity to the etheric shell of the Earth which helps to build up conflict and strife where it breaks out on the material level. A place of power and light helps enormously to neutralise this negativity and transmute it, helping to re-establish the equilibrium and maintain it. To do this requires close attunement to the God within and to each other, bringing about the sense of oneness. It requires a high level of positive thinking so that the love, light, understanding, and wisdom radiated may have the maximum effect.

The world we live in is a dualistic world; so far, no one has disproved this in a satisfactory manner. It would seem that we must accept it; of higher planes we do not know. It may be that only on the highest level, in God himself, is the duality finally resolved to become total unity.

Protection from Evil Influences

Much of ROC's work sought to prevent the ingress of negative and evil influences to both people and places (such as the nascent Findhorn Community). This took the form of the creation of a protective shell or dome, etheric in nature, which acted as a kind of wall or reflective mirror-like surface around that which was being protected; negativity impacting on such surfaces would be prevented from penetrating inwards.

Nonetheless, such a shield was capable of being breached, most often because of the presence of an "evil" person physically within the shell of the place protected, or a heavy attack launched from "outside". The shell itself would in any case gradually weaken with time, and required therefore to be reinforced on a regular basis. ROC generally performed this task out-of-body, and in consort with his "aspects", and also often with others from the invisible worlds. There are many instances of these episodes recorded in his diaries, two examples of which follow:

> 670719. Findhorn. As soon as I was in bed I was out of my body and walking round the site in my Saturnian Aspect with St. Germain. We walked clockwise three times round the site. Then I was standing on top of the dome of protection as a very tall figure in blue and silver robes.

> 700927. Edinburgh. Last night on the protective dome over Findhorn, as Saturn aspect. An enormous being pale blue in colour. Great energy coming down through me into the dome, giving the effect of blue and silver robes flaming over the dome, which grew thicker and thicker and glowed golden. The dome extended under the ground to form a complete sphere of

R. Ogilvie Crombie

protection. Magenta ray and cosmic fire called into it, and power from the cosmic power point.

The Occult Diaries of

R. Ogilvie Crombie

Chapter 11
Music
'Music is the Breathing of the Soul'

Positive Aspects of Music

ROC's spiritual and magical work most definitely included music and drew on his musical talents and knowledge. His take on modern music and its importance in the New Age is expressed in a treatise which he first wrote in 1966 and later updated. In this adaptation, aspects of music are considered in regards to meditation, healing, the etheric body, the creation of certain feeling tones, moods and "atmospheres" in an area, the drawing down of cosmic energy, and the dispersal of negative thought forms:

> 660301. Music is organised sound; vibrations set up by the various instruments producing it—strings, wind, percussion, etc.—and transmitted to the ear drums by means of sound waves in the air, producing effects on the feelings and emotions of the listeners. These effects vary enormously according to the kind of music, from, for instance, the gentle soothing lullaby which sends the infant to sleep, such as Brahm's "Cradle Song," to the excitement and exultation produced by the violent rhythmic stimulation of a work like Stravinsky's "Sacre du Printemps."
>
> Music covers every possible feeling and emotion and can have a profound effect on the listener, good or bad as the case may be. It is not surprising, therefore, to find that considerable attention is being paid to the possibility of using music as a therapeutic agent. This is not a new idea, as it was known to the peoples of the past. Dr. Roberto Assagioli in a chapter on music in his book *Psychosynthesis* says: "Among primitive peoples, songs and musical instruments such as the drum and the rattle were used not only in order to increase the effect of herbs or drugs, but also as an independent means of healing."
>
> Many examples of this can be found throughout the ages. One we might instance is David playing the harp to King Saul: "And it came to pass, when the evil spirit from God was upon Saul, that David took an harp, and played with his hand; so Saul was refreshed, and was well, and the evil spirit departed from him." According to Porphyry, Pythagoras "based musical education in

the first place on certain melodies and rhythms which exercised a healing, purifying influence on human actions and passions, restoring the pristine harmony of the soul's faculties. He applied the same means to curing of diseases of both body and mind."

During the nineteenth century, a very material age, the use of music in psychotherapy was neglected, but there is now a revived interest in the possibility, mainly in three ways: 1. as a means of soothing pain; 2. through collective application in hospitals—especially psychiatric clinics—with the aim of producing calming or tonic effects; and 3. as a means of occupational therapy. Assagioli quotes the New York Times a few years back: "The University of Chicago clinics experimentally introduced music to alleviate tensions of patients undergoing surgery. So successful was the experiment that the University of Chicago medical research centre will introduce music with anaesthesia in its six major operating rooms and its six preparation rooms when it opens Chicago's first cancer research institution. Music with anaesthesia has been used in almost all types of operation. It is very important in cases where the patient is too old or ill to receive sedatives."

The whole subject is too vast to more than touch on at the moment, but it is one that deserves very careful study. Assagioli suggests that "the development of musical therapy may make it possible for musicians who are also psychologists or doctors to compose special music aiming at definite therapeutic effects." This is one of the aspects of music that may well have an increasing part to play.

This raises the important question, however, as to the most suitable kind of music for the purpose. Who is to decide what this is? Taste in music is a very individual matter and varies from person to person. In the use of music as a healing agent, it is very important that the selection of a suitable composition should take into account the individual taste of the subject or patient and not be a dogmatically laid down selection—one particular piece for all, for one particular trouble—otherwise no great progress will be made with musical therapy. Unfortunately, Assagioli himself is apt to be rather dogmatic in this respect.

Similar care must be used in the selection of suitable music to act as a background to meditation, another of the possible uses of music. Meditation is often best performed in complete silence, but there are times when a suitably chosen piece of music may be of great help in obtaining the maximum benefit; it can help to produce the necessary calmness and relaxation so vital to the act. One might suggest certain music by Bach, Mozart and Beethoven as suitable for this purpose. For example, the final movement, the Arietta, of Beethoven's last sonata, Opus 111, considered by some musicians to be the most "sublime piece of music ever written," would be an ideal choice for this purpose. But, as before, the music must be matched to the individual.

Some people belonging to New Age and similar groups and to Spiritual healing centres practice radiating out "light" or sending helpful thoughts towards those in need of aid or treatment. In such cases, the person radiating acts as a channel for spiritual or cosmic forces which are directed towards the subject. Music is a powerful agent in the evocation of the type of energy involved and can be of the greatest assistance in such work. Experiments in this field have shown me that the impressionist music of composers such as Debussy and Ravel is most effective here. The former's pianoforte prelude "La Cathedral Engloutie," for instance, can call up a tremendous surge of cosmic energy, which then becomes available for "projection" in the manner mentioned, but there are many other works that would be equally evocative.

Still on the subject of spiritual and cosmic energies, it is possible to call down spiritual energy from higher spheres in such a way as to act as an uplifting and vitalising force to all listeners who lay themselves open to it. Obviously, the listener to music must play his part. This does not mean that he need have musical knowledge or training, but simply that he must really listen to the music without his thoughts straying off in other directions, and so allow it to have the maximum effect. All musical people have experienced that wonderful feeling of exultation that accompanies the hearing of a great masterpiece well performed by understanding artists. With certain types of music, there is a tremendous sense of spiritual awareness produced as well. This is all to the good in an age that still leans too much towards a sterile materialism.

No one doubts the greatness of the classical masters in

the evocation of spiritual awareness, but some musical people deny that the contemporary composer has this power. This is a great pity, as contemporary music speaks for the age we live in and has a great deal to say to those who really try to make the effort to come to terms with it. Surely nobody who has heard works like the Britten "War Requiem," or, possibly one of the greatest masterpieces of the twentieth century, Bartok's "Music for Strings, Percussion and Celeste," can doubt the ability of the contemporary composer to evoke spiritual awareness to a very high degree. Passages of the Bartok are the true music of the spheres.

Unfortunately, the inspired composer is usually ahead of his time by something like fifty years. The last Beethoven String Quartets and Piano Sonatas were considered to be quite outrageous by his contemporaries who said unkindly, "It is obvious that he is deaf!" At the beginning of the twentieth century, the music of Bartok and Stravinsky, for instance, was dismissed as rubbish with no lasting life. "In five or ten years it will be forgotten." One recalls the riot that took place at the first performance of the ballet "Sacre du Printemps" in Paris in 1913 when fights broke out in the auditorium, and the so-called "cultured" audience made such a noise that the music could not be heard, a fact that did not prevent people from criticising it severely. Today, this work is universally accepted as a major masterpiece, and some musicians consider that the six Bartok String Quartets will take equal place with the last Beethoven ones in the view of posterity.

Many people are sincerely puzzled by what they call the discordant nature and lack of harmony and melody of much contemporary music, as well as by the odd fragmentation and absence of tonality in so-called serial music such as that of the later Schonberg and Webern. Some even believe that it is deliberately done simply to annoy and is a leg-pull with no meaning. This is very far from being the case, though there may have been one or two feeble examples of it which soon faded into oblivion. No serious dedicated composer would be guilty of such behaviour. He writes music in this way because he must. He is inspired to do so because this kind of music is necessary in an age such as ours.

R. Ogilvie Crombie

I do not wish to go into the technical reasons why composers have departed, in many cases, from the diatonic scales and started to explore and use other types of harmony and melody. Suffice it to say that it is not, as some people think, simply to reflect the ugly, violent times we live in. It is more than that; it has a very definite purpose, otherwise it would not be written.

That much neglected composer, Cyril Scott gives us a clue to this purpose in a book he wrote, *Music: Its Secret Influence throughout the Ages*. Scott, who died in 1970, was a theosophist and mystic and well versed in occult studies. I have not been able to consult a copy of the book, but I understand that he suggests that one function of the so-called discordant and harsh music produced by contemporary composers is to disintegrate and disperse wrong and undesirable thoughts and thought-forms, and help us to think differently and so create more wholesome ones. From my own experience, I am certain that he is right. Because of the widespread materialism, wrong thinking and violence of our present period, the world is over-run and haunted by wrong and evil thought-forms which invade every corner of life. Certain inspired—possibly great—contemporary composers have been guided to produce the right type of music to counter these evil forces. It is a cathartic type of music—it is like the surgeon's knife or the radio-active needle, attacking the cancers of modern life. Looked at in this way, even the diehard enemies of contemporary music might come in time to see at least its purpose, if not the real beauty in it, provided an open mind is kept. There is no greater obstacle to spiritual development than the biased and prejudiced mind.

I have used music such as the Webern "Variations for Pianoforte" and late Schonberg piano pieces to disintegrate and disperse undesirable and malign forces with great efficacy. This is due to the concentrated nature of this music. I am therefore satisfied that Scott is right in his suggestion. I know that this is a highly controversial matter which may well be a new idea to many. If it gives rise to thought and discussion, and perhaps leads to someone, listening to the radio and on the point of switching off a horrid noise that they think to be masquerading as music, pausing for a moment to wonder if it is perhaps performing the very necessary function of helping to combat evil, this script will have fulfilled its function.

While I have kept entirely to the positive effects of music on the individual, there is a negative side to the question. Some people believe that music of a certain type can do harm in certain circumstances, but that is another story.

The positive impact that "appropriate" music can have is described in the following diary entry written at Findhorn:

> 680917. Inspired to play La Mer at evening session. I have rarely had such an extraordinary experience as what happened during the music. Brilliant colour visions, and then still hearing the music, I was on the beach and then in the sea, much aware of the spirit of the Moray Firth. I identified with the sea in all its moods, so well depicted in Debussy's music. Aware of a calm, a sort of brooding calm, and then of great exultation and a tremendous ecstatic feeling which persisted. It was a remarkable experience, very difficult to put into words, and lasted the whole of the music.

Negative Aspects of Music

ROC produced a short draft outline of a talk intended to be delivered at Findhorn. While re-emphasising the above points, he now considers the dangers of music, especially of "the wrong type of music"—however that might be defined—played back at extreme volume levels. ROC's wording pulls no punches here and though they may seem a bit "over the top," the implications are clear:

> 740804. Music played above a certain decibel level is dangerous on many levels. Even if played on the very finest hi-fi equipment with absolutely minimum distortion, it is dangerous. Played on the average commercial equipment, it is most dangerous because the distortion inevitable on such equipment played loud increases the damage. Dangers are:
>
> 1 – Causes deafness which to begin with may be temporary but becomes permanent. Sensitivity to the high frequencies is cut and the audibility range is reduced.

2 - The loudness has to be such that the effect produced is purely physical in the body, not the ears. One does not listen to the music; one feels it, chiefly in the solar plexus. It turns people into robots; in other words they lose control of themselves, becoming automatons, open to control from outside sources.

3 - Though it is mainly infra sound that produces internal haemorrhage (Le Vavoureur in Paris with his infra sound whistle), if the loudspeakers are large enough, there might be a slight danger of this happening.

4 - A great deal of pop music is good and in itself harmless, but some of it is not, being lived out by groups in some cases practising black magic and using negative rhythms in the percussion, or even doing so inadvertently. This kind of music played at excessive volumes can be lethal.

The chief danger is brought about on higher levels:

A. It puts the etheric body out of register with the physical one.

B. It brings about unseen stimulation of the centres [chakras] which upsets the balance, and over-stimulation of the solar plexus and lower centres takes place to such an extent that it opens one completely to being controlled by negative and evil energies. Unbalance of the centres produces imbalance in the endocrine gland system, seriously affecting the physical health of the body by bringing about malfunction and upsetting of the metabolism.

C. As in the case of drugs, it damages the physical aura of the body, blasting holes through it and destroying the natural protection this aura gives. Listening to too loud music becomes an addiction and, like taking drugs, can do long term, if not permanent damage to the higher bodies, as well as to the physical one. Those addicted open themselves to negative energies and surrender themselves to being used, even if unconsciously, by the enemies of the light.

This is a very serious matter in places like the Findhorn community, which are under continual attacks from those working against the light (black magicians, etc.). These are not figments of the imagination of thriller writers like Dennis Wheatley; they have developed techniques that give these attacks a terrifying power.

Apart from these human enemies of the light, there are the discarnate entities working for the powers of darkness, inspiring these human tools in their works of anarchy and destruction.

People who open themselves to being used either consciously or unconsciously by such powers can be highly dangerous, especially at aspiring light centres. The way in which the opposing forces work is subtle and insidious, and when channels are opened within a protective dome such as exists at Findhorn, they can function as focal points for the entry of such forces. No amount of so-called protection can keep them out.

Playing records or tapes too loud is one of the sure methods of bringing negative energies into such a community and is, therefore, however innocent the intentions, subversive. It is working for the enemy. Promptings which lead to this kind of selfish stupidity are coming from a wrong source.

It can be the workings of a power complex—the desire to make the loudest possible noise—to make the whole district aware that some great egotistical "I" is functioning, an "I" that must make itself felt, e.g. "the Who." They claim to produce the highest decibel level possible. Anyone doing such a thing is obviously mentally unbalanced.

It can be a strong frustration leading to the desire to escape from reality by trying to overwhelm it by volume of sound. Or fear of thinking, fear of silence because it leads to thinking—the reason why so many people today must have a noise background; whatever they are doing, they must be accompanied by a radio or records. What is that but drug addiction? And of a dangerous kind.

Such music, as well as filling the neighbourhood with physical sound, also fills the etheric shell of the earth with a more or less permanent field of energy. Is it surprising that entities in the higher places are appalled at the incredible stupidity of mankind? The development of super power amplifiers, and consequent use of the high levels was inspired by the dark powers. The pity is that so many people have fallen into the trap and become addicts, joining the ranks of the enemy.

R. Ogilvie Crombie

Scriabin Sonatas

The ability of certain music to produce positive or negative results is further considered in the following, where strong elements of magic ritual appear in some of Scriabin's works. Golu, his teacher, answers some of ROC's discomfiture in the following script:

> 641023. Question: Am I right in my feeling about the Scriabin sonatas?
>
> G: Yes, you are right. Both the sixth and the ninth are powerful ritual and a not very advisable kind of magic. They should never he played too often, and though you have developed counter forces around yourself, the effect could be bad, especially at the moment when strong psychic forces are being built up in your flat. You are advised to cease playing either of the two sonatas mentioned until you are told you may do so. Do not play Vers la flamme either. The rest of Scriabin's music is permissible. Music is a powerful means of calling up forces. In particular play Bach, Beethoven, Debussy, Bloch and the Jarnach Sonatina. Schonberg and Webern are also helpful. Another phase in psychic development is beginning. Do not worry at any strange occurrences. You are in safe hands. As you know I can communicate directly with you, but if you feel inspired to try writing, do so.
>
> ROC: This question was mainly asked because of the strange effect sometimes brought on by playing the sixth sonata. One night, possibly about the year 1955, I was alone in the flat and felt an impulse to play the sonata. I seemed to be very much in key with the music and felt my playing was inspired. Partly through the work, I suddenly felt the presence of a strange power building up in the room. It was very powerful and sent a cold shiver down my back, and I began to feel afraid. It almost seemed as if some baleful being was about to materialise. I stopped playing and began to play a quite different type of music to disperse the atmosphere. The thing was very unexpected, as I had at that time no reason to think of this music as evocative in this way.
>
> Later in the year I spoke about it to Willie Johnston, a great student of Scriabin and an advanced occultist. He told me that Scriabin had studied magic and possibly black magic and that

he believed he had put black magic formulae into some of his music. Once or twice I have played this sonata to people and it invariably produced strange reactions. It always caused an almost chilling silence, and some people had strange and frightening visions. The ninth sonata is called the Black Mass. Because of recent strong reactions to this music, though I have not felt any presence, I [had] asked the above question.

About three months later, the question of Scriabin's sonatas was again raised. Golu's comments here are instructive:

> 650131. Question: What is the present situation regarding Scriabin's Sixth sonata. You advised me not to play it until told I could. I have twice played it since then with permission. Is it likely to do harm to any listener. Am I right in refusing to record it as I have done?
>
> G: You may now play the sonata if you feel you wish to and are asked to do so. As you were told, there is a form of magic ritual implanted in the music to which certain powerful mental psychic forces may respond. These forces are not in themselves evil but could be used for evil purposes. No evil entities are likely to he summoned unless there is someone present who deliberately tries to use the music to call them up. The psychic forces mentioned in the last script have now been so well established that you are completely protected. This also applies to your listeners.
>
> You are advised not to play the sonata anywhere else [than in the flat]. On no account record it for the reasons you already know. It is not likely to do harm to your listeners unless they are evil in themselves and have evil intentions. If the forces respond strongly to the call of the music, they are likely to cause disturbing feelings in the listeners, mainly because the forces are unknown and strange and not because they are evil. Because of the feeling of discomfort, some people have decided that the sonata is black magic ritual. To them it might well prove to be so.
>
> It is not right to be afraid of psychic forces because they are strange and often terrifying. They can he directed in the right way. As you know the sonata has depths of spiritual beauty in it which can be inspiring. It is a conflict, but so is life. And the conflicts of life cannot be evaded. Use your discretion and trust

me to guide you.

Almost ten years on, there is a further sequel to information about the Scriabin 6th:

> 740806. Played records – Falla's "Nights in the garden of Spain" and Rodriguez "Guitar Concerto," followed by Scriabin's piano sonata 3—a posthumous fantasia—and the 6th and 7th. The 6th is the one I had the odd feeling about in the 30's and stopped playing, feeling it had evil ritual in it. Later in the 50's, I was guided to play it only in the flat and with care. I have not played it for some time and recently read that Scriabin himself refused to play it in public, as he thought it was evil.
> Recently when I have played it, I have only been aware of its beauty. This time again it did invoke an entity—the same as what I had been aware of in the 30's as black or very dark grey and negative. This time the entity was red and did not feel evil, though the sonata is still strange—very elemental.

Mahler

On a more positive note, Mahler made an appearance to ROC at a concert during the Edinburgh Festival in 1967.

> 670907. During the performance of Mahler's 10th Symphony, I was aware of the presence of Mahler behind and above me. This was utterly unexpected, as I do not as a rule have any awareness of people who have passed on from earth incarnations. He spoke to me:
> M. "Isn't this a really beautiful passage? (referring to a bit in the adagio 1st movement). I poured my whole heart and soul into my music!"
> He approved of this version, saying he might not have written it that way if he had lived to finish it, but it was acceptable and good that his sketches and ideas for the rest of the symphony had been realised in this way.
> M. "Alma was a fool (referring to her ban on performance and publication of this version). She never really understood my music - she was jealous of it. But I understand and fully forgive

her. I am glad she changed her mind about this. It was more of the whole musical world was against her. I know some people think me long-winded, but I had a great deal to say."

Could all this have been imagination?

Chapter 12
Power Points

In the extracts from ROC's diaries quoted earlier in this book, reference is made to "power points." The term *power points* in this context is an esoteric concept and refers to places on the ground around the earth which have localised "force fields" which sensitives can detect as "vibrations" or "power." These have psychic and/or physiological effects on the person which allow them to home in on their epicentre. In general, these points are more or less fixed, but they can be moved somewhat, intensified, or even shut down by those with the know-how. Many power points are believed to have existed for aeons of time but have no doubt shifted in location as a result of continental drift and the accompanying rise and fall of the land masses and changes in ocean cover. There are an enormous number of such points, and it is believed that they are connected energetically by straight lines, referred to as ley lines, which, it is claimed, can be traced out by the usual dowsing techniques. The points therefore appear as a complex grid or net circling the planet.

In conformity to the principle of duality in general, these points may be positive (having good "vibrations), neutral, or negative, and thus they may be utilised for promoting and intensifying "good" or "bad" effects by manipulation through white or black magic ritual. The points themselves may be sensed as "Cosmic Power Points," "Nature Power Points," "Religious Power Points," and so forth.

In Roc's rather lyrical, dramatic but beautifully poetic vision which follows, some of the recognised power points around the UK which he previously visited in the flesh are stepped through in largely symbolic fashion. Such is the nature of visions in general, that they present themselves in archetypal language, superficially nonsensical but with a deeper (and, dare I say it) enigmatic meaning. In the first paragraph, the strong physiological effect on ROC of the Findhorn power point can be judged. In this particular case, he was able to simultaneously experience the vision and commit it to paper.

> 660912. Findhorn. This was the first night I spent in Naomi's caravan, which is almost on top of the power point, and shortly after going to bed, I felt physically ill. There was tremendous power flowing through me which affected my heart very strongly, causing acute discomfort and a feeling of suffocation. A voice urged me to get up and go out and stand on the power point. For some time I resisted this, but as the voice kept on urging me to

get up, I finally did so and went out and stood on the power point which is in the centre of the lawn, outside the caravan. There was a tremendous surge of power, which affected my legs strongly, and was accompanied by an intense feeling of heat. I returned to the caravan and went back to bed. I lay for some time without sleeping, still suffering considerable discomfort. Presently I sat up, propped against the pillows, hoping to ease the discomfort. My heart was thumping and felt as if it was swelling up. I sat up for some time and began to feel much better. A strong sense of something impending came over me, and I was prompted to get a notebook and pen and recorded the following. As I experienced it, part of me remained detached and wrote down what was happening.

I become a vast vortex of power on the Findhorn power point, a tall soaring flame, a being. Every part of me becomes a part of it. I myself am nothing, but I experience and am the vortex. I am now on Cluny Hill, a giant intangible something rising up from the power point. I am, and become, the pulsating rhythm. I am, and become, the mound. I am now in Pluscarden Priory, a huge something filling the building, expanding into the stones. I become the priory; the building and I are one. Within me is the sound of chanting monks. I feel the rhythm of the stones, and a quiet and wonderful peace fills me. I am a three-sided pyramid, the base points resting on Findhorn, Cluny Hill and Pluscarden. This is complete identification and becoming, and yet the recording part of me is separate and detached, the physical me is nothing. The sense of colour cannot be adequately recorded—it surpasses human perception. All the colours of the rainbow are here and more. Purple, gold, magenta and green predominate, but there are all shades intermingled, shimmering in constantly changing shapes. The pyramid which I have become is fixed and immovable for all eternity and yet is so tenuous that it cannot be seen or touched. Within it I am the flame, the mound, the building. This is utter identification, yet the physical I is nothing.

There is now a sense of soaring upwards and I am detached from the pyramid. I am Columba, my head is resting on a stone in Columba's cell. Now I am writing, there is a blue radiance round my hand giving enough light to see, and there is a feeling of striving. Now there is peace, utter peace. Now a sense of movement, and I become a figure standing in a ring of stones in the hermit's cell. I grow and grow and become immense. I look down on the Island which lies below at my feet.

My feet are cloven hooves, my legs are shaggy, I have horns on my forehead, I am Pan surveying his universe. I become one with Nature. I am all the elemental spirits and earth spirits, they are within me. They are me and yet not me. I feel the disbelief and the fear and the hatred of mankind, and I am filled with sadness. I feel the weight of the anathema of the Church. It is infinite. Yet there is One who calls me brother and gives me infinite love. He is the Christ. Now I feel a stirring within mankind, a new turning towards me and my kingdom. Perhaps mankind is beginning to turn towards us and we can work with him, though he still fears me and my shape. If this fear does not go, must I turn sadly away? Again, this is total identification. The physical I is nothing.

I am now a lotus blossom, peaceful and serene (Jessica Ferriera's Sanctuary). I am the petals; I am the essence of the flower. I become tenuous, a faint perfume, subtle and ineffable. I seem to spread into infinite space. I now condense together and become a figure sitting under a tree. I am the Buddha. There is a sense of utter peace, a sense of both nothingness and all things, of all eternity in the everlasting now. I am the scent of incense, the sound of the OM. I am the East, yet the physical I is nothing.

I am the island of Iona, breathing in the rhythm of the earth in the midst of a calm sea. Now there are rumblings. I hear the sound of the wind and the waves. I am the wind, raging in fury, lashing the waves. I am the waves buffeting the island. I feel a wild exhilaration. I know the necessity for the storm, I feel the cleansing power.

All dissolves into a soaring sensation, and I become the tower on Glastonbury Tor, rugged and old. I suddenly disintegrate into a soaring shape of immense size. I am Michael holding the sword in readiness. Round the base of the Tor is coiled the dragon, black and horrible. It moves slowly in a circle, breathing out a poisonous smoke which curls in wisps about the Tor and the tower. But the sword is ready. This again is total identification, and yet detached observation. The physical I is nothing.

I am now limpid and liquid. I am the water in a well, cool and pure, yet little curls of mud rise up now and again to mar the purity. All is not as it should be, could be, and will be. I am now a little flame in the centre of a quiet place. There is great holiness, and peace and strength, and yet there is a faint disquiet, a slight feeling of tension, all is not perfect yet, but it will be. I am all these things that I have been, all separate and yet all one.

And now I am sitting up in bed in Naomi's caravan, a very ordinary, fallible human being. It is nearly 2.30 am. I had better try to sleep.

NOTE: It is essential to understand that I do not think I was any of the beings or things I became in this vision, but for some reason or other, it was a complete momentary identification.

Coming down to earth a bit, the following is a more typical experience of power points and the finding of them. The visit on this occasion was to "Williamston," a country house near Insch, in Aberdeenshire.

680911. Walking up the avenue of trees and beautiful grass, I felt great power and spirituality, and began to find it difficult to walk—the thicker-than-air feelings as usual, and the backs of my legs were affected. Going up three stone steps onto the lawn, the power intensified, and I felt great heat. There are three rowan trees with tiny shrubs in front. In the middle of which was the power point—very strong. I knew at once that it was a cosmic power point. Standing on it, I was aware of a shaft of energy being channelled through me as in the "journey," probably both linking up and activating the point.

At right angles [to this point], is a beautiful "vista" avenue. Walking up this, the power kept increasing until I found the greatest difficulty in walking. The heart and throat chakras were activated. I had great difficulty breathing. This kept increasing. The power here was as great as I felt at any of the points on the power point journeys. I began to feel that it could not increase any more without causing intense discomfort. Shortly after this, the power began to diminish, and I knew I had passed the point. I turned back, and found an area between four trees. Armine located the exact point with a pendulum—almost where I had found it.

We went on. Again the power increased and reached a peak just after the path was crossed by a drive, but this was not a power point. We went on, and I presently located a second point just off the path, which was again right [according to Armine].

The final point was out in a field beyond the end of the path (through a gate); with only a slight indication from Armine, I again found it. I felt that there were three power points of almost equal strength but varying in the type of energy or power which was used in certain rituals and ceremonies.

On the uses of energy from power points, pertinent especially to ROC's own case, the following script was obtained from St. Germain. The power point in the flat in Edinburgh was brought into existence through ROC's nightly rituals, and was not, I understand, a pre-existing power point. It would gradually dissipate when ROC "moved on." Reference has already been made to the "Illustrious Doctors," but it is included here again for the sake of completeness:

> 670207e. Findhorn. You may be told a little more about the work you are doing during the night. Because of development and training, you can be used as a channel for many kinds of power, and as you are closely linked in with the Power Point [at Findhorn], you can draw power from it. You can also draw cosmic fire from its living centre, and the strong bond with ancient Egypt is another source. Your training as a Healer Priest has given you a depth of medical knowledge that you are quite unaware of. It is being used while out of the body. A group of what Ali called "Illustrious doctors," who can at different times incarnate on earth and in different races, gather round you when you leave your body. You travel with them to certain places where healing is needed, and to certain people—at the moment we will not tell you why or how these people are chosen. Using you as a source of power and as an intermediary link between themselves and the earth patient, they are able to bring about many cases of cure, sometimes by etheric operations, sometimes by other means. Instead of working through a non-physical earth medium, they work through a physical earth medium. They work through your etheric body and at the same time can draw power through it.
>
> When you wake during the night, you sometimes feel tired, but you can replenish yourself by drawing power from the Power Point network. You can do this best here at Findhorn, but

you can also do it in Edinburgh. This is one of the reasons why your flat is linked in with the network through St. Margaret's chapel. You already know much of the other work you are also used for. Certain channels can be used for different purposes, sometimes simultaneously. This is all part of Divine Economy. You are blest in being chosen for this work. Accept it with joy. Be humble but realise the importance and value of the work you are being used for.

To round off this chapter on power points, recorded below is a visit made by ROC to Cairnpapple and a subsequent visit during the night, out-of-the-body. In this state, he re-experiences some of the ritualistic history and early appearance of the site and the attire of the people.

> 670628. Cairnpapple, West Lothian. Yesterday I went [to] the ancient worship and burial ground which is between Bathgate and Linlithgow. There are at least five different periods, each with different peoples and burial customs. The earliest dates back to 2,500 to 2,000 B.C., late Neolithic. There is great power here. I was aware of it on the way up to the hill. It is a cosmic power point with no later Christian overlay. In the dome beside the Beaker People tomb and the crouch burial cist, there is great peace. The dome is a modern concrete one placed over the tombs to protect them and give some idea of the original cairn of stones that covered them and was flattened by later developments. Outside the dome there is tremendous power, especially about the holes where the original standing stones had been. These had been removed and broken up to make stones for the cairn. But in any place like this which is being preserved as a national monument and is visited by people, there is usually a certain lowering of the power. Here it is still very strong. I had an impression of sun worship and no doubt its associated fire worship and, from the intense stimulation of the sixth and seventh chakras, of a powerful fertility cult. There is no trace here of any unpleasant vibrations such as are associated with any place where human sacrifice has taken place. I think it unlikely that it happened here.
> From the wonderful position of the hill, a tremendous circular panorama is seen. On a clear day the custodian said that the Bass Rock could be seen to the east [and to the west, Goat Fell,

R. Ogilvie Crombie

on the island of Arran], and even yesterday, which was a little hazy, a wonderful view of the mountains and hills was much appreciated. This is a place of great significance and feels like an axis of some sort. I am not clear on this yet.

During the night, I was again on the hill out-of-the-body and apparently watching and taking part in a festival. It must have been in the first period as only the original standing stones were there in a great complete circle like a smaller version of Stonehenge. It seemed to be the day of the summer solstice and the rising of the sun was being awaited with great expectation by a crowd of people both male and female. They were short and of stocky build, with broad, fairly low foreheads. Their hair was long and the skin of a brownish tint. Some were naked, but most of them wore skin kilts. Others, who were probably priests, wore robes of what look like a woollen material, but like most out-of-the-body experiences, it is not easy to recall details. The attention is held by certain definite things, in this case the stones themselves, which were at least ten feet high. The sky was very clear and lightening in the east. I seemed to be looking at the scene from different angles. As the sun rose there was a murmur from the people, and a curious kind of chanting began.

The Occult Diaries of

Chapter 13
Conclusions

In examining the life, times and teachings of ROC, I have tried my best to establish who he was: not simply the physical man with its corresponding physical history—that was the easy bit—but the inner man and his spiritual ancestry. He was a man who went about an intense and varied spiritual work quietly and, for the most part, anonymously. This work had at its core the process of integration between the human Ogilvie and the higher worlds, and in particular with his higher self. The ritual drawing down of energies was a virtually daily event seemingly required to keep the "energy" topped up for out-of-body work when he was called upon to perform such. He was thus prepared for whatever inner activities came his way: anchoring spiritual energies, protecting where necessary (such as the work he did creating a protective dome over the Findhorn community), contacting the nature forces, book reading to improve his knowledge, writing up and analysing the inner events in which he participated, and so forth. He was available, in other words, to serve and to be used however, whenever, and wherever needed, both in and out of his physical body. All of this together constituted his "real work," as St. Germain at times referred to it.

To do this spiritual and magical work effectively, he chose to work privately behind the scenes, drawing as little notice to himself as possible. The one great exception to this was his work with both the Findhorn community and the adult education programs of Sir George Trevelyan, first at the adult education college at Attingham Park and later through Sir George's own non-profit organisation, the Wrekin Trust. Through these relationships and venues, ROC brought to the world the story of Pan and the nature spirits and the urgent need for human acceptance of and reconciliation with these inner intelligences. However, although ROC's purpose was to focus attention on the inner kingdoms of nature, the spotlight of public awareness and recognition also spilled over onto him, the messenger.

One result of this was that his anonymity was breached, and the needed privacy of his flat--his *sanctum sanctorum* where he built up and held the subtle energies needed for his work--could be invaded by the advent of people seeking him out, sometimes due to ROC's own kind-heartedness and compassion. He was a warm and friendly person—certainly not a solitary recluse spurning human contact—but he also had boundaries he needed to maintain to preserve the integrity of his energy. At one point, St. Germain addressed this issue with him:

> St G.: The main trouble will be visitors; some are right for you, and some others are time wasters and energy drainers. They will have to be coped with; you will have to be firm and learn to say "no," especially as the publicity you are receiving on the nature spirit side may well bring many more visitors.
>
> You have already been told that personal relationships must not be allowed to interfere with your real work. Be adamant. You are sensible in the way you handle your relationships with others, though still a bit too ready to rush to people's assistance when they call for help. You must go your own way, which you know to be right. Allow nobody to possess you--some try as you know--or to dictate to you what you must do. You are the only one who knows how far you can drive yourself. Your way of life has brought you to the age of 75. However pig-headed some people may think you, stick to it.

By the age of 75, by virtue of doing his "real work," he had reached the peak of this particular earthly incarnation and the process of integration with his higher self was complete. He (they) have this to say:

> 740713c. As you have been discovering in analysing and studying your material, your whole life has been following a plan; the apparent misfortune, the worries and suffering, which have been great, were all necessary. Now you have come to the fruition of your life, when the results of your life work will become evident. A great deal of what you have written down is a concentrated account of happenings and experiences; many repetitions of building up protection, cleansing, and neutralising negative places and energies.
>
> You know who you are and to a great extent why you are here, but you are wise enough to make no claims. This is as it should be. And it is best that other people make no claims for you. The work is best performed quietly, in secret, in the background.
>
> One or two people recognise you—they have been allowed to do so, but they keep the knowledge to themselves. Some have thought they recognised you and have changed their minds. This is no doubt a good thing. No man can change who you are because he thinks it politic or expedient to do so. No man can

change the truth, however much he might wish to do so. God himself would not try to do so, since it is his truth.

Your position is difficult. It usually has been. You can make no claims; you must be modest, and yet you must have a real sense of the importance of your work. You regard yourself as no more than a channel, rightly so, but you are in yourself important as a channel. Long training and devotion to the true path has gained you great respect from higher levels. You have never been afraid to accept full responsibility for your every action from quite an early age.

Of course, you are not the only one. There are very many, but that is something you know well. Your position is not easy. What are you to do with some of your material? Quite a lot cannot be given out, at least not yet—mankind is not ready for it in spite of what some people say. He would abuse it. Some was for you alone and will never be given out. You will be told to destroy it as you write. A great deal of to you new information is now available to you, which will have to be held in reserve.

What are you to do with this script, for instance, and for the others which make your identity clear to the perceptive ones? Is it to let them read this making a claim you should not make? This is a difficult problem which you will have to tackle and face up to.

Of course, your true identity refers to your higher self who is dictating this now. The integration is very complete now. Naturally, I am not always in evidence, though I am always there. Your conscious ego must play a part in your everyday material life and face its own problems. It will no doubt delight you, when you do shed your physical body, to see how beautifully simple it all is.

Taken at face value from all the information presented in this book, ROC would indeed, I believe, fit easily into the category of sage, an enlightened and illumined soul. Had he proclaimed himself as such, we would have had good cause to doubt his spiritual pedigree, but on the other hand, his modesty and humility, while totally consistent with spiritual worthiness, tends to obscure any revelations of "Greatness," as any indications of such are played down in his writings. If you can't tell people you are a highly evolved spiritual being, how are they going to know this? If, on the other hand, you do tell people that you are and how important your work is, then few will believe you anyway because you then lack the expected humility. It's a bit of an impasse. Fortunately, this embargo does not affect me, and I am free to review ROC's status from his most private of notes; something that he could not do, nor could others, while he was still alive.

I think the evidence, largely anecdotal though it is, does indicate that ROC possessed considerable psychic abilities and that the visions and other-worldly experiences he had were real to him, in much the same way as the physical world is real to us. Because we cannot touch his world does not necessarily prove that that world is illusory. We do have the support of those describing their out-of-body experiences and those who have returned following their near-death-experiences, but above all we have detailed "inside information" of the soul world from Newton's and others' life-between-life studies. If nothing else, all these seem to indicate, or even prove, that we have an existence apart from the body and that when death takes us, it is simply our release to return to our perennial home and prepare for the next "big push." Life continues—eternally!

Throughout ROC's spiritual "downloads," he was constantly made aware of the dangers of channel colouration, both his own and of others—without exception. Nonetheless, recognising this danger in itself diminishes its effect, and I must conclude from my own dealings with him that colouration appeared to be minimal; he was forever analysing, doubting and questioning, which was a good by-product of his scientific training. As pointed out below, with the proper approach, nonetheless, the "core of truth can be recognised."

> 670725. No human is perfect, so all such have imperfections and are liable to error. No human channel is a hundred percent pure; there is always a certain colouration, however small it may be, at times coming mainly from the personality, from wishful thinking and desires and so on. This can usually be stripped away when one becomes familiar with what is coming through any particular channel.
>
> Where there is sincerity and faith, there is always a core of truth which can be recognised.

In summary, therefore, having known Ogilvie personally over many years, I am convinced that he is reporting exactly what he has experienced. From his most private writings, it is soon evident that he clearly has a powerful claim to have been the reincarnation of the Compte de St Germain.

R. Ogilvie Crombie

In addition, his remarkable dealings with the representatives of the elemental Nature Kingdoms as mediator for mankind has resulted in these two factions being brought closer together, helping to heal the rifts created by humanity's abuses of nature. It is to be hoped that this new understanding is not further violated by our species in the years to come. But we have freewill—the path can go upwards or downwards; it is our choice!

Bibliography

Some of ROC's encounters with the nature spirits and Pan have been previously published by Findhorn Press and are included here with kind permission. Presently available through Findhorn Press are the following titles:

The Gentleman and the Faun — Encounters with Pan and the Elemental Kingdom, R. Ogilvie Crombie. © Findhorn Foundation et al., 2009. (Also published by Allen & Unwin in North America and Australia as *Meeting Fairies*.)

The Findhorn Garden Story, The Findhorn Community. © Findhorn Foundation 1975, 2008.

Encounters with Pan and the Elemental Kingdom, R. Ogilvie Crombie (ROC). Double CD. ©Findhorn Foundation, 1972 - 74, 2009.

Buhlman, William. *Adventures Beyond the Body*. HarperCollins, 1996
Buhlman, William. *The Secret of the Soul*. HarperCollins, 2001
Bruce, Robert. *Astral Dynamics*. Hampton Roads Publishing, 1999
Compte de Saint Germain & Manly Hall. *The Most Holy Triosophia*. Phoenix Press, 1933
Hasted, John. *The Metal Benders*. Routledge & Keegan Paul, 1981
Hopkins, Budd. *Intruders:The Incredible Visitations at Copley Woods*. Random House, 1987
Hopkins, Budd. *Witnessed*. Bloomsbury Publishing Plc, 1997
Jacobs, David. *The Threat*. Simon & Schuster, 1998
Jung, C. G. *Memories, Dreams, Reflections*. Collins and Routledge & Kegan Paul, 1963
Lawton, Ian. *The Wisdom of the Soul: Profound Insights from the Life between Lives*. Rational Spirituality Press, 2007
Lawton, Ian. *The Big Book of the Soul: Rational Spirituality for the Twenty-First Century*. Rational Spirituality Press, 2008
Mack, John E. *Abduction:Human Encounters with Aliens*. Pocket Books, 1995
Maltz, Maxwell. *Psycho-Cybernetics*. Pocket books, 1969
Monroe, Robert A. *Journeys out of the Body*. Anchor Press Edition, 1977
Moody, Raymond A. *Life after Life*. Bantam edition, 1976

R. Ogilvie Crombie

Newton, Michael. *Destiny of Souls*. Llewellyn, 1st edition, 16th printing, 2009

Newton, Michael. *Journey of Souls*. Llewellyn, 5th edition, 1996

Ring, Ken. *Lessons from the Light: What We Can Learn from the Near-death Experience*. Moment Point Press Inc, US, 2009

Sartori, Penny. *The Near-death Experiences of Hospitalised Intensive Care Patients*. Edwin Mellen Press Ltd., 2008

Sculthorp, Frederick C. *Excursions to the Spirit World*. Almorris Press Ltd., 1981

Smith, Gordon. *The Unbelievable Truth*. Hay House, Inc. 2004.

Tomlinson, Andy. *Exploring the Eternal Soul: Insights from the Life between Lives*. O Books, 2007

Tomlinson, Andy. *Healing the Eternal Soul*. O Books, 2nd publication, 2008

Tudor Pole, W. *The Silent Road*. Neville Spearman Ltd., 1960

Yogananda, Paramhansa. *Autobigraphy of a Yogi*. Rider and Company, 1965

Lightning Source UK Ltd.
Milton Keynes UK
UKHW040605091118
332047UK00001B/106/P